THE EVERYTHING.
Hinduism
Book

Dear Reader,

My introduction to Hinduism came through the music of The Beatles, and one Beatle in particular—George Harrison. It didn't require much spiritual advancement to figure out that songs such as "My Sweet Lord," "Within You Without You," "Beware of Darkness," "Awaiting on You All," and others were the product of a soul-searching man with a genuine yearning to know and seek union with God. Even the title of Harrison's masterpiece, "All Things Must Pass," (by the way, the only three-record set by a single artist in rock history) implied that even before the age of thirty he understood a central tenet of Hindu thought: All the processed and material things of this world will perish, so we should not get too attached to them.

I became more familiar with Hinduism in another indirect manner. I wrote a story about a group of devotees in the Hare Krishna movement who took up residence in my hometown on Long Island for the local newspaper. From there, I moved into their temple on West 54th Street in Manhattan and commuted to my job in lower Manhattan. I occasionally wrote and edited for them.

Later, as a professor of philosophy, I studied and taught more about the history and central metaphysical, theological, and moral ideas. Hinduism is the oldest of the major religions, I learned, dating back over 3,500 years. It offers up a vast landscape of history, myth, religion, and philosophy. If you don't like the taste of one item on the spiritual smorgasbord, you will probably savor another. I learned about the beginnings of the religion in ancient India and the practical, life-oriented philosophy that it serves up as a plan for living.

Kenneth Shouler

Welcome to the EVERYTHING® Series!

These handy, accessible books give you all you need to tackle a difficult project, gain a new hobby, comprehend a fascinating topic, prepare for an exam, or even brush up on something you learned back in school but have since forgotten.

You can choose to read an *Everything*® book from cover to cover or just pick out the information you want from our four useful boxes: e-questions, e-facts, e-alerts, and e-ssentials.

We give you everything you need to know on the subject, but throw in a lot of fun stuff along the way, too.

We now have more than 400 *Everything*® books in print, spanning such wide-ranging categories as weddings, pregnancy, cooking, music instruction, foreign language, crafts, pets, New Age, and so much more. When you're done reading them all, you can finally say you know *Everything*®!

QUESTIONS?

Answers to
common questions

F A C T S

Important snippets
of information

INSIGHT

A revealing look at
an issue

ESSENTIALS

Quick
handy tips

PUBLISHER Karen Cooper

DIRECTOR OF ACQUISITIONS AND INNOVATION Paula Munier

MANAGING EDITOR, EVERYTHING SERIES Lisa Laing

COPY CHIEF Casey Ebert

ACQUISITIONS EDITOR Lisa Laing

DEVELOPMENT EDITOR Elizabeth Kassab

EDITORIAL ASSISTANT Hillary Thompson

Visit the entire Everything® series at *www.everything.com*

THE
EVERYTHING®
Hinduism
Book

Learn the traditions and rituals
of the "religion of peace"

Kenneth Shouler, Ph.D. and Susai Anthony

Avon, Massachusetts

An Everything® Series Book.
Everything® and everything.com® are registered trademarks of F+W Media, Inc.

Published by Adams Media, an F+W Media Company
57 Littlefield Street, Avon, MA 02322 U.S.A.
www.adamsmedia.com

ISBN 10: 1-59869-862-1
ISBN 13: 978-1-59869-862-6

Printed in the United States of America.

J   I   H   G   F   E   D   C   B   A

Library of Congress Cataloging-in-Publication Data
is available from the publisher.

This publication is designed to provide accurate and authoritative information with regard to the subject matter covered. It is sold with the understanding that the publisher is not engaged in rendering legal, accounting, or other professional advice. If legal advice or other expert assistance is required, the services of a competent professional person should be sought.

—From a *Declaration of Principles* jointly adopted by a Committee of the American Bar Association and a Committee of Publishers and Associations

Many of the designations used by manufacturers and sellers to distinguish their products are claimed as trademarks. Where those designations appear in this book and Adams Media was aware of a trademark claim, the designations have been printed with initial capital letters.

Unless otherwise indicated, translations of scriptural writings
come from the following sources:
De Bary, William Theodore. *Sources of Indian Tradition*. New York:
Columbia University Press, 1958.
Doniger O'Flaherty, Wendy, tr. *The Rig Veda*. New York: Penguin, 1981.
Easwaran, Eknath, tr. *The Upanishads*. Tomales, California: 2007.
Klostermaier, Kalus K. *A Survey of Hinduism*. New York: State of New York Press, 1989.
Mascaro, Juan, ed. *The Bhagavad Gita*. New York: Penguin Classic, 1962.
Mascaro, Juan, tr. *The Dhammapada*. New York: Penguin Classics, 1973.
Muller, Max, tr. *The Upanishads, Parts 1 and 2*. Mineola, New York: Dover Publications, 1962.
Sattar, Arshia, tr. *The Ramayana by Valmiki*. New York: Penguin Books, 1996.

This book is available at quantity discounts for bulk purchases.
For information, please call 1-800-289-0963.

For my mother and father, who made everything possible.

Contents

Acknowledgments

I am grateful to Fr. Paul John, a Catholic priest who was born in India and knows so much about the culture and ideas, present and past. My conversations with him have been invaluable. I am very fortunate to have known him for these last six years. I have also benefited from exchanging ideas with my coauthor (and an author in his own right), Susai Anthony, who sees Hinduism clearly for what it is, not romantically for what some would turn it into.

Finally, I appreciate the patience and equanimity of my editor Lisa Laing, who gave me the time I needed to learn what I know about this ancient way of life.

Top Ten Quotes about Hinduism

1. "The lower animals are our brethren. I include among them the lion and the tiger. We do not know how to live with these carnivorous beasts and poisonous reptiles because of our ignorance."—Mohandas K. Gandhi

2. "The fullest life is impossible without an immovable belief in a Living Law in obedience to which the whole universe moves."—Mohandas K. Gandhi

3. "It is fitting that at this solemn moment we take the pledge of dedication to the service of India and her people and to the still larger cause of humanity." —Jawaharlal Nehru, Inaugural Address as Prime Minister, August 15, 1947

4. "The seeker of God is the real lover of vidya, unchangeable truth; all else is avidya, relative knowledge."—Paramahansa Yogananda

5. "Doubtless, oh great warrior, the mind is difficult to subdue. It is restless all the time. But oh! Son of Kunti, the mind can be conquered by repeated exercises and dispassion to sensual objects."—Krishna to Arjuna, Bhagavad Gita 6:34

6. "It made me high. It really did."—John Lennon, reflecting on cruising the Adriatic Sea while chanting "Hare Krishna" with George Harrison

7. "When a chunk of salt is thrown into water, it dissolves into that very water, and it cannot be picked up in any way. Yet, from whatever place one may take a sip, the salt is there! In the same way, this Immense Being has no limit or boundary and is a single mass of perception."—Upanishads, 2.4.12

8. "Owing to ignorance of the rope, the rope appears to be a snake; owing to ignorance of the Self, the transient state arises of the individualized, limited, phenomenal aspect of the Self."—Shankara

9. "By chanting the names of the Lord you will be free/The Lord is awaiting on you all to awaken and see"—George Harrison, "Awaiting on You All"

10. "I believe what it says in the scriptures and in the Bhagavad Gita: 'Never was there a time when you did not exist, and there never will be a time when you cease to exist.'"—George Harrison

Introduction

▶ HINDUISM CAN ATTRACT you in many ways. There are enough rituals, philosophy, and interesting doctrines to draw most anyone in. For those who enjoy the subtle pleasures of metaphysics, there is the philosophy of monism—that all things, however varied, are Brahman. Those drawn to lasting moral and political ideas can trace a continuous thread from the nonviolence that runs from the fifth-century B.C.E. Jains—who believed that no living thing should be harmed—all the way to Mohandas K. Gandhi—who was inspired by the Jains and embraced a philosophy of *ahimsa*, or nonviolence.

For more than 2,000 years, Yoga has taught concentration and meditation techniques as a means to know God. Hinduism created offshoots such as Jainism and Buddhism, which prescribed their own *dharma*, or set of duties, for living a proper life.

In all of the ages of Hindu thought there are kernels of insight. Consider this one: The great king Yudhishthira once said that the most wonderful and truly startling thing in life is that every moment we see people dying around us, and yet we think we shall never die.

For those seeking common ground between Eastern and Western thought, you need only look at the Hindu emphasis on a reality beyond the world of our senses. The following passage is from the ancient *Katha Upanishad* (3.3–7, 10–14). The metaphor of the chariot here also makes an appearance in Plato as he discusses the virtue of self-control.

Think of the soul as the master of a chariot. The body is the chariot itself, the faculty of reason is the rider, and the mind is the reins. The senses are the horses, and desires are the roads on which they travel.

When the master of a chariot has full control of the chariot, the rider, the reins, and the horses, then the chariot moves swiftly and smoothly. In the same way, when the soul controls the body, the mind, and the senses, life is joyful and happy. But when the master lacks control, the horses run wild. In the same way, when the body, the mind, and the senses are not controlled by the soul, there is misery and pain.

The objects of desire guide the senses. The senses supply information to the mind, and so influence what the mind thinks. The thoughts of the mind are ordered by the faculty of reason. And reason only operates successfully when it is guided by the soul. Reason and the mind can be trained to hear the guidance of the soul, and obey it. The training takes the form of meditation, by which the reason and the mind rise to a higher level of consciousness.

So wake up, rise to your feet, and seek a teacher who can train you.

Plato and the Upanishads started in two different places but arrived at the same truth: Genuine happiness can only be attained when reason steers the desires, not the other way around. The idea is more than 2,500 years old.

CHAPTER 1

The Goal of Living: Hinduism and the Four Aims of Life

Hinduism presents us with a plan for living. It offers an ethic with goals—and stages for meeting those goals—for what it considers a proper life. Hinduism is not an otherworldly philosophy that demands its adherents subscribe to exotic doctrines. On the contrary, it is a most practical religion, complete with purposes for living, which is much of what this book is about. What are these goals for living? They are presented in a doctrine called The Four Ends of Life.

The Dutiful Way to Live

One of the essential doctrines that prescribe how a good Hindu should live is the Four aims, or ends, of human life. The four ends of life, or goals of humanity, are called *purusharthas*. In Hindu tradition, these four comprise a scheme, or set of goals, that tell us what life is for. The scheme has been maintained in its current form for more than 2,000 years. Each of these four aims prescribes a value or manner of conduct that is a piece of a larger moral view. Each is therefore appropriate for a proper Hindu upbringing.

FACT

Recent evidence shows that followers of Hinduism are more likely to stay with their religion than followers of any other major religion. According to a Pew forum poll, 90 percent of all people who are raised Hindu remain Hindu. This ranks first among the major religions, with Catholics (89 percent) and Jewish people (85 percent) running second and third.

To be sure, there are activities in a person's life where he tries to gain an advantage or pursue some pleasure. When the object of this pursuit is material well-being, the end is *artha*. When it is love or pleasure, it is *kama*. At the end of life, there is a renunciation of all these activities in order to devote oneself to religious or spiritual activities. Here, the goal is *moksha*, the liberation or release of oneself from the concerns and activities of worldly life. We will consider each stage in turn. While the four are emphasized at different stages of life, one seems to reign above the rest: *dharma*. Dharma is one of the four ends, but it is also like an umbrella that covers the other three ends.

Why Dharma Is the Principal End

At times, Hindu texts reduce our aspirations to three: *dharma* ("virtue"), material gain, and love or pleasure. Dharma is the one that provides the underpinning for the others, for the concept of dharma establishes an ideal of behavior, religion, and ethics. As such, if we are living appropriately at the various stages of life, we are always doing our dharma. Etymologists might be interested to find that the word comes from the root *dhr*, meaning "to sustain." This is fitting; dharma is the moral law that sustains the individual and, ultimately, human society.

Hinduism teaches that the ultimate goal of life is to keep from being reborn. It is only by transcending selfishness that one can achieve that destiny. According to the Bhagavad Gita, the way to the cessation of the cycle of rebirth is to perform all of our actions just because such actions are our dharma, without egotistical concern for their fruits.

The great Hindu epic *Mahabharata* states the essence of its teachings: "With uplifted arms I cry, none heeds; from dharma, material gain and pleasure flow; then, why is not dharma pursued? Neither for the sake of pleasure, nor out of avarice, no, not even for the sake of one's life should one give up dharma; dharma stands alone for all time; pleasure and pain are transitory." The passage is meaningful on several levels.

When the *Mahabharata* states that fulfilling ethical duties will lead to material rewards and pleasures, it means not only in this life, but in heaven, too. In the epic *Ramayana*, attributed to the sage Valmiki, it says, "From dharma issue profit and pleasure; one attains everything by dharma; it is dharma which is the essence and strength of the world."

Plato maintained that reason should be that faculty in the soul that controls appetite and desire. A healthy soul exhibited this kind of order. In Hinduism, dharma plays the same role that reason plays for Plato. Whatever else you are chasing in life, your dharma functions as a supervisor and ranks first among the four ends because it is a supervisor.

Even those who live large lives of outsized pleasure are called upon to follow the duties of dharma. Kings must observe dharma and enforce it among their subjects. A king who follows the injunctions of dharma is called a royal sage, for his rule is based on moral principles. The *Lawbook of Yajnavalkya* states that where there is a conflict between righteousness and material advantage, dharma, and artha, dharma comes first.

According to Hinduism, our many loves and or pleasures (kama) are also subject to dharma. A well-known passage in the Bhagavad Gita (7.11) shows that desire is consistent with dharma. Lord Krishna speaks, "I am the power of those who are strong when this power is free from passions and selfish desires. I am desire when this is pure, when this desire is not against righteousness."

The Hindu ideal does not preach abstinence from pleasure; but love should be chaste, regulated by considerations of morality and material well-being.

FACT

Hinduism maintains that there are four stages of gurus. Parents provide us with this body and acquaint us with the problems of life. Worldly teachers at schools and universities help educate us. The spiritual master knows the purpose of life and explains the way to self-realization. The fully enlightened cosmic guru is the final guru, and we are introduced to this guru through the spiritual master.

Artha

Artha is the first aim of life. It signifies material prosperity and achieving worldly well-being. The word literally means "thing, object, or substance." It signifies the whole range of tangible objects that can be possessed, enjoyed, and lost and that we require in our lives for the upkeep of a household, raising of a family, and discharge of religious duties. Wealth and material well-being are not ends in themselves, but the means to an enriched life.

Hinduism recognizes that people have a desire for wealth and, in many cases, fame and power. Here, the satisfactions last longer than they do with kama, for success is a personal, and usually social, achievement that involves the lives of others. For this reason, success here has an importance of which pleasure cannot boast.

Successes in the stage of artha are means to ends, since they help us support a household and discharge our civic duties. But there are limitations even at this stage, since success can be very private: my dollar is not your dollar. So success here is private, not cooperative. There is another problem: Wealth, fame, and power do not survive death and are, therefore, ephemeral.

FACT

For Brahmins, the ritual donning of the *janeu*, or "sacred thread," is an important ceremony symbolizing their upper-caste standing and also marking the beginning of their stage of life as students. It is usually done between the ages of eight and twelve and is considered a second birth.

What draws many people into Hinduism is the testimony of others who have let the fulfillment of pleasure guide their life and have found that life to be incomplete. There may be no better example than George Harrison, guitarist for The Beatles. By the time he had reached the age of twenty-four, he knew that there must be more to life than the fame and material well-being he had already achieved.

Kama

Kama, the second aim of life, has to do with fun or, more generally, pleasure. In Indian mythology, Kama is the counterpart of Cupid; he is the Hindu god of love. Kama refers to the emotional being, the feelings and desires of a person.

According to Indian philosophy, people who are denied their emotional lives and the fulfillment of pleasurable desires are repressed and live under a continual strain. All of this is ruinous to their sanity and well-being.

Kama teaching is exciting because it runs counter to the frustrations that result from arranged marriages of convenience. Traditional Hindu marriages became more and more family-managed affairs. There were no limits as to how meddlesome the parents might be. Bargains struck by the heads of families, based on the horoscopes cast by astrologers and on economic and social considerations, determined the fate of the young bride and groom.

Hinduism acknowledges that seeking pleasures and avoiding pain are fundamental to human psychology, and therefore pleasure is one of the ends—or goals—of existence. But people do come to the realization that pleasure is not all there is. In fact, the nonstop pursuit of pleasure is rather trivial and ultimately boring; people desire something more lasting.

The principal surviving classic of India's kama teaching is Vatsayana's celebrated Kama Sutra. This sensual work has earned India a reputation for sensuality that is rather misleading; the subject of sex is treated on a secular and technical level. The Kama Sutra is more or less a textbook for lovers and courtesans. In such a planned environment, with its arranged marriages, there have been plenty of dull and painful households where a copy of the Kama Sutra would come in handy.

FACT

Despite the sensuality described—and depicted—in the lovemaking classic Kama Sutra, the average Hindu holds an austere, chaste, and extremely restrained attitude about sexual activity. The goal of the ideal life is to be immersed in spiritual pursuits and to have mystical experiences that result in a union with God.

Not all Indian literature is imbued with a hankering for increased spirituality. Vatsayana also gives a veritable guide for the "man about town" who enjoys "the good things of life, has a cultured taste, and moves in the most refined social and artistic circles."

After acquisition of learning, a person should with the help of the material resources obtained by him through gifts from others, personal gain, commerce or service, marry and set up a home, and then follow the ways of the man of taste and culture.

He may make his abode, in accordance with the calling chosen by him, in a city, in a commercial center, or a town; any of these that he chooses should be inhabited by good people. There he should make for himself a house, with water nearby, having a garden, provided with separate apartments for different activities.

—Kama Sutra 1.4

QUESTION?

Who was the Kama Sutra written for?
There is little doubt that the Kama Sutra was written for a predominantly male audience, setting out to cater to their sexual desires. Some passages refer to how men might better satisfy women's sexual pleasure, but even this is framed in a male-centered way.

The text continues that the retiring room shall have a "fine couch" with two pillows, not to mention a swing in the garden. The sensual life should be replete with a bath every day, a massage every second day, and a salve every third day to ward off stiffness of the legs. A male's aesthetic will also include excursions to attending festivals, salons for enjoying literature and art, drinking parties, excursions to parks, and group games.

Dharma

The third of the four aims, dharma, includes, in essence, the sum and substance of the religious and moral duties that comprise our righteousness. Indian literature contains rituals and numerous social regulations of the three upper castes—Brahmin (priest), Kshatriya (noble), and Vaishya (merchant and agriculturalist)—meticulously formulated according to the teaching of the Creator (in the *Vedas*).

Dharma is the doctrine of the duties and rights of each group and person in the ideal society, and as such, the law or mirror of all moral action. Ethical life is the means to spiritual freedom, as well as its expression on

Earth. At this stage, the individual undertakes a kind of religion of duty. Energy is directed toward helping others, but this service is also finite, and so will come to an end.

Moksha

Moksha is last in the Hindu scheme of values, for it ought to be the final and supreme aspiration of man. In a well-lived life, young boys and girls attend to accomplishments like learning; in youth, enjoyment should be the principal aim; in later life, one should pursue the ideals of virtue and spiritual liberation. Moksha is this desire to be free of the endless cycle of transmigration that traps the spirit. The Upanishads tell us that there is nothing higher than people, but people are not mere assemblages of body, life, and mind born of and subject to physical nature.

The natural half-animal being is not a person's whole or real being; it is but the instrument for the use of spirit that is the truth of their being. It is the ultimate aim, the final good, and as such is set over and above the other three. Artha, kama, and dharma, known as the *trivarga*, or "group of three," are the pursuits of the world; each implies its own orientation or life philosophy, and to each a special literature is dedicated.

But by far the greatest measure of Indian thought, research, teaching, and writing has been concerned with the supreme spiritual theme of liberation from ignorance and the passions of the world's general illusion. Moksha, from the root *muc,* "to loose, set free, let go, release, liberate, deliver, to leave, abandon, quit," means "liberation." These terms suggest the highest end of man as conceived by Hinduism.

CHAPTER 2

Paths to Uniting with God

When a westerner hears the word "yoga," his mind goes immediately to a person locked in meditation, sitting upright, cross-legged, palms upward, likely chanting the sound "Om." In Hinduism, yoga is a spiritual path, a discipline that leads one to actualize his potential. In other words, it is a means to the end of spiritual enlightenment discussed in our first chapter.

Yoga

Yoga is a well-known word in the West, and is connected etymologically with the English word "yoke," or "union" of the individual consciousness with the Infinite Consciousness. The term can be loosely translated as "spiritual discipline" or "application." Yoga is taught by all sects of Hinduism, and it is taught as a means of salvation.

There are four kinds of yoga, and it is the combination of the four disciplines that leads us from release to rebirth. The Bhagavad Gita is a classic Hindu text that presents a variety of options for those who desire release from rebirth. There the god Krishna talks about the ways in which humans can find release. One is by fulfilling their caste duties. Another is by practicing the philosophy known as yoga.

The significance of the term yoga is profound: Yoga is a method of spiritual training whose purpose is to integrate or unite the self. A physical exercise, its goal is nonphysical—uniting with God. Yoga teaches that people should attempt to yoke the individual spirit to God, to atman—the individual soul or essence of a person—and to Brahman.

What is essential to all yoga is meditation. Meditation is valuable insofar as it enables its practitioners to find release from the endless cycle of birth, death, and rebirth. The early practice concentrated on "yoking in," or restraining, the senses. Later the word yoga was seen as a metaphor for or "yoking" to God or the divine.

Since there are different types of people, different spiritual personality types, Hinduism recognizes a different path for each. Every human being possesses a talent or attribute that could be emphasized in approaching God. As a consequence, there are several forms of yoga, each having different features.

Before a person can even begin on any of the paths, they must undertake some moral preliminaries. This means casting aside bad habits and acquiring good ones, including nonviolence, truthfulness, self-discipline, cleanliness, contentment, and a genuine desire to reach the goal.

Yoga over Time

People today are tempted to think of yoga as the brainchild of some new-wave philosophy. They might think it originated with some recent guru. In actuality, yoga is about 3,000 years old.

Statues and seals depicting persons in various yogic positions have been found in remains dating back to the third millennium B.C.E.; but the earliest form of yoga as we know it was probably Jain yoga (900 B.C.E.). Jain yoga involved severe sensual denial and restraint. To free the soul from birth and rebirth, Jains felt it was necessary to restrain the senses completely to be beyond both love and hate. In reality, this means to be in control of all positive or negative emotions.

As early as 900 B.C.E., the Jain monks and Tirthankaras (perfected beings) would train themselves to ignore the pains and longings of the body completely. Nearly 3,000 years later, the details of such practices are lost to us. Jain yoga today has evolved; it is now focused more on restraining oneself to prevent injury to any living being.

Patanjali and the Yoga Sutras

The current philosophy of yoga was developed by the sage Patanjali, who lived in the second century B.C.E. and regulated the teachings of yoga in the Yoga Sutras. The Yoga Sutras are the most important text of hatha yoga, or "posture yoga" tradition. "Sutra" refers to the text style: a collection of concise lines—what are commonly called aphorisms—often requiring further explanation to be fully understood.

QUESTION?

What is known about the sage Patanjali?
According to tradition, Patanjali was an incarnation of the divine serpent Adishesha. Patanjali is often depicted with the lower body of a snake and a canopy of five serpent heads.

The Yoga Sutras contain 193 sutras divided into four books. Book I is on concentration and its spiritual uses; Book II outlines the practice and means of reaching the highest goals; Book III details the "powers" gained in the practice of yoga. Book IV is titled "Independence"; it describes various aspects of the nature of things, especially the nature of the liberated state. Scholars believe that the four chapters might have been composed at various times, but they nonetheless comprise a single authoritative text.

The Yoga Sutras on Concentration: Books I and II

The Yoga Sutras begin with a simple sutra numbered one: "Now concentration is explained." Sutra two says yoga is a restraining of the individual consciousness (*chitta*) to control *vrittis* (thoughts, feelings, and emotions). Book I begins with a definition: "Yoga is the practice of ceasing the false identification with the fluctuations of the mind." What could this mean?

Yoga is a method of restraining the natural turbulence and agitation of our thoughts. Without slowing down the mind's agitation, we cannot glimpse our true nature; as soon as the ripples or waves in a lake have stopped, we see its true nature. So with the mind; when it is calm, we see what our nature is. The third sutra says, "At the time of concentration the seer rests in his own state." According to Hinduism, the mind is continually transforming itself into the shapes and objects it becomes aware of, a power of transformation that is never at rest.

According to Patanjali, a person who has attained certain powers through medicines, words, or mortifications (self-denial) still has desires. But the man who has attained *samadhi*, which is the highest level of concentration and absorption in yoga, is free from all desires.

Yoga philosophy teaches that the whole of nature consists of three qualities, or forces. These three show up in the spiritual world as darkness or inactivity (*tamas*), attraction or repulsion (*rajas*), and the equilibrium of the two (*sattva*).

Your mind may be distracted by the desire to rest by playing a game of solitaire. Or your important conversation may be halted by your eyes trailing the form of a beautiful woman as she walks by. A line of music may send you into reverie about a person and a time long past. The yogi knows that a person in samadhi, or the highest state of concentration, is indifferent to such external stimuli.

How does this come about? The control of the mind comes about by practice and nonattachment to objects, according to the twelfth sutra. It has been said that habit is second nature, but this truth is not the whole truth. Habit is first nature, too, and the whole nature of man. Everything that we are is the result of our habits.

The philosophy is positive, even hopeful: We can remedy bad habits with counter habits. In this sense, no person is ever hopeless, because his character—a combination of his habits—can always be replaced by newer and better habits. With practice, you can achieve what the thirteenth sutra counsels: "Constant struggle to keep them [the vrittis, or forms of the world] perfectly restrained in practice." Nonattachment is the reward of long, continued practice: "That effect which comes to those who have given up their thirst after objects, either seen or heard, and which wills to control the objects, is nonattachment."

In concentrating, you must work toward yoga. An analogy is made between a man and his senses and a charioteer controlling his horses. The sense organs are like horses, the mind the reins, the intellect the charioteer, the soul the rider, and the body the chariot. If the horses are very strong and do not obey the reins, if the charioteer—the intellect—does not know how to control the horses; then the chariot will come to grief.

Book II

Book II of the Yoga Sutras prescribes methods for overcoming the mental "afflictions," which means all of those things that cause distractions. The real root of ignorance, or having the wrong idea about reality, is discussed here. As the fifth sutra of the second book says, "Ignorance is taking the noneternal, the impure, the painful, and the non-self for the eternal, the pure, the happy, and the atman, or self." In short, ignorance is treating unimportant, temporal things as truly important, eternal things. Among the things people mistake for being important are pleasures and pains.

Yogis say that the person who has discriminating powers sees through everything called pleasures and pains. Pleasures and pains come to all persons; they are transient, with one passing easily into the other.

All people follow an ignis fatuus all their lives, and never succeed in fulfilling their desires. The great king Yudhishthira once said that the most wonderful and truly startling thing in life is that every moment we see people dying around us, and yet we think we shall never die.

A yogi observes that even the love between husbands and wives, children and friends, slowly decays. The desires of this world are vain and dreamlike. Frustrated with the ephemeral nature of this world and its continued disappointments, the yogi then glimpses *vairagya* (renunciation). Freedom from attachment brings with it the promise of what lies beyond. If the yogi leaves this world of the senses, then there is hope of bringing the eternal into this life.

The sound *"Om"* is believed to be the supreme symbol of God and the sound that expresses all truth. Thus, the priest begins worship and spiritual leaders begin their lessons with *Om*. In addition, disciples open themselves to those lessons with Om. It is claimed that those in whom the sound resides are unified with God.

Holding on to this world will not do; attachment does not serve spiritual advancement. Never did a great soul exist who did not turn his back on sense pleasures and enjoyments. The cause of misery is the clash between the forces of nature—one dragging one way, another dragging the other way, rendering permanent happiness impossible.

The yogi realizes the cause of pain or pleasure is always joining ourselves with the body (sutra 23). It is our ignorance of this that has led to our misery (sutra 24), which is due to our joining ourselves to a particular body. But this idea of body is a superstition caused by ignorance, and leads us to feel heat and cold, pleasure and pain. Yogis teach that it is our task to rise above this superstition. Some people do, so at times, we see a person who is burned but feels no pain. We can get hold of the upheavals of the mind and permanently attain to the separation of self from the body.

In essence, one must conquer one's own ignorance. This can be done by work, worship, psychic control, philosophy, or some combination of them. To overcome this bondage of nature over us is to achieve freedom. This is the whole of religion. The rest of religion—its metaphysical doctrines, dogmas, rituals, books, and artifacts—rank far behind in importance. Nature versus self: it is a pitched battle for control. What are the stakes?

The stakes are high, indeed. The yogi contends that he who controls mind controls matter, too. The internal nature is much higher than the external; in addition, this internal nature is more difficult to control. If you conquer your internal nature, you can control the entire universe. Book II stresses the goal of practice: discriminating between the real and the unreal.

FACT

Yoga practice includes truthfulness, continence, and not stealing, killing, or receiving gifts. These are eternal vows, uninterrupted by time, place, caste rules, or other circumstances. They must be observed by every man, woman, and child, regardless of their nation of origin or position in life.

Each can be considered in turn. Falsehoods, no matter how small, are sinful. Even mild lies are still lies. The yogi must be true in thought, word, and deed.

A yogi must practice the ideal of nonviolence, toward animals as well as people; if you injure animals without concern, you become callous. The sutras say even animals at odds, such as tigers and lambs, will play together in the presence of a nonviolent yogi.

QUESTION?

What is a yogi's view of sex?
A yogi must be continent, meaning self-controlled, specifically with regard to sexual appetites; thus, a perfect yogi must renounce sexual ideas. The soul has no sex, so why should it degrade itself by being sexually preoccupied? Chastity yields tremendous energy; without it there can be no spiritual strength.

As regards the giving and receiving of gifts, receiving gifts is prone to undercut the independence of the mind and make individuals slavish. A man who does not make a practice of receiving gifts does not become beholden to others; rather, he remains independent and free.

There are other virtues for the yogi: he should practice cleanliness, and he should be cheerful, not gloomy.

Powers: The Yoga Sutras Book III

The third book of the Yoga Sutras begins with a discussion of the internal practices of yoga, including meditation and various levels of concentration, including samadhi, the highest. Concentration is of the utmost importance to quiet the mind.

The mind by its nature is in constant agitation; yoga stops this agitation. One metaphor explains the mind as being in a continuous ripple, like the surface of a pond being stirred by a breeze. Like this pond, the mind is ever changing, shimmering with every different influence that captures it at distinct moments.

The mind can never be still—all the impressions our senses experience coming from without would have to cease. In addition, all the impulses from within must also grind to a halt. Memories, emotional pressures, and incitements of the imagination—which are like internal springs, as opposed to the external springs of the objects of sense—are forever active. What can the mind do in the face of this continual onslaught of internal and external stimuli?

Patanjali's yoga has the power to still the mind, which is at the center of a cauldron. His yoga is a technique to rid your mind of the torments, afflictions, and sufferings and bring out the inner perfection of the essential person.

There are five impairments for the mind:

1. *Avidya:* Avidya is commonly translated as ignorance. It is the fundamental ignorance that causes us to misperceive the phenomenal world. This ignorance makes us believe that what we see is the only reality, when in actuality there is an underlying reality that transcends the mundane sphere, though it is not apparent to ordinary vision.
2. *Asmita:* Asmita means "I am." This impairment leads a person to think his self is separate from reality and is the essence of his being.
3. *Raja:* Raja is one of the three *gunas* of worldly existence. It refers to attachment, sympathy, and interest or affection of every kind. Yogic practice tries to realize the self beyond and untouched by the three gunas of worldly existence.
4. *Dvesa:* Dvesa is the feeling contrary to raja. Instead of attachment, it is disinclination, distaste, dislike, repugnance, and hatred. Dvesa and raja together tear the soul this way and that, upsetting its balance.
5. *Abhinivesa:* Abhinivesa is a clinging to life as a process that should go on without end.

Among the five hindrances, ignorance is the one that underlies the rest. What are called the goods of life are intrinsically impure, yet people value them as if they were permanent. Nothing could be further from the truth.

The Yoga Sutras teach that through a life perfectly conducted according to these principles, a person can attain a mental level where the five impairments are reduced to practically nothing. Once the impairments have been removed, illumination comes to the mind.

Raja Yoga: Mental and Spiritual Development

According to the Yoga Sutras, there are eight steps a person must take to achieve the superconscious mental level in raja yoga. This is a "sitting" yoga, which focuses on breathing. As one observes the breath, one develops ways of concentrating the mind and eventually controlling it. Postures are stressed in today's versions of Patanjali yoga, but Patanjali's Yoga Sutras do not list any postures.

Raja yoga is known in India as "the royal (*raj*) road to reintegration." The goal of the meditative exercise is to achieve "the beyond within." The yogi or yogini (female) is involved in introspection, the result of which is to uncover the four layers of the self. This self is composed of a body; next comes the conscious layer of our minds; underlying these two is an individual subconscious, which contains bits of our own personal histories. The fourth layer is being itself—infinite and eternal.

Employing a method that might be called willed introversion, one can drive the psychic energy of the self inward, to its deepest base.

QUESTION?

What is the most common posture during yoga?
The most frequent of all yoga postures used in meditation is the so-called lotus position. A person sits cross-legged—right foot upon the left thigh, the left foot upon the right thigh, with back erect. Concentration is thought to be easier in such a centered or balanced position, where you are not attending to the comforts and discomforts of the body.

The following eight steps achieve the goal of raja yoga—a trance state:

1. Before you can progress, you must take certain vows of restraint (*yama*). These vows include not harming living creatures, and chastity.

2. At this stage, you attempt to achieve internal control, calmness, and equanimity (*niyama*).
3. In the third stage, you learn and practice certain bodily postures (*asana*) designed to help achieve the aims of yoga.
4. Once the postures have been mastered, you work on breath control (*pranayama*).
5. The fifth stage is control of the senses (*pratyahara*), in which you seek to shut out the outside world.
6. The sixth stage is extreme concentration on a single object (*dharana*).
7. Then one seeks to achieve meditation (*dhyana*).
8. Finally, you seek a trance (*samadhi*), in which you become one with the Brahman.

Breaking Down the Eight Steps

What does each step mean? The first two steps involve the required moral preliminaries common to all four yogas.

Unless a meditator's mind is clear and her life—that is, her relationships to others and herself—follows some semblance of order, self-knowledge is difficult, if not possible, to attain. Thus, step one involves the practice of five moral abstentions—from injury, lying, stealing, sensuality, and greed. Step two includes an additional five observances: cleanliness, contentment, self-control, studiousness, and contemplation of the divine.

The third step demands precision regarding the physical requirements of yoga. This means the lotus position: the yogi sits, ideally on a tiger skin—symbolizing energy—covered by a deerskin—symbolizing calm—with legs crossed so each foot rests sole up on its opposing thigh. The spine is now in a natural position, nearly erect, with hands placed palms up in the lap, thumbs touching lightly. The eyes should not be looking off; instead, they should be closed or allowed to fall, unfocused, to the ground.

The fourth step focuses on breath control (*pranayama*). Having achieved relaxation in your body, you now turn to controlling your breath. It is believed that if the mind is breathing randomly it might be perturbed, so evenness of breath is one ideal. Another is breath reduction. Ideally, breathing should be gentle and sparse; abstention from breathing can lead the body to be still, allowing the mind to achieve a state where it seems disembodied. This facilitates the effectiveness of the meditation. As it is written in the Bhagavad Gita, "The light of a lamp does not flicker in a windless place."

The fifth step of controlling the senses (*pratyahara*) cannot be overemphasized. In order to contemplate effectively, you cannot be distracted by the passing parade, that steady stream of sights and sounds that interrupt your calm repose. How can you fight the onslaught of objects and sensory stimuli that unsettle you and split your concentration?

INSIGHT

"Restless the mind is, so strongly shaken by the grip of the senses. Truly I think that the wind is no wilder," it is written in the Bhagavad Gita.

This step counsels that the constant din of sensory input must be quieted. You hear sounds you ought not to hear and wouldn't hear if you were concentrating correctly. On the other hand, we don't hear directives and requests that were intended for us, since we are distracted with other matters. Your spouse tells you to shut off the stove after you've boiled the eggs, but you were thinking of the day's schedule at the time and didn't hear the directive.

Then there is that environmental clatter; the steady, shrill drivel of nonsense from the television or the gossip at the dinner table after a meal. All of this is inviting to an undisciplined mind. But a disciplined mind set on spiritual advancement must tune it out, as if shutting off a switch. For the yogi bent on making progress, concentration must cease to be a random occurrence and commence to be a controlled skill.

The sixth step involves extreme concentration, or what is more often called focus (dharana). The Katha Upanishad says, "When all the senses are stilled, when the mind is at rest, when the intellect wavers not—that, say the wise, is the highest state."

Stated thus, it is easier said than done. Our minds are routinely unwieldy, more prone to activity than stillness. No sooner do we concentrate on some bit of music, dialogue, or calculation, than poof—off our mind goes, exploring the landscape of some other matter. From there it is distracted once again, foraging over the surface of some new matter. You find yourself in conversation with a person and suddenly their head snaps left or right, eyes trained on someone walking by.

The would-be yogi, or even advanced yogi, is in need of a mental tune-up, always struggling to cultivate stronger powers of concentration. To attain this end, some dedicated work is required. The method has two parts. The first is relaxing the mind in order to free thoughts and feelings formerly repressed. With the hornet's nest of the unconscious now stirred up, try your skill at concentrating on some object.

You can concentration on anything: a billiard ball sitting on the green baize, the relentless waves pounding the shore. The choice of an object matters less than the ability of the mind to stay focused on the object.

In step seven, one goes beyond step six in an important way. In step six, you focused on some object, all the while aware that you were doing so—you were aware of your awareness. But in the seventh step, you drop out of the equation. The object now occupies your attention utterly, with no room remaining for self-consciousness or awareness that you are doing so. In essence, there is no split between self and other; at this point, you have achieved meditation (dhyana).

What is meditation?
The word comes from the Latin root *meditare,* with the Latin *mederi* meaning "to heal." So, meditation is the art of healing all physical and mental ailments. Hinduism talks about twenty different levels of consciousness or mental stages. Meditation is the art of making the mind still.

In step eight, you finally achieve the sought-after union with a supreme being. In this stage, known as samadhi, even the object of contemplation disappears. The limited object of your contemplation now gone, your mind finds union with the infinite, with the Brahman. This infinite substance excludes nothing—it is formless. It is "separated from all qualities, neither this nor that, without form, without a name," as the Upanishads say. You have contacted total being.

Jnana Yoga: The Way to God Through Knowledge

The term derives from a root *jna* which means "to know." The knowledge being referred to in jnana yoga has to do with the unity between the highest realization, or Brahman and the individual self, or *Jivatman*. The role of jnana is explained in the Upanishads and is most clearly outlined in the *advaita* (nondualist) philosophy of Shankara.

Jnana knowledge is not factual information or book knowledge; it has more to do with discernment, reflection, and intuition. The intuitive knowledge in question transforms the knower into the likeness of what he knows. self-knowledge is most important, and the realization of this comes after three stages.

The Three Stages of Knowing

self-realization will come about only after distinguishing between the surface of reality and the true reality that lies underneath. The first stage is hearing. You listen to sages and scriptures and you come to realize that your essential nature is being itself. Your second step is thinking. It is by prolonged, intensive introspection that you can become hyperaware of your own thought processes and language and how they might lead you astray.

For example, the words "me" or "my" imply a duality, a separation between the possessor and what is possessed. A person is misled to embrace this dual thinking when she uses other possessive language—such as "my body," "my mind," "my personality," all of which imply her separation from the world around her.

Further, even as almost everything about her physical self has changed over time, there is some enduring part of her that is unchanging. There is an enduring self, even as a surface, transient self undergoes change. The third step then becomes her identification with this enduring part of herself, as opposed to her surface self. In this way, she comes closer to her fuller self— the self that is identical with Brahman.

Bhakti Yoga: The Path to God Through Love

The road to God through knowledge may be a direct path for many seekers of wisdom, but it is also a steep path. The word *bhakti* means "to adore, honor, worship." In the Vedic tradition, going back to 1500 B.C.E., the religious practice of Hinduism relied on chanting the name of God and making offerings to various divinities. In current times, those who praise Krishna or some other manifestation of God might chant "Hare Krishna, Hare Krishna" repeatedly, which means "Praise Krishna."

The bhakti yogi believes that, "The utterance of the Lord's name completely destroys all sin." The *japa* discipline includes the repetitive recitation of the "mantra of the sixteen names," the "great mantra" for the japa of Krishna bhaktas: "Hare Rama Hare Rama Hare Rama Hare Rama Hare Krishna Hare Krishna Hare Krishna Hare Krishna."

Repetition of the divine name is essential for complete self-surrender to God. There are calamities aplenty in the world—Earthquakes, hurricanes, floods, plagues, famines, food scarcity—but there is no calamity that will not yield to the divine name. Therefore, for the good of India and the world at large, everyone should repeat and sing the divine name, both for worldly gains and otherworldly peace and happiness.

The yoga developed in the Bhagavad Gita was called devotional yoga; in bhakti yoga, our lives are steered less by reason than by emotion, with the strongest emotion by far being love. The goal of bhakti yoga is to approach God with love and devotion. Perhaps because it draws on the emotion found in all persons, bhakti yoga is the most popular of the four yogas.

In jnana yoga, God is the infinite, a constant being beneath the fluctuations of day-to-day reality. This God is impersonal—or transpersonal;

but to the bhakti aspirant, feelings bear greater importance than thoughts.

Even if yoga's steps don't lead you to a union with God, they may aid you in uniting with the task at hand, whatever it happens to be. All of us require concentration—and at times supreme concentration—to achieve our separate ends. Yoga can aid and abet the achievement of those objectives; in this sense, yoga is a supremely practical enterprise.

It is the bhakti yogi's goal not to identify with God, but to adore God. If you love God dearly, love God only, and love for no ulterior reason but for love's sake alone, you can know joy. But this is an objective only—how can you achieve it? At first it may seem like a very difficult thing to do; and yes, you must undertake a few measures to fully attain love of God.

One of these measures is to enter Hinduism's myths and symbols. It could be that a symbol of Krishna might remind you of God's awe-inspiring power. Stories and legends about the gods impart ideals and morals, hopefully leading readers to imitate what they learn. Prayer, meditation, purifying, worshiping, devotion, reading—all of these activities should move us in God's direction.

Three Bhakti Yoga Activities

Religious author Houston Smith maintains that three activities in particular may aid and abet our approach to God. The bhakta's approach should involve *japam*, ringing the changes on love, and the worship of one's chosen ideal. Japam is the practice of repeating God's name. If you keep the name of the Lord before you, the very repetition of the sound can penetrate the subconscious mind and fill it with holiness. Whatever the swirl of your daily activities happens to be, the name of the Lord can be summoned to mind and kept on your lips.

Ringing the changes on love is the second activity, encouraging all bhaktas to behold the vast differences in the kinds of love in our lives. Love takes many forms. There is the love of a parent for children, which of necessity includes a spirit of protectiveness. The reverse, of course, is not true; a child's love is shaped around his dependency on his parents. The love between friends can be platonic or based on some kind of reciprocity, or take any number of other forms. This contrasts with the conjugal love between woman and man. Awe may describe the feelings of a servant for a master, while the master may return this with a paternal spirit. A bhakta who understands these varieties of love may well increase his love of God as a consequence.

Finally, one involved in bhakti yoga will worship God in the form of his chosen ideal or *ishta*. *Ishta devata*—or "desired divinity"—is an invaluable concept in theistic Hinduism. Each person has a divinity that best suits his personal inclinations and way of life. It is highly likely that he will choose an ishta devata according to the sectarian mode of Hinduism he grew up with.

Thus, one who grew up in a Shaivite family will likely choose a Shaivite deity to worship. Shiva is the Destroyer, Nataraja—Lord of the Dance— known to all India, since his form is found in most temples. He is also the Lord of Chaos, who destroys the universe with his final dance. But the name Shiva means "the beneficent one," and he can just as easily dance that same universe back into existence again if he so desires.

It is not unusual for worshippers to choose divinities outside their sectarian context. Thus, it is not impossible for a Bengali Vaishnavite (devotee of Vishnu) to choose Kali, the fierce goddess, as ishta devata. Whatever the choice, the most effective ishta will be one of God's incarnations, for the human heart is naturally turned to loving people.

Karma Yoga: The Way to God Through Work

A last way of approaching God is through work. If you work not only to survive but also because you enjoy your work, you can find God in this manner. What is required is that the work takes you in a direction toward God, not away from God. Indian philosophy contrasts the *karma kanda* (action aspect) of tradition with *jnana kanda* (the knowledge aspect).

The term "karma" refers to the law of action. According to this ethical concept, the actions or karmas of people in their current births shape their lives in their next births. Another sense of the term comes from the Bhaga-vad Gita, where karma yoga refers to a yoga of action in the world without regard to its fruits. To find a famous exemplar of this concept you needn't look further than Mohandas K. Gandhi. Gandhi embodied karma yoga and made the term well known, since his political actions were undertaken in the name of karma yoga.

But everything depends on how the yogi approaches work. One possibility is to approach work reflectively; another possibility is to approach it in a spirit of love. The first mode would be jnana yoga, the second, bhakti. What difference will it make?

Hinduism proclaims that every action directed toward the external world reacts on the doer. For instance, if you performed all work for your private benefit, you have only succeeded in bolstering your own ego and increased your distance from God. On the other hand, selfless action takes you out of yourself and toward the divine.

The mode of the philosopher is one of detachment. A person acting in jnana mode accepts the notion of an infinite being at the center of her being, rather than a providential father.

In bhakti mode, personal rewards are not first and foremost in the mind; instead, acts are now performed as a service to God. Moreover, when this working for God takes hold of the individual, she is transformed; she is powered by God's will and prompted by God's energy. A spirit of "Thou art the Doer, I am the instrument" imbues the individual.

Yoga Today

What is the meaning of the term "yoga" as it is popularly used today? First, how much has the yoga landscape changed over the last two millennia? The short answer is that much is the same, and there are some differences. The practices for increasing *sattvic*, or pure, qualities are known collectively as yoga. Yoga, the tradition with which Sankhya is paired, still sets out the principles of discipline required for achieving liberation.

The methods of yoga are called *sadhanas*. The different methods to achieve liberation remain, such as hatha yoga, kundalini yoga, mantra yoga, jnana yoga, karma yoga, and bhakti yoga. The means to the ends, therefore, are much the same as ever.

Yoga developed in special ways, especially by the tantric schools of the Middle Ages. The "yoga of dissolution," laya yoga, is often identified with hatha yoga, based on ancient Indian physiological notions that play a major part in the form of yoga taught by Western practitioners. Hatha yoga emphasizes the importance of physical means, such as special acrobatic exercises and very difficult postures, and sometimes advocates sexual union as a means of salvation.

Kundalini Yoga and Chakras

In kundalini yoga, the body is thought to exist within a field of energy that is most concentrated in the seven major *chakras* (wheels), that is, subtle centers along the chief vein of the body, known as *susumna* (channel).

In the first chakra, *muladhara*, the lowest "wheel," behind the genitals, is the *kundalini*, the "serpent power," which is generally in a quiescent state. By yogic practices, however, the kundalini is awakened, rises through the susumna, passes through all the seven "wheels" of psychic force, and unites with the topmost, sahasrara. By awakening and raising his kundalini, the yogi gains spiritual power, and by uniting it with sahasrara, he wins salvation.

The *sadhaka,* or devotee, in the tantric rite imagines the divine power (*shakti*) asleep within him, coiled away like a sleeping serpent (kundalini) at the root of his spine. While carefully controlling his inhalations, the sadhaka breaths deeply first through one nostril and then the other (*pranayama*), to clear the way for the kundalini in the spiritual channel. He then thinks of her as aroused; she lifts her head and begins to move up the susumna, touching a number of "centers" or "lotuses" (the chakras) regarded as the seats of the elements of the body. The muladhara is the seat of "Earth"; it is pictured as a crimson lotus of four petals.

The second chakra, called *svadhisthana* (Shakti's own abode), is at the level of the genitals and is the seat of the element water. It is often depicted as a vermilion lotus of six petals.

The third chakra lies at the level of the navel and is known as *manipura*, the city of the lustrous gem, so called because it is the seat of element fire. It is sometimes pictured as a blue-black lotus of ten petals. According to the psychology of this system of lotuses, muladhara, svadhisthana, and manipura are the centers from which the lives of most people are governed.

Superior Centers

The rest of the centers are superior centers. The fourth chakra lies at the level of the heart, and is the lotus in which the first realization of the divinity of the world is experienced. Here, the god reaches down to touch his devotee.

The fifth chakra, ether, the ultimate element in the universe, is a smoky purple hue and is made of sixteen petals, at the level of the throat. This is the *visuddha* chakra, which means "the completely purified."

The sixth chakra is called the third eye. Beyond this point between the eyebrows, is the lotus of command (*ajna*), where the mind is free of limitations. This is when the devotee sees the Lord. It is considered the center that manifests the power of the will and allows spiritual insight.

The seventh chakra, the crown, is considered the seat of cosmic consciousness. In its fully opened state, it is perceived as a thousand-petal lotus effulgent with light. The tantric worshipper is supposed to imagine himself as having purified his body by suffusing all the lotuses with the awakened kundalini in this way.

The awakened kundalini gives the yogi superhuman power and knowledge, and many yogis have practiced yoga for this rather than for salvation. Some adepts of this form of yoga have developed powers that cannot fully be accounted for by modern medical science and that cannot be explained away as subjective, but the physiological basis of laya and hatha yoga is certainly false; there is no physical kundalini, susumna or sahasrara.

As A. L. Basham exhorts, "The ancient mystical physiology of India needs study, not only by Indologists, but by open-minded biologists and psychologists, who may reveal the true secret of the yogi."

CHAPTER 3

Hinduism: History and Central Ideas

Hinduism is a Western term for the religious beliefs and practices of the vast majority of the people of India. Hinduism is one of the oldest religions in the world. It is also unique in that it lacks a single founder but grew over a span of some 4,000 years, drawing on the cultural movements of the Indian subcontinent.

The Evolution of Hindu Thought

Hinduism today stands as an endless, borderless amalgam, composed as it is of innumerable sects. It also lacks a well-defined ecclesiastical organization. Its two most general features are the caste system and the acceptance of the Vedas (meaning "wisdom" or "knowledge") as the most sacred scriptures.

FACT

Hinduism is not the strange religion it appears to be to some westerners; it is one of the oldest religions of the world and, according to a 2007 study, has about 886,279,172 adherents. Roughly 13 percent of the world's population and its followers reside in all the continents of the world.

A contemporary reader may ask, "Why is it worth learning about something as strange and far away as Hinduism?" Hinduism is also called Santana Dharma, a Sanskrit phrase meaning "the eternal law"; if that is true, then it is surely something that every human should be interested in.

FACT

Countries with sizable Hindu populations include India, Nepal, Bangladesh, Sri Lanka, Pakistan, Indonesia, Malaysia, Singapore, Mauritius, Fiji, Suriname, Guyana, Trinidad and Tobago, the United Kingdom, Canada, and the United States of America. Hinduism is not a religion that can be defined as *just* a religion; it is a way of life, and therefore, it is to be understood as a cultural and philosophical practice.

To understand people, one should understand people's respective religions, cultures, languages, political philosophies, ethical value systems, and so on. Unlike in the past, in the present global setting, countries and peoples are interwoven in many ways. Changes occurring in one part of the world affect the lives of other people all around the world. Hence, we need to know about others. There is no such thing as separation of religion and state in India because Hinduism encompasses all walks of life, so it is impossible to keep them apart. This pervasiveness with all the aspects of Indian life makes learning about this religion especially worthwhile.

A Philosophy and Feel for Hinduism

Hinduism is not just a religion with a long history. Nor is it just the religion that gave birth to Jainism and Buddhism. It is more than a set of dates and related ideas. Hinduism is also a different way of sensing and seeing reality. It is a different mindset, illustrated by evocative stories.

There is a symbolic story from the religious book known as the Upanishads, the most philosophical of the Hindu texts. In the following passage, a boy, Shvetaketu, is asking his father Uddalaka about the true nature of reality.

> *"My teachers must not have known this wisdom," the boy says, "for*
> *if they had known, how could they have failed to teach it to me?*
> *Please instruct me in this wisdom, father."*
> *"Yes, dear one, I will" replied the father.*
> *"In the beginning was only Being,*
> *One without a second*
> *Out of himself he brought forth the cosmos*
> *And entered into everything in it.*
> *There is nothing that does not come from him.*
> *Of everything he is the inmost Self.*
> *He is the truth; he is the Self supreme.*
> *You are that, Shvetaketu, you are that."*
>
> —Upanishads, 1.7–2.3

The boy desires to learn more, so the father instructs him in a more concrete way.

> *"Please, Father, tell me more about this Self."*
> *"Yes, dear one, I will," Uddalaka said.*
> *"Place this salt in water and bring it here Tomorrow morning."*
> *The boy did.*

"Where is that salt?" his father asked.
"I do not see it."
"Sip here. How does it taste?"
"Salty, Father."
"And here? And there?"
"I taste salt everywhere."
"It is everywhere, though we see him not.
There is nothing that does not come from him
Of everything he is the inmost Self.
He is the truth; he is the Self supreme.
You are that, Shvetaketu; you are that."

—Upanishads, 12.3–13.3

This salt-in-the-water analogy shows that Brahman is everywhere, in all things. Despite all of the variety in the world, one reality pervades all of it, just as salt is everywhere in the water.

The exchange between father and son instructs us about the spirituality through which Hindus perceive reality. To Hindu eyes, the most ordinary occurrences possess spiritual significance. The salt is there in the water, though we cannot see it. Reality, too, is all spiritual, alive with Brahman, this "Immense Being" (as he is called in some translations) part of each thing, without limit or boundaries. All of reality is one.

Images of Hinduism

Aside from being the world's oldest religion, aside from being the third largest religion, Hinduism is a way of seeing and a way of being. It is full of rituals. Just close your eyes and think of it and it conjures images of stone deities, depictions of elephants. We picture ordinary citizens practicing *puja*, or purification, at home or in the sacred waters of the Ganges.

Thinking of Hindusim, our minds might go to yogis, eyes closed, palms up, meditating in the lotus position. We might conjure Brahmin priests—the religious leaders, scholars, and philosophers of Hinduism—sitting cross-legged in orange robes, books open and studying. Or we might think of incense and candles in a Hindu temple.

Not all the exotic elements of the religion are visual; the ideas are rich, too. The idea of reincarnation reminds us of the cyclical nature of existence. We think of sacred cows, protected because they play an important role in traditional Hindu life. We learn of karma, that law of cause and effect produced by all human actions. We think of birth, death, and cremation, with human ashes being spread over sacred waters. We think of the caste system, that social hierarchy into which Hindus are born. We think of the "stages of life" that prescribe their behavior from the time they are students right through retirement and detachment from the material world. We think of thriving rituals and festivals, celebrated in India and in cities in the United States.

FACT

Hinduism is a broad, elastic term for the religious beliefs and customs that originated in India. The beliefs themselves are a rich blend of elements from the Indo-European culture brought by the Aryan invasions of 1500 B.C.E. onward, and from the indigenous pre-Aryan and Dravidian societies.

Because of its evolution over such a long period, Hinduism ranges over a landscape of religious beliefs and practices of unparalleled vastness, and it is neither dogmatic nor evangelical.

Because Hinduism lacks a creedal longitude and latitude, it has always seemed inclusive rather than exclusive. Despite its amorphous nature, despite a lack of a binding theological creed, Hindu consciousness is known by a family of elements. One of these elements is respect for the Vedas, the earliest Hindu sacred texts.

A History of Ancient India Before the Aryan Migration

Perhaps because Hinduism traces the beginning of some of its religious themes and forms to the third millennium B.C.E., it has drawn in and adopted many influences. As a result, no religion can claim to be as diverse and varied as Hinduism. Its scope ranges from a simple animism—the belief that every living creature, inanimate object, and wishful thought has a spirit—to some of the most elaborate philosophical systems. Hinduism's diversity is such that it allows for literally millions of major and minor gods, their temples, and their priests. As a consequence of this openness, the possible religious views for Hindus are virtually infinite.

Where and when did Hinduism begin? Did it have a founder like Jesus or Mohammad or Buddha? Unlike most of the other major religions of the world, Hinduism has no identifiable founder. However, there was a mythological founder, Brahma, of the Vedic religion, a denomination of Hinduism.

The word "Hindu" is as much geographical as anything else. It comes from the Sanskrit name for the river Indus, which flows through northern India. The word "Hinduism" is a generic term and did not come into popular use until the eighteenth century, coined by the British to simplify the work of the census takers.

FACT

In ancient times, the Indus river was called the Sindhu, but the Persians who eventually migrated to India called the river Hindu. They also came to call the land Hindustan and its inhabitants Hindus. So, the term applies generally to the religion of the people of India.

The British wanted to classify those who were not Christians, Muslims, Jains, Sikhs, or Buddhists as Hindus. Historically, this term is a Persian word referring to the people living around the Sindhu or Indus River. The Rig Veda mentions the land of the Indo-Aryans as Sapta Sindhu (the land of seven rivers in northwestern South Asia, one of them being the Indus River).

There are different denominations of Hinduism, such as Vedism, Brahmanism, Shaivism, Vaishnavism, Shaktism, Smartism, Tantrism, Lingayatism, and many other variations of local religious traditions. Some proponents of the religion take the source to mythological ages. Historically speaking, the Vedic religion evolved from 1500 B.C.E. Shaivite religion was practiced by the Dravidians from 2000 B.C.E.

Hinduism is most likely a synthesis of the religion that came into India with the migratory wave of Aryans in the second millennium B.C.E. and the indigenous religion of the native people. The resulting culture became classical Hinduism.

The first task is to describe pre-Aryan Indians. The problem is that it is not easy to know much about them. Prior to the 1920s, the only source that spoke of the pre-Aryan people was the Vedic literature of early Hinduism. Since this was the religious literature of the Aryans, it is decidedly biased, with negative references to India and its religions. The Indian people themselves were portrayed as uncivilized and barbaric.

The new evidence of the 1920s told a different story. It was then that excavations in northwestern India revealed complexes of cities along the Indus River. Indeed, as early as 2500 B.C.E., there were signs of an advanced civilization in the Indus Valley. This civilization—including smaller villages and cities—sprawled over 100 square miles of the region. By some estimates, it may be the largest political community prior to the Roman Empire. Cities were elaborate, laid out in rectangular blocks, with drainage systems, and some 40,000 people per city.

The advancement of the region was impressive. Homes, constructed of firebrick, were often two stories high and included bathrooms with running water. Adjacent to the cities were agricultural communities with irrigation systems. Further evidence of modern amenities is evident from the large granaries that existed for the storage and distribution of food.

Archaeological evidence reveals that pre-Aryan Indians of the third and second millennium B.C.E. had a written language. Unfortunately, their language has not been translated. As a result, much information about the everyday lives and religion of the native people remains hidden.

Other physical evidence—especially in the form of statues and amulets—reveals the images of fertility gods and goddesses. Some of the figures sit cross-legged, in the familiar lotus position of the practice of yoga and other forms of meditation. In sum, the picture that emerges of pre-Aryan India is not one of a primitive people living in an ancient backwater; rather, the pre-Aryans were urban and technologically advanced, and they furnished some of the religious content for latter-day Hinduism.

Aryan India

It would surprise many to learn that the word "Aryan" is of Sanskrit origin and means "the noble ones." It originally applied to the group that migrated to the Indus Valley in the second millennium from the region now known as Iran. The largest migratory waves of Aryans came into India between 1750 and 1200 B.C.E. It is hard to know whether the Aryans invaded and conquered the Indian culture or whether the pre-Aryan culture was already in decline.

"Aryan" conjures up images of blue-eyed, blond-haired males for the modern reader, due to Adolf Hitler calling people of this description his "master race." According to the Nazis, people fitting this physical description were historically superior; by contrast, Semitic Jews and Africans were deemed inferior, despite the lack of any historical or scientific evidence to support this view.

But Hitler didn't coin the term "Aryan," even in the modern era. It was current in the nineteenth century, applying at that time to a family of languages. Thereafter, it often appeared as an adjective to describe biological or racial units, but it has also been used to describe North Indians, Asians (at least from the west), and Europeans.

Little is known for sure of the Aryans, but references in the Vedic texts themselves suggests that the Aryans were nomadic herders, shepherding flocks. They were tribal and led by chieftains called *rajas*. By the sixth century B.C.E. they had settled in cities in the Indus valley and begun to build minor kingdoms.

In time, Aryan society was divided into three classes, or *varnas*. Sitting atop this pecking order were the Brahmins, a priestly set held in high regard for their knowledge. After the priests came the esteemed Kshatriyas, the chieftains and their loyal warriors. Commoners and merchants, known as Vaishyas, were subservient to the two classes above them. The Shudras, consisting of conquered pre-Aryans, were the fourth group. The Shudras did not enjoy full membership in society, since they were servants to the Aryans. These divisions originating with the Aryans would cut across Indian society for centuries to come.

Aryan Religion: Gateway to the Vedas

Vedic literature is probably the best sourcebook for an understanding of early Indian philosophy. But as authoritative as the Vedas are, even the best scholars are confused trying to separate the Aryan from the Indian contribution to the religion. After all, the Vedas were composed *after* the Aryan migration, not before it. Thus, we cannot ascertain what portions of these great scriptures are Aryan and what portions are pre-Aryan.

What can we know about the religion the Aryans brought with them? It seems to have been polytheistic and probably bore more than a little resemblance with the religions of other Indo-Europeans; comparisons have been made between the Aryan gods and those of Greece and Rome. The connection is a natural once, since the Aryans, like the Greeks, personified gods as natural forces and objects, such as the sun, the moon, and the fertility of the soil. A connection, then, between Hinduism and animism is likely.

Due to their nomadic ways, in the early years of their occupation, the Aryans built no temples to their gods; instead, they made animal sacrifices in open places. They also sacrificed dairy products like butter or milk, which was poured out to the gods. Also used in sacrifices was the juice of the soma plant. In ancient texts, this is described as a sacred plant, since it was sent to Earth by the god Indra.

Not only was the juice of the soma plant delicious, it was invigorating to whoever drank it and shared it with the gods. Since the time of the Aryans, people have speculated that the plant might have been a kind of mushroom capable of inducing hallucinations.

No doubt the most elaborate of all these primitive sacrifices was the horse sacrifice. It was believed that this sacrifice helped the ruler atone for past misdeeds and provided religious power to participants. It was also believed that the sacrifice helped rulers expand their territories, which made the idea attractive to Indian rulers.

The sacrifice commenced with releasing a young male horse to roam the countryside for one year. The ruler's attendants followed the horse, and if the horse covered any territory not in the domain of the ruler, that raja laid claim to that territory. When after a year the horse returned, some 600 other living beings—ranging from bees to elephants—were sacrificed to the gods. The sacred horse was strangled, and the rulers' wives participated in fertility rights with the carcass. It was then butchered and devoured by the ruler and his kin. One legend held that if a man performed 100 horse sacrifices, he would be master over all the gods and the universe. This rite belonged not only to the Aryans, but was performed as recently as the eighteenth century by an Indian ruler.

CHAPTER 4

Ancient Scriptures: The Vedas

"Veda" is a Sanskrit word meaning "wisdom" or "knowledge." The meanings are appropriate, since these were the oldest scriptures of Hinduism and also the most authoritative of the Hindu sacred texts. In fact, all later texts are considered to be mere commentary on the Vedas. For Hindus, they are the basic source for understanding the universe. Indeed, the Vedas are regarded as *sruti*, the products of divine revelation. In addition, the content of the hymns was influenced by the indigenous traditions of the Indus Valley and from legends born of the Aryan warrior aristocracy.

4

The Vedas

The Vedas developed from a group of sages and *rishis* (in the Vedic sense, a seer or inspired poet), who discovered the truths and realities that lie behind human existence and formulated a set of rules for good living. These rules, known as dharma and anti-dharma (*adharma*), are components of Hinduism. They are eternal truths and applicable to all times. The Vedas are highly developed mythology. These sacred texts are divided into two groups: *sruti* ("revealed ") and *smriti* ("remembered"), and were kept by people through oral tradition, from one generation to the next.

People disagree over what is included in the Vedas. Some believe the Vedas comprise only the ancient collection of hymns to the Aryan gods. Others believe they comprise the entire literature, including the hymns as well as the later additions of the Brahmanas, Aranyakas, and the Upanishads.

Estimates about the time the Vedas were written vary widely, with some scholars maintaining they were recorded prior to 2000 B.C.E., before the arrival of the Aryans, and were still being developed as late as the sixth century B.C.E. Other estimates contend that the Vedas were composed anywhere from 1500 to 400 B.C.E. They were composed and transmitted orally before they were committed to writing, and centuries lapsed between their origin and completion. The four basic collections of Vedas include the Rig Veda, Yajur Veda, Sama Veda, and Atharva Veda.

The Four Vedas

The earliest written document is the Rig Veda, a collection of 1,017 Sanskrit poems addressed to various gods, as well as three other collections (*Samhitas*) —the Sama, Yajur, and Atharva Vedas—a collection of hymns used in the ritual services, all written in archaic poetic texts.

The Rig Veda, also known as The Veda of Verses, is the first portion of the Vedas and consists of 1,028 hymns covering 10,600 stanzas of praise to the nature gods, particularly Agni—the fire god—and Indra—the warrior god.

The purpose of the Vedas was to teach people their dharma—their conduct and duty in the present life. The Vedas also serve a special purpose: They are used for sacrifices. These hymns are to be intoned with special tunes, and the pronunciations of the words must be accurate, since they are addressed to special gods thanking the deities and asking for material favors.

In the Vedic cosmology, the universe is divided into three parts—Earth, atmosphere, and heaven—and the gods are assigned to these parts. The gods mentioned in the Rig Veda are related to forces of nature: Varuna is related to the heavens; Usha is the goddess of dawn; and Surya is related to the sun. Indra is the most important of all atmospheric gods.

In later years, commentaries on these hymns, called Brahmanas, were written. Still later, in the sixth century B.C.E., mystical philosophical works were developed that differed from previous Brahmanas and Samhitas. These works are called Vedanta Upanishads. The Bhagavad Gita (a later addition to the Upanishads) and the Upanishads themselves form the basis for the sacred scriptures of Hinduism. The Vedas and Upanishads are the foremost scriptures in antiquity, both in authority and importance. Other major scriptures include the Tantras, the sectarian Agamas, the Puranas (legends), and the epics Mahabharata and Ramayana. The Bhagavad Gita, which comes later, is a treatise from the Mahabharata and is sometimes called a summary of the spiritual teachings of the Vedas.

FACT

One Aryan religious practice was to drink the juice of the soma, a deified plant. After Indra and Agni, this is the most important god in the Rig Veda. One verse about the soma reads: "I, of good understanding, have partaken of the sweet potion, the well-minded, the best finder of bliss, which all the gods and mortals, calling it 'honey,' seek."

Creation in the Vedas

What are the most important traditional Hindu views on the origin and structure of the universe, of physical reality? The origin of the universe and man is found in the Hindu mythical realm, and there are several stories depicting the creation, some of which overlap. These views were expressed by rishis of the Vedic period. In later years, embellishments were added to these stories.

The Vedic text on "Hymn of Creation" contains the most ancient traces of cosmogenic speculation. The Rig Veda poets began to wonder about creation, which was not adequately explained by the mythology of the time.

The Golden Embryo

One story suggests that the universe originated in a "golden embryo." In the beginning, the universe was all waters, and God wanted to divide them. In the division of the water, there appeared a golden egg, and this egg produced the first man, Prajapati, "the Lord of Beings," later called Brahma. Prajapati created gods in the sky with light, and *asura* (demons) in the Earth with darkness, thereby creating day and night. His breath brought about air (sky), a woman, a cow, a mare, and so on. He created power of reproduction into his self; he divided himself into two persons, male and female. They copulated and produced sons. She became a cow and he became a bull. These two copulated and produced calves. She became a mare and he became a horse, and they produced colts. This story went on and on, and thus, the whole Earth was populated with animals. This is the second story of creation.

The Yajur Veda, the Sama Veda, and the Atharva Veda

The Rig Veda is the most important, but the other three Vedas are also significant. Each of the Vedic books is subdivided into four parts. Each contains a section of hymns to the gods, which recall the period when statements about the gods were memorized, chanted, and passed on from one generation to another; ritual instructions (Brahmanas), in which worshipers are given instructions about how to perform their sacrifices; the so-called Forest Treatises (Aranyakas), which give instructions to hermits in their religious pursuits; and the Upanishads, composed of philosophical materials.

Again, it is believed that the Vedas are revealed to the sages by God. The other possibility is that the Vedas revealed themselves to the seers or *mantradrasta* of the hymns. The Vedas were compiled by Vyasa Krishma Dwaipayana around the time of the Lord Krishna, around 1500 B.C.E. Just as the gospels have four writers, there are four primary seers—Atri, Kanwa, Vashistha, and Vishwamitra.

The Yajur Veda

The second book is the Yajur Veda, known as the Veda of Sacrificial Texts, a collection of sacrificial rites. It is also sometimes called a book of rituals. Simply put, it is a liturgical collection including the materials to be recited during sacrifices to the gods.

The Yajur Veda serves as a practical guidebook for the priests who execute sacrificial acts, simultaneously muttering the prose prayers and the sacrificial formulas (yajus). It is similar to ancient Egypt's Book of the Dead. There are no less than six complete recensions of the Yajur Veda—Madyandina, Kanva, Taittiriya, Kathaka, Maitrayani, and Kapishthala.

The Yajur Veda inspires humans to walk on the path of karma (deeds), so it is also called Karma Veda. It comprises hymns taken from the Rig Veda and adds explanatory notes in prose form. It contains fifty chapters each, which are subdivided into *kandikas*, or paragraphs, numbering 1,975 mantras.

FACT

The contents of the Vedas include the Principle of Dharma (ethics or duties), which are closely associated with the Principle of Karma—duty in life (action and subsequent reaction) according to one's caste for the betterment of society—and the principle of *samsara* (the continuing cycle of birth, life, death, and rebirth).

The Sama Veda

The third book, the Sama Veda, is also known as The Veda of Chants or Book of Songs. It contains the required melodies and chants recited by priests for special sacrifices. It is a collection of spiritual hymns, used as musical notes, which were almost completely drawn from the Rig Veda and have no distinctive lessons of their own. One Vedic scholar said that if the Rig Veda is the word, Sama Veda is the song or the meaning; if Rig Veda is the knowledge, Sama Veda is its realization; if Rig Veda is the wife, the Sama Veda is her husband.

The Sama Veda resembles the Rig Veda. Most of its mantras are taken from the Rig Veda, but the order is modified for chanting. It is divided into two books called *ankas*. It has twenty-one chapters and contains 1,875 mantras. These mantras are addressed to Agni, Indra, and Sama.

The Atharva Veda

The Atharva Veda is the Veda of the Fire Priest, consisting of occult formulas and spells. This Book of Spells, the last of the Vedas, is completely different from the other three Vedas and is next in importance to Rig Veda with regard to history and sociology.

A different spirit pervades this Veda. Its hymns are of a more diverse character than the Rig Veda and are simpler in language. In fact, many scholars do not consider it part of the Vedas at all. This Veda consists of spells and charms prevalent at the time it was written, and it portrays a clearer picture of the Vedic society.

Gods of the Rig Veda

The Vedas include basic descriptions and mythology of the various Aryan and pre-Aryan gods, but there are more hymns devoted to Indra than to any other god. Of the 1,028 hymns of the Rig Veda, no fewer than a quarter are dedicated to Indra.

Indra is the god of the thunderbolt, clouds, and rain, the ruler of heaven. Indra is also significant as the conqueror of Vitra, the personification of chaos. Indra slays other demons, but preserves humans and gods. He quenches his thirst with soma. Here is a sampling of the verses to Indra; the first pays homage to his heroism:

> *I.32*
>
> 1 *Now I shall proclaim the heroic feats of Indra, which the holder of the thunderbolt performed first: he slew the serpent, bored after the waters, split open the flanks of the mountains*

Several verses that follow extol his might:

> 3 *Desiring manly strength, he chose the Soma: he drank the extract in three brown vessels. Maghavan took his missile, the thunderbolt, slew him, the first-born of serpents.*
>
> 4 *When, Indra, you slew the first-born of serpents and then reduced to naught the wiles of the wily, causing to be born the sun, the heaven and the dawn, since then you have found no enemy at all.*

Agni: The God of Fire

Since the Vedas offer varying explanations of the beginnings of reality, many passages address the gods who function actively in this. Agni, the god of fire, is mentioned in over 200 hymns. Agni is also the god of the priests and the priest of the gods. He leads the gods in proper sacrifice and, as the god of fire, brings the burnt sacrifices to the other gods.

> *I.1.*
>
> 7 *You we approach every day, O Agni, you who gleam in the darkness, with devotion and bearing homage:*
>
> 8 *—you who are of the sacrifices, guardian of the Order, brightly shining, growing in your own abode.*
>
> 9 *Be accessible unto us, O Agni, as a father unto his son! Accompany us for our well-being.*

Gods such as Vishnu and Rudra—later known as Shiva, the god of death and destruction—are also mentioned briefly in the Vedas. But they did not possess the importance they would later have in Hinduism, when they became two of the most popular gods.

FACT

Many verses in the Vedas praise the might of Indra, considered the most important deity of the hymns. This is evident in the conflict with the demon Vitra: "With his thunderbolt, his great weapon, Indra slew Vitra, the arch-Vitra, the shoulderless; like a tree-trunk split asunder with an axe, the serpent lay flat on the ground."

In thinking of Agni, the god of fire, you should bear in mind that "agni" in Sanskrit means "fire." In the course of the rites, Agni accepts sacrifices and delivers to the gods because he is the messenger from and to the other gods. In art, he is depicted as possessing two or seven hands, two heads, and three legs. He has seven fiery tongues, thus he is also called Saptajithva (having seven tongues). He rides a ram or a chariot pulled by goats, or, rarely, by parrots.

Varuna: The God of the Sky

Varuna is a god of the sky, rain, and the celestial ocean. He is also the god of law and of the underworld. He is more concerned about the moral and social well-being of men. He is identified with Mitra, the god of oath. In the Rig Veda, he is entwined with Indra.

The Atharva Veda portrays Varuna as omniscient, catching liars as he has the stars of the sky for eyes. Varuna is classified as an asura in the Rig Veda. In later years, Varuna becomes the god of oceans and rivers and keeper of the souls of the drowned. Thus, he becomes the god of the dead and can grant immortality. Varuna may be compared with Poseidon in Greek mythology.

CHAPTER 5

Ancient Scriptures: The Upanishads

For those whose appetites run more to philosophy than to hymns about the gods, there are the Upanishads. The Upanishads are the fourth section of each of the Vedas. The word "Upanishads" means "sitting near," as in being near enough to listen to your sage or master. The conversations in the Upanishads took place between gurus and their students as they sat and ruminated over the philosophical implications of the Vedas.

Vedanta: The End of the Vedas

There are reasons for the transition from the Vedas to the Upanishads. During the Vedic period, the rituals consisted of sacrifices; they became so elaborate that only rich people could afford them. As Sanskrit (the refined language) was not used or understood by the masses, the Vedic religion became the exclusive milieu of the rich and priestly class of people, thus losing the following of the masses. The priestly class made the rituals too cumbersome and used the legal system—Manusmrti—to regulate society; Brahmanism replaced the Vedic religion, and the masses were excluded from the Vedic gods and the sacrifices. As a result of these two problems, the common people lost their connection to the religion.

FACT

There are about 200 Upanishads, ranging in length from one to fifty pages. About fourteen, or less than 10 percent, of these are known as principal Upanishads. The earliest likely originated in the ninth century B.C.E.

Opposition to the Vedic religion came from two directions. The common people did not like the hierarchical structure of the society—the caste system—imposed on them; they also opposed the hold the priestly class had on the religion. This social unrest resulted in the rise of Buddhism and Jainism during the lifetimes of Gautama Buddha and Mahavira.

Buddha's doctrine of universal charity, liberty, equality, and fraternity was increasingly attractive to the masses. Buddhism and Jainism assailed the very core of Vedic religion, and Brahmanism was faced with the difficult dilemma of recognizing and assimilating the current popular cults and creeds or facing extinction. To survive, Brahmanism had to expand; otherwise, it risked shrinking numbers of adherents, and eventual death.

The designation of Upanishads (Approaches) as the end of Veda (also Vedanta), indicates both their place in the sequence of Vedic literature and their position in the canon of Hindu scriptures. In a sense, Vedanta is the summary of Vedic religion. There is an important principle that atman and Brahman are identical and undifferentiated. The principle contained in the

Upanishads is encapsulated in the formula "that art thou." "That" stands for universal Brahman, and "thou" stands for individual atman.

The following are the main ideas of Vedanta:

- God is one, without a second, absolute and indivisible. God assumes various personal forms to reveal itself to us.
- All of the incarnations (manifestations of God on Earth) are actual embodiments of Divinity.
- There are no accidents in the cosmic universe; human destiny is governed by the law of cause and effect.
- We are born on Earth repeatedly to finish the unfinished work of realizing our divinity.
- There is a higher state of consciousness that can be achieved in this human birth.
- There are many ways to achieve union with God: through the intellect, emotions, actions, and the will.

A special type of Vedanta, Adavaita Vedanta, needs some more explanation.

Advaita Vedanta

This Vedantic nondualism is a subschool of the Vedanta. The word "Advaita" essentially refers to the identity of the self (atman) and the whole (Brahman). The key source texts for all schools of Vedanta are the Prasthanatrayi, the canonical texts consisting of the Upanishads, the Bhagavad Gita, and the Brahma Sutras. The first person to consolidate the principles of Advaita was Adi Shankara (or Sankara), and the first historical proponent was Gaudapada, the guru of Shankara's guru Bhagavatpada.

Vedanta is considered the summary of the Vedas or an appendix to the Vedas; it did not bring about an end to Hinduism, but acted as a bridge between the Vedic and modern Hindu traditions. The developments that followed Vedanta were Puranas, Agamas, and the epics Ramayana and Mahabharata. Agama literature was the most suitable for making images.

Although this assertion of the ultimate identity of Brahman and atman seems to be the dominating theme of the Upanishads, there are other ways to interpret the relationship between the two principles. One of the Upanishads, Svetasvatara, speaks of Brahman as God, making a distinction between this and the external world. In addition to this theistic interpretation, there is also a movement toward pantheism, a tendency to think of the natural universe and the individual soul as God.

The Upanishads are a collection of more than 100 Hindu sacred texts composed in Sanskrit. In content, these texts are a distillation of the teachings of the Vedas and Brahmanas, or commentaries on the hymns and rituals of the Vedas. Therefore, they are known as the Vedanta, or end of the Vedas.

The Nature of the Upanishads

The Upanishads are more philosophical and mystical in character than the Vedas. In the Upanishads, scholars observe for the first time a concept of a single, supreme God (Brahman) who is knowable by the human self (atman).

Another school of thought disagrees, saying that polytheism pervades the earlier Vedic material, with its stress on the proper manner of worshipping many gods. By way of contrast, the Upanishads are monistic; that is, all reality is one, not many. This reality is an impersonal being known as Brahman. All other entities that exist in nature—and even beyond nature—are a manifestation of this omnipresent Brahman. Trees, sky, Earth, water, spiritual entities—all things material and immaterial are not diverse, but express a single reality: Brahman.

This philosophical monism of the Upanishads is not only an exercise in metaphysics—that branch of philosophy that studies the true nature of reality—but epistemology, too. Epistemology is the branch of philosophy that involves the study of knowledge. In the way of knowing that pertains to Brahman, the highest kind of knowledge is to recognize that only Brahman is real. By logical implication, all that is not Brahman is unreal.

Here, the concept of *maya* rears its head. To be in maya is to be laboring under an illusion, the illusion that Brahman and the rest of reality are separate. No object, not even our own selves, is separate from Brahman. The greatest illusion is not understanding that.

This emphasis on philosophy, in this case monism, sets the Upanishads apart from the Vedas. In the Vedas, the stress was on how to worship the various Aryan gods by means of sacrifice, but the Upanishads emphasize dispassionate meditation on the ultimate nature of reality.

According to the Upanishads, the proper diagnosis of our human illness is that we live in ignorance (*avidya*) of the true nature of reality, which is but another way of saying that we live and breathe in maya, or illusion. The prescription for this philosophical illness is to arrive at true knowledge. In Hinduism, liberation only comes with right thinking.

Much of this philosophy is a metaphysical search for Brahman, the absolute ground of all being. "Brahman" is a Sanskrit word meaning "the eternal, imperishable, absolute." This being is also unknowable and has no past, present, or future. Brahman is also impersonal, not completely unlike the god of the deists at the time of the European Enlightenment. In fact, "Brahman" also means "ever growing."

To illustrate the idea that all is Brahman, consider this verse from the Shvetashvatara Upanishad:

> *All this is full. All that is full.*
> *From fullness, fullness comes.*
> *When fullness is taken from fullness,*
> *Fullness still remains.*

In short, if we remove all the materials and living things from the universe, strip away all its furniture, and empty it of all being, fullness will still be left behind. That is because even without material objects, there will always be Brahman.

Separateness Is an Illusion

If all of reality is one, then the idea that things are separate is an illusion. The Shvetashvatara Upanishad emphasizes the idea that separateness is an illusion.

It proceeds as follows:

[1]
1 What is the cause of the cosmos? Is it Brahman?
From where do we come? By what live?
Where shall we find peace at last?
What power governs the duality
Of pleasure and pain by which we are driven?
2 Time, nature, necessity, accident,
Elements, energy, intelligence—
None of these can be the First Cause
They are effects, whose only purpose is
To help the self rise above pleasure and pain.
3 In the depths of meditation, sages
Saw within themselves the Lord of Love,
Who dwells in the heart of every creature.
Deep in the hearts of all he dwells, hidden
Behind the gunas of law, energy,
And inertia. He is One. He it is
Who rules over time, space, and causality.
4 The world is the wheel of God, turning round
And round with all living creatures upon its rim.
5 The world is the river of God,
Flowing from him and flowing back to him.
6 On this ever-revolving wheel of life
The individual self goes round and round
Through life after life, believing itself
To be a separate creature, until
It sees its identity with the Lord of Love

And attains immortality in the indivisible whole.
7 He is the eternal reality, sing
The scriptures, and the ground of existence.
Those who perceive him in every creature
Merge in him and are released from the wheel
Of birth and death.
8 The Lord of Love holds in his hand the world,
Composed of the changing and the changeless,
The manifest and the unmanifest.
The separate self, not yet aware of the Lord,
Goes after pleasure, only to become
Bound more and more, When it sees the Lord,
There comes an end to its bondage.
9 Conscious spirit and unconscious matter
Both have existed since the dawn of time,
With maya appearing to connect them,
Misrepresenting joy as outside us.
When all these three are seen as one, the Self
Reveals his universal form and serves
As an instrument of the divine will.
10 All is change in the world of the senses,
But changeless is the supreme Lord of Love.
Meditate on him, be absorbed in him,
Wake up from this dream of separateness.
11 Know God and all fetters will fall away.
No longer identifying yourself
With the body, go beyond birth and death.
All your desires will be fulfilled in him.
Who is One without a second.
12 Know him to be enshrined in your heart always.
Truly there is nothing more in life to know.
Meditate and realize that this world
Is filled with the presence of God.

All Is Brahman

The underlying monism of the Upanishads says that all of the living beings that inhabit the world are manifestations of Brahman. These living things bear souls (atman) that, when taken together, make up Brahman. The world of senses (tenth stanza) tells us of the separateness of the world. But to see the phenomenal world as separate is to see the world in an illusory fashion. To see Brahman is to see one, not many; to see changeless being, not superficial differences; to see unity, not separation.

The ultimate knowledge for all individuals is the knowledge of Brahman, the principle of the universe. The world is not dual, and this realization is the beginning of wisdom.

> *Whoever sees all beings in the soul*
> *And the soul in all beings*
> *Does not shrink away from this.*
> *In whom all beings have become one with the knowing soul*
> *what delusion or sorrow is there for the one who sees unity?*
> *It has filled all.*
> *It is radiant, incorporeal, invulnerable,*
> *Without tendons, pure, untouched by evil.*
> *Wise, intelligent, encompassing, self-existent,*
> *It organizes objects throughout eternity.*

Brahman is a state of pure transcendence that cannot be grasped by thought or speech; hence Sri Ramskrishna's statement, "No tongue has ever defiled Brahman." The Vedic utterance "Kham Brahm" ("All is Brahman") means that Brahman alone exits, while we project upon it an imaginary world of motions, like superimposing a snake on a rope; a person who sees a snake while looking at the rope is being deceived by his senses.

Our Spiritual Illness

The greatest spiritual ill of human beings is that they fail to recognize reality for what it is. "Those who worship ignorance enter blinding darkness," says the Upanishads. The ignorance might best be illustrated by the parable of the tiger.

The tiger was orphaned as a cub and reared by goats. For his entire life, he believed he was a goat, even eating grass and bleating like a goat. Then one day he met another tiger who took him to a pool of water, and the first tiger saw his true image in the reflection of the water. The second tiger urged him to eat meat for the first time. Soon, he realized his true tiger nature.

Similarly, human beings are often deceived about their true nature. If so, they are living in maya. It is the task of religion to reveal the divine within us, and the connectedness of all human beings and living things.

CHAPTER 6

Central Concepts of Hinduism: Karma and Samsara

After the completion of the Upanishads, the inter-connected doctrines of karma and samsara became prominent in Hindu thinking and persist even today. Both have to do with a philosophy of action and the results of that action. According to the ethical concept of karma (often spelled kharma), the actions or karmas of individuals in their current births shape their lives in their next births. This is connected to reincarnation, or the cycles of lives. Souls are believed to cycle through human or animal lives until they are liberated and merge with a higher reality.

Karma

The Sanskrit word "karma" comes from a root that means "to do or act." The law of karma says that people reap what they sow. In essence, the law of karma is a law of justice that implies that every thought or deed, whether good or bad, counts in determining how a person will be born in his next life on Earth.

The idea of karma is that every thought, word, or deed will influence whether individuals achieve liberation or will have to repeat the cycle of birth and death. Karma might be understood as the spiritual or ethical residue of every action; in other words, beyond its external, visible effects, every action has a deep impact on our spiritual relationship.

At the dawn of Indian philosophy, Indians came to believe that every action and every thought had a consequence, which would show up in the present life or in a succeeding one. Most Indian sects believed karma operated as an automatic moral sanction, ensuring the evildoer suffered and the righteous prospered.

A person with bad karma could suffer being reborn many times into lower castes of humans—or even lower animals—and then could not be released until she had been reborn in the Brahmin, or priestly, caste. The doctrine that traces back to the Upanishads maintains that all living creatures are responsible for their karma. To be more specific, they are responsible for their actions and the effects of their actions. They themselves can control their release from the cycle of birth and rebirth.

Karma and Good Qualities

In our own time, when an individual is described as talented, kind, or intelligent, it is believed he has genetics or his environment to thank. But ancient thinkers preferred to think that a person possessed or lacked particular qualities due to choices he made in past lives.

A person's good qualities were attributed to good actions he had taken in a past life. On the other hand, a person possessing bad qualities—such as hatred of others, antisocial tendencies, or even criminal behavior—was also the product of his past choices. Every thought, word, and action—and even nonaction—was believed to have deep effects on a person's spiritual relationships.

FACT

Jawaharal Nehru, the first prime minister of India, wrote in his autobiography, *The Discovery of India,* "The environment in which I have grown up takes the soul (or rather the *atma*) and a future life, and the *karma* theory of cause and effect, and reincarnation for granted. I have been affected by this and so, in a sense, am favorably disposed toward these assumptions."

On the one hand, karma stresses recurrence—continual renewal and rebirth. On the other hand, the doctrine of the identity of atman and the Brahman stresses the permanent and unchanging. This apparent contradiction between the two concepts was solved by the understanding that the cycle of rebirth is caused by ignorance of the true nature of the self and the failure to realize that it never changes.

QUESTION?

What is the Hindu concept of moksha?
In Hinduism, moksha is the release of the soul from a cycle of rebirths. It is one of the four acceptable goals of life, according to Hinduism. But for people seeking spiritual advancement, it is the ultimate goal of life.

Emancipation becomes, therefore, a process of coming to an awareness of that state of being that is beyond process, the identity of atman and Brahman. To have that intuitive knowledge is to become immortal, for "knowing All, he becomes All." While in one sense it is true to say that this search is defined in terms of escape from the cycle of rebirth, on a higher level it is to be understood as the realization of the soul's true nature.

You must recall that the ultimate goal of life, according to Hinduism, was to attain moksha, instead of going back to human life on Earth. This being the case, a person's actions must be pure in order for those actions to have pure effects.

Some sects in ancient times appear to have believed that every soul must travel through a fixed number of births. One text puts the number at 8,400,000. The Ajivika sect believed that these births were inevitable; a person could reach liberation only after they were all completed.

Samsara

Samsara is the round or cycle of birth and rebirth that all Hindus are subject to in the Hindu worldview. Each person at the time of death possesses a karmic account balance; whether the actions are good or bad determines that agent's future destiny.

The literal meaning of the word "samsara" is "to wander across." It signifies that, in Indian thought, a person's life force does not pass on with the death of the body, but instead wanders across. That is, the life force migrates to another time and body, where it continues to live.

An illustration of the interrelation of the concepts of karma and samsara occurs in the Bhagavad Gita (Chapter IX, verses 30–31). Krishna says: "Even he with the worst karma who ceaselessly meditates on me quickly loses the effects of his past actions. Becoming a high-souled being, he soon attains perennial peace. Know this for certain: the devotee who puts his trust in me never perishes."

The term samsara also finds a home in Jainism, Buddhism, and Sikhism. To a Western way of thinking, this is known as reincarnation. Reincarnation carries with it a burden; the agent will have to live through generations over and over again. This is contrary to the goals of Indian religions, which stress that individuals must break the cycle of karma and samsara to be free of the burden of life. This release from life is the goal of life, and is called moksha.

In *Autobiography of a Yogi*, Paramahansa Yogananda writes, "Life by life man progresses (at his own pace be it ever so erratic) toward the goal of his own apotheosis. Death, no interruption in this onward sleep, simply offers man the more congenial environment of an astral world in which to purify his dross."

Such spiritual release is only possible when an individual has a true knowledge of the illusion of life. As it's written in the Svetasvatara Upanishad, "By knowing God man is free from all bonds." Atman, or self, returning to God is overcoming a separation. The doctrine of Brahman-Atman recognizes that self and God are ultimately a unity.

Karma and Dharma

Good karma is created by obeying one's dharma, or larger ethical and religious duty. Humans are reminded that the solution to human problems, according to Hinduism, is in the hands of the deities, whom devotees can cultivate through proper ritual action, or karma.

Of the relationship between karma and samsara, Paramahansa Yogananda is full of insight:

> *Various great Jain teachers of India have been called tirthakaras, "ford makers," because they reveal the passage by which bewildered humanity may cross over and beyond the stormy seas of samsara (the karmic wheel, the recurrence of lives and deaths). Samsara (literally, "a flowing with" the phenomenal flux) induces man to take*

the line of least resistance. "Whosoever therefore will be a friend of the world is the enemy of God." (James 4:4)

To become the friend of God, man must overcome the devils or evils of his own karma or actions that ever urge him to spineless acquiescence in the mayic delusions of the world. A knowledge of the iron law of karma encourages the earnest seeker to find the way of final escape from its bonds. Because the karmic slavery of human beings is rooted in the desires of maya-darkened minds, it is with mind control that the yogi concerns himself.

CHAPTER 7

Hinduism Creates Jainism

In the sixth century B.C.E., two exciting new schools of thought emerged. Jainism practiced reverence for life, celibacy, and moral conduct. It stressed a life of the mind and a turning from a life of bodily pleasures. The other school of thought was Buddhism. Siddhartha Gautama (563–483 B.C.E.) also sought a way of release that did not depend upon the teachings of the Vedas and the rituals of the Brahmins. His essential teaching was that enlightenment came from a monkish existence and nonattachment to anything of this world.

Jainism Carving Its Own Path

The name Jain derives from *jina* ("victory."); Jainism is literally the religion of the "victorious one"—a tag befitting any human being who by her own effort has conquered the lower passions and thus become free of attachments to things.

The Tirthankaras

Many Jains believe that their faith was founded by a lineage of twenty-four teacher-saints, known as the Tirthankaras. The Tirthankaras have offered human beings a means to cross the ocean of samsara (the cycle of existence), which was the subject of the last chapter. Chief among these Tirthankaras—in fact, he was the last of the twenty-four—was the Jain leader Mahavira, who lived 599–527 B.C.E. An ascetic, Mahavira was esteemed among his followers as one whose life and example could release them from the wheel of rebirth. If the animal drives of the body could be left behind and the higher intellectual and spiritual potentialities of human beings unlocked, a path of release was possible for the soul in this life.

Tenets of Jainism

According to Jainism, spiritual progress is made through accomplishments in a person's own life. For one, Jainism rejects the idea of castes. Like Buddhism, Jainism broke free from the restraints of the Vedas and emphasized that no matter what a person's station in life—no matter what level of the caste she occupied—if she lived properly, she might find release.

Jainism's views on the Vedas differ from those of Hindus, and should be viewed as a separate religion unto itself. At the same time, its views of karma and samsara give its doctrine more than a little in common with the Indian thought that preceded it. Jainism rejected the idea that persons achieved release from life by offering sacrifices to the gods or by other forms of worship.

Jainism redirected the focus from attention to the gods to a personal philosophy. One such philosophy was asceticism. Asceticism is the belief that people should deny and even conquer their desires. The strong version of this belief is that people should deny all desires without exception. The weaker version of this doctrine is that people should only deny the base desires of the body, like extreme lust, lasciviousness, and sensuousness, and of the world, such as the desire for material possessions, fame, and achievement.

According to Jainism, the more someone denies pleasures and satisfactions of the body, the more she is able to achieve freedom from the endless cycle of birth and rebirth. The founders of Jainism went beyond the traditional Indian moral concern for cattle. They taught that all forms of life were sacred; all manner of life should be loved and preserved wherever possible. This doctrine of love and nonviolence toward all things is known as *ahimsa*.

INSIGHT

"Ahimsa" means "nonkilling." This concept is primarily associated with the Jains. The notion of ahimsa is applied toward animal life primarily, but in Jain philosophy is recognized in the case of plants also. Mohandas Gandhi admitted that his regard for all life was inspired by the Jain's practice of ahimsa toward all things.

The Amazing Mahavira

Mahavira's real name was Nataputta Vardhamana, but he was better known to his followers as Mahavira, or "great hero." He is traditionally identified as the founder of Jainism. As stated, Mahavira and the twenty-three prior to him who established Jainism are Tirthankaras, or "crossing builders," so called because they forged a bridge between this life and Nirvana, or release from this world.

Mahavira's birth and death dates of 599 and 527 make him a contemporary of Siddhartha Gautama, Confucius, Lao-Tzu, and the great Hebrew prophets of the sixth century B.C.E., including Jeremiah, Ezekiel, and the anonymous author or authors of Isaiah 40–60. Like Buddha, Mahavira was born to parents of the Kshatriya or priestly caste. His father was a ruler and the family possessed great wealth and lived in luxury. He married and had a daughter, but his social standing and wealth left him unhappy, and he sought a spiritual answer to that unhappiness.

For a time he joined an order of wandering ascetics. First, however, he waited until his parents had died and the business affairs of his family had been successfully taken over by his older brother. Then he bade farewell to his family, turned his back upon his wealth and luxury, tore out his hair and beard by the handfuls, and went off to join the ascetics.

A peerless ascetic, the Jain leader Mahavira lived most of his life without clothes, the most visible symbol of a renounced life. After some twelve years as an ascetic, he managed to overcome worldly desires and passions and become the "victor," which is the meaning of jina. Jains describe this state of mind as *kevalajnana,* or perfect perception, knowledge, power, and bliss.

Mahavira concluded that their asceticism was not extreme enough. For the soul to find release from this life, the asceticism must be more extreme. Extreme asceticism was necessary, but still not sufficient. Mahavira eventually thought that one must practice ahimsa (noninjury), so he carved his own path to find release.

This combination of ahimsa and extreme renunciation gave rise to practices that form the legend of Mahavira's life. In an effort to stay detached from things and people, he never stayed more than one night in any place when he traveled.

QUESTION?

How was Mahavira recognized upon his death?
A number of kings decided to recognize his passing with a festival of lights in 527 B.C.E. Jains believe that Mahavira entered the blissful state of *ishatpragbhara,* beyond life and death.

Once he had attained enlightenment, Mahavira had conquered his weaknesses, escaping the cycle of human biological and psychological needs. The story goes that he now sat in a lotus posture, in a steady omniscient trance, and sent forth only a divine sound. Above his head at all times was a white umbrella, symbolizing that no mortal was higher or holier. His nature as a Tirthankara, or spiritual leader, attracted all of the Jain community around him, including monks, nuns, laymen, and laywomen.

QUESTION?

What kinds of precautions did Mahavira take to avoid harming living things?
When it rained, Mahavira stayed off the roads so that he would not trample on insects. In dry season, he swept the roads before him as he walked to avoid crushing insects. He strained his drinking water to keep from swallowing any living entity.

After his renunciation and detachment from the world, Mahavira attracted a very large congregation of devotees. The Shvetambaras claim that there were 14,000 monks, 36,000 nuns, 159,000 laymen, and 318,000 laywomen.

ESSENTIAL

Mahavira earned the title of Jina, or "conqueror," denoting a person who had heroically conquered himself and faced the harshest inconveniences of life. He was a renunciant, able to ignore the inconveniences of body longing and pain in order to achieve spiritual realization. Though achieving moksha at the age of forty-two, he lived until seventy-two.

The Jain community originated because of the efforts of Mahavira's closest disciples. A Brahmin, Indrabhuti Gautama, came to him seeking an interpretation of a revelation of Jain teachings, sent by the king of gods, Indra. All the teachings became clear in the presence of Mahavira. As a result, Gautama and ten other Brahmins converted to become his followers. He continued teaching for thirty more years.

As with many ascetics, Mahavira begged for his food. He preferred leftover food from people's meals rather than raw food, so that he didn't consume food that might cause his death. To heighten his self-torment, he sought out the coldest locations in the winter months and the most sweltering environments in the summer—always naked!

The Problem and Solution of Living

According to the Jains, the earlier Hindu idea that you must learn how to shake off the repetition of reincarnation is true. You are born, live your life, die, and then are born again. But how does one get away from this endless wheel of life (samsara)? Despite its rebellion against Hinduism, a philosophy out of which it grew, the Jains agree with Hindus, and Buddhists, in embracing the law of karma. If people are stuck in the wheel of birth and rebirth, it is because of the karma they possess as a result of their last actions.

Karma in an individual was not only created by actions so good they were saintly on the one hand or so bad they were monstrous on the other. Mahavira taught that karma was built up as a result of even seemingly trivial action or inaction. So, the ideal existence was to live detached from life, thereby freeing oneself, as far as one could, from karma.

The Jains also accept the omnipresence of the soul. Soul inhabits even the lowest forms of life, no matter how weighed down with the weight of karma. As such, the soul can descend from the weight of karma and can rise from the release of karma.

In one sense, the term "karma" means the consequences of mental or physical actions. An individual accumulates bad karma as a result of his selfish desires. He sheds such karma by unselfish deeds. Karma has the greatest effect on an individual's recurring rebirth. The only way to obtain release from the human form that he might inhabit for eons of drudgery is to have the right thoughts and actions. Seeking glory and honor is not the right way to happiness and wisdom. In addition, a person who causes pain on Earth or who permits others to harm Earth is deprived of happiness and wisdom.

Salvation can only come about through individual effort. A person who follows the example of Mahavira and performs good works will achieve final liberation. In order to achieve liberation, Jain monks typically take five vows.

The Five Vows of Jainism

In the earliest Sanskrit, the term *vrata* meant not just a "temporary vow," but more of a dedication of oneself on a permanent basis to a single purpose. The adoption of the five *mahavratas*, or Great Vows, was the defining set of characteristics of monks and nuns after their ascetic initiation. The vows were to govern their behavior and provide a structure for their spiritual guidance.

FACT

The Jain custom was for an ascetic at a ceremony of initiation to read out the scriptural story of Rohini, the girl who was distinguished from her unwise sisters because she planted and reaped the rewards of five rice grains given to her by her father. Her story was told to demonstrate how the five Great Vows could be put to good use.

The traditional description of the Great Vows can be found in the second book of the Acaranga or scriptures. Each of the five vows or renunciations is first stated, then followed by realizations describing the further implications of the vow, ensuring that the vow will be correctly executed.

The Vow of the Noninjury of Life (Ahimsa)

This is sometimes referred to as nonviolence, especially by Mohandas K. Gandhi, who in the twentieth century credited the Jains with his own practice of nonviolence. But this way of putting the matter is inaccurate. For the term nonviolence in ordinary usage involves only human beings. The Sanskrit term ahimsa appeared in the Upanishads in about 500 B.C.E., when many people among the Brahmins, Buddhists, and Jains emphasized reverence for all life, rather than the sacrifice of animals.

The "realizations" then describes ways in which the ascetic must take care. First, he must observe how and where he walks lest he injure life forms on the way. This is especially relevant during the four-month rain retreat, for it is during the monsoon season that there is a great burgeoning of plant and insect life that might otherwise be injured by wandering ascetics.

When it comes to nonviolence, the Jains taught the wrongness of killing of any life form and undertook this vow for the rest of their lives. Mahavira taught that it is "sinful" to act badly toward animals; a "wise man" should not act sinfully toward animals, nor even cause or allow others to do so.

The ascetic must also get hold of her own mind and speech, for these may be agents of violence. Further directions concern how an ascetic is to put down her alms bowl and how she must inspect all food and drink to ensure there are no life forms in it.

The noninjury of other life forms is perhaps best known among all Jain traits. Jains are vegetarians, and they will not own leather goods, since these require the killing of animals. They go to such extremes with vegetarianism that they will not even eat from pans in which meat has been cooked. They follow Mahavira's example of sweeping a path before them to avoid stepping on insects. Jains routinely shun occupations that might bring harm or death to another living thing. For this reason, they even avoid agricultural professions (not to mention livelihoods that involve hunting for or handling meat).

FACT

The nonviolence of Jains is so extreme that they practice it toward animals that are considered pests, even creatures such as rodents and rats. When a rat infestation occurred in Bombay, Jains captured them and provided hospices for them, feeding and caring for them until their natural deaths.

Further, some scholars have emphasized a Vedic belief in an "inverted" order in the world to come. In this new order, an individual would have to endure the very pain that she inflicted on other beings. If a person accepts the doctrine that Brahman is connected with atman, the metaphysical implication is clear: we have a fellowship with all living creatures.

Jains must show care toward living things even in the consumption of food, and the notion goes beyond simple vegetarianism; food is only acceptable if it does not cost a life. It is not just animal flesh, fish, and eggs that are prohibited, but also types of vegetables that were thought to contain life forms. Even though total consistency of diet is not to be expected, the Jains prohibit vegetables such as onions, garlic, potatoes, and fruits with large numbers of seeds in them. Most holy men and women survive on fruits that have fallen naturally from the trees.

FACT

The Jain principle of ahimsa, or noninjury of all living things, has been embraced by non-Jains, too. Ordinary citizens in and out of India have embraced the Jain principles of noninjury. Jain ideas have been especially attractive to Mohandas K. Gandhi and Albert Schweitzer.

A story illustrates the Jain respect for life. The story is from the Akaranga Sutra, I.1, which serves to illustrate the Jain respect for all life.

Earth is afflicted and wretched, it is hard to teach, it has no discrimination. Unenlightened men, who suffer from the effect of past deeds, cause great pain in a world full of pain already, for in Earth souls are individually embodied. If, thinking to gain praise, honor, or respect . . . or to achieve a good rebirth . . . or to win salvation, or to escape pain, a man sins against Earth or causes or permits others to do so, . . . he will not gain joy or wisdom . . . Injury to the Earth is like striking, cutting, maiming, or killing a blind man. . . . Knowing this, man should not sin against Earth or cause or permit others to do so. He who understands the nature of sin against Earth is called a true sage who understands karma.

And there are many souls embodied in water. Truly water . . . is alive. He who injures the lives in water does not understand the nature of sin or renounce it. . . . Knowing this, a man should not sin against water, or cause or permit others to do so. He who understands the nature of sin against water is called a true sage who understands karma.

And just as it is in the nature of a man to be born and grow old, so is it the nature of a plant to be born and grow old. . . . One is endowed with reason, and so is the other; one is sick, if injured, and so is the other; one grows larger, and so does the other; one changes with time, and so does the other. . . . He who understands the nature of sin against plants is called a true sage who understands karma.

All beings with two, three, four, or five senses, . . . in fact all creation, know individually pleasure and displeasure, pain, terror, and sorrow. All are full of fears which come from all directions. And yet there exist people who could cause greater pain to them . . . Some kill animals for sacrifice, some for their skin, flesh, blood, . . . feathers, teeth, or tusks; . . . some kill them intentionally and some unintentionally; some kill because they have been previously injured by them, . . . and some because they expect to be injured. He who harms animals has not understood or renounced deeds of sin . . . He who understands the nature of sin against animals is called a true sage who understands karma.

A man who is averse from harming even the wind knows the sorrow of all things living. . . . He who knows what is bad for himself knows what is bad for others, and he who knows what is bad for others knows what is bad for himself. This reciprocity should always be borne in mind. Those whose minds are at peace and who are free from passions do not desire to live (at the expense of others). . . . He who understands the nature of sin against wind is called a true sage who understands karma.

In short, he who understands the nature of sin in respect to all six types of living beings is called a true sage who understands karma.

The Vow Not to Speak Untruth

Jains are widely respected for their truthfulness. The second Great Vow says an ascetic must abstain from lying. The realization here is that she must be deliberate in her speech and not given to anger, greed, fear, or mirth.

Philosophically, the Jains are relativists; they allow that there are truths in the doctrines of other philosophies. There is a well-known story of the blind men and the elephant that is told to illustrate this point. In this tale, several blind men are asked to describe an elephant. Each touches a different part of the elephant's body, and thus each describes it in a different way. To one man, the elephant is like a stone wall because he has touched the side. Another thinks the elephant is like a fan since he has touched its wide ear. Each man truthfully described the elephant, but since each had touched a different part, their descriptions varied. Truth here is relative to their perspectives and positions. Human knowledge, then, is likely to be misleading. Despite this position about the relativity of truth, it is speaking what you know to be false that breaks the vow of the Jains.

The Vow Not to Steal

The third of the great vows says that an ascetic should not take what has not been given. Jain monks are forbidden from taking anything that doesn't belong to them. Like their observance of the second vow, this one aids and abets their reputation for honesty.

The Vow to Renounce Sexual Pleasures

This Great Vow states that an ascetic must renounce all sexual activity. Since asceticism has always viewed the pleasures of the flesh as evil, and since sex is one of the greatest pleasures of the flesh, it must be forsaken.

The vow to renounce sexual pleasures denounced any contact, mental or physical, with women, or eating or drinking anything likely to stimulate the sexual drive. Mahavira did not only renounce sexual pleasures, he renounced women for good. His renunciation of all external pleasures and things was due to the admonition that, "Women are the greatest temptation in the world."

The Vow to Renounce all Attachments

The fifth Great Vow counsels the renunciation of any attachment to objects of the senses. This refers to possessions in general. Of all the things that bind human beings to this life, the love for other persons and things is among the strongest bonds. Thus, Mahavira left behind his family and possessions and didn't remain in one place for more than a day, lest he form attachments to people and things. At the age of thirty-two, he became a wandering monk, at which point the sky glowed like a lake covered in lotus flowers. A sixth vow was later added to the list of five.

No Eating after Dark

The first appearance of this vow describes it as a supplement to the Great Vows. In reality, it is but a subdivision of the first Great Vow of non-violence. The apparent reason for prohibiting eating at night is that ascetics cannot go out and seek alms at night, since this activity would involve trampling upon small life forms. In addition, cooking of food by the laity would attract insects, which would be drawn into the flames. According to popular belief, the proper digestion of food can only take place in sunlight.

Do all Jains practice all five vows?

Here is where the matter becomes philosophically interesting. If an individual becomes a monk, he holds to all five. On the other hand, a Jain layperson integrates this philosophy with marriage, family, and the material well-being that accompanies such a life. But this sort of life will not lead to spiritual release.

The purpose of the Great Vows, and indeed of the other ancillary vows that a Jain ascetic undertakes, is to bring about a state of internal purification. The first of the five—the renunciation of violence—is fundamental according to the Jains. For instance, not speaking falsely (the second vow) is important because of the connection between truth and violence. While lying should be avoided, truths which harm others should not be spoken. Also, the third Great Vow of not taking what has not been given concerns the ascetic's honesty in dealing with all people, but also includes not taking the lives of other beings. Likewise, the attachment to possessions and sense objects, which is rejected by the fourth Great Vow, stirs the passions in people, one of the primary causes of violence. In addition, sexual activity is prohibited not only because of the distraction and passion it causes, but because innumerable life forms are destroyed in each ejaculation of semen.

The World and Its Inhabitants

The word *loka* is Sanskrit for "world," and recalls the traditional division of the universe into various worlds, specifically a three-fold division (*triloka*) into heaven, Earth, and hell. These are frequently referred to as the three worlds. Humans reside in the Middle World; below is hell; above is Ishat-pragbhara, where liberated souls live.

QUESTION?

What is animism and how does it apply to Jainism?
The earliest forms of Hinduism seem to have roots in animism. Animism is the belief that nature is not comprised of dead matter, but is alive and filled with unseen spirits. Animists are likely to see a soul or self existing in trees, stones, rivers, and even heavenly bodies.

Five kinds of existents—or beings—reside in the loka. The most important is the *jiva*, translatable as "soul" or "life monad." All that is nonsoul is divided into four kinds of being—motion, rest, atoms, and space. Jiva is eternal consciousness and is intermingled with *ajiva* or "nonjiva." Karma binds jiva to nonjiva. It is jiva's goal to act in such a way that it wears away nonsoul, including karma.

How difficult is it for humans to shed the bonds of karma? There is an allegory that captures the futility and misery of human existence in *The Story of Samaraditya*, by Haridhadra, of the seventh century. In the story, a man leaves his home in quest of another country, promising new life and new experiences. In time, he is lost, hungry, and thirsty. A mad elephant charges at him, then a demoness with a sharp sword appears in his path. He seeks refuge in a distant banyan tree, whereupon he finds that he cannot climb the tree and dives into a well instead, only to be beset by a series of calamities.

The story proceeds:

A clump of reeds grew from its deep wall, and to this he clung,
While below him he saw terrible snakes, enraged at the sound of his
*   falling;*
And at the very bottom, known from the hiss of his breath, was a
*   black and mighty python*
With mouth agape, its body thick as the trunk of a heavenly elephant,
*   with terrible red eyes*
He thought, "My life will only last as long as these reeds hold fast,"
And he raised his head; and there, on the clump of reeds, he saw two
*   large mice,*
One white, one black, their sharp teeth ever gnawing at the roots of
*   the reed-clump.*
Then up came the wild elephant, and enraged the more at not catch-
*   ing him,*
Charged time and again at the trunk of the banyan tree.
At the shock of his charge a honeycomb on a large branch
Which hung over the old well, shook loose and fell.
The man's whole body was stung by a swarm of angry bees,
But just by a chance, a drop of honey fell on his head,
Rolled down his brow, and somehow reached his lips,
And gave him a moment's sweetness. He longed for other drops,
And he thought nothing of the python, the snakes, the elephant, the
*   mice, the well, or the bees,*
In his excited craving for yet more drops of honey.

The meaning of the story? Against the myriad evils of the world, against its many hardships, human beings hanker for the most trivial pleasures of life.

Jain Division

By 80 B.C.E., a divide had occurred in Jain teachings. The more liberal interpretation of Jain teachings comes from the Svetambara (meaning "white
clad"). This sect, mainly inhabiting the northern part of India, are called
white clad because they regard clothing as permissible, allowing the monks
to wear simple white garments. Further, they allow women to practice religion, to enter the monasteries, and see no reason why a woman cannot find
release. The Svetambara has popular appeal.

The Digambara (meaning "sky clad") are a second Jain sect. It is by
far the more conservative of the two. Inhabiting southern India, this group
embraces a purer Jainism, living closer to the paradigm established by
Mahavira. The Digambara mandate that monks adhere to the old ideals.
This includes that they go about nearly nude; only the holiest individuals
are totally nude. Women cannot hope for the same aspirations. They have
no chance for release. In addition, they serve only to distract men from
their spiritual advancement, since they are such a temptation. They are
even denied entry into the monasteries and temples. According to this sect,
Mahavira was never married.

Both groups believe that before Mahavira, there had been twenty-
three Tirthankaras or spiritual leaders. They also agree that Mahavira had
renounced the world at the age of thirty. As stated, they disagree about
whether woman could attain such a lofty position. They also disagree on
another matter that has divided them for all times.

The Digambaras think the gods took Mahavira's clothes away during
his travels, which would make him a naked wanderer. The Shvetambaras
disagree; they believe his tattered garment was torn away by a thorn bush
thirteen months after his wanderings began. Thus had Mahavira become
"sky clad."

Why is the issue of clothing so important? The Digambaras say that
although the absence of clothing doesn't signify a true monk, the presence of clothing indicates some residual shame, a deficit of character that
wouldn't be found in a true monk. They believe that only previous Tirthankaras were nude and only Digambaras can attain moksha, freedom from
bondage to the world.

The Jains in Our Time

While Jainism emerged as a protest against the Hindu caste system, Hinduism came to accept Jain asceticism and ahimsa. Still, Jainism doesn't claim many adherents, with slightly less than 4 million followers in the world today. Perhaps the strict requirements of Jainism keep it a minority religion.

Jains acknowledge no transcendent beings. In fact, they have no need for gods, since they embrace a secular ethic. They worship the twenty-four spiritual leaders, or Tirthankaras, who embody their philosophy. To what extent are they still worshipped? Some 40,000 temples in India worship these figures. One of the temples—erected on Mount Abu—is considered one of the seven wonders of India. In addition to temple worship, Jain worship extends to rituals in the home. This includes a broad variety of activities, including reciting the names of the first Jinas (or saints), bathing their idols, and making offerings of flowers and perfume to these idols. Home ceremonies typically include meditation and the observance of vows, too.

Dualism

Much of the moral content of karma and Jainism is due to its dualistic metaphysics. According to Jainism, the world is comprised of two kinds of substances: soul (jiva) and matter (ajiva). The two substances—as Western philosopher René Descartes would elaborate on in his *Meditations* two millennia later—possess opposite attributes. Soul is vital, alive, immaterial, eternal, and valuable; matter, by contrast, is lifeless, material, and evil. People themselves are the best example of this combination of attributes.

In one way, people can be looked at as spiritual selves surrounded by a material shell. If a person's soul cannot separate from the body, it is because of past actions weighing it down, keeping it sealed in the prison of the body. Jainism is about getting the soul liberated from evil flesh. The answer is a life of hyperausterity and renunciation of the flesh.

If a Jain has too many worldly responsibilities and is thus unable to dedicate himself to an ascetic life, he has less chance for liberation than one who practices asceticism. Because he was able to turn his back on wealth and because of his indifference to pleasure, Mahavira is the Jain model for spiritual advancement.

One story tells that Mahavira, whose name means "great hero," was meditating one day when people lit a fire beneath him to test his powers of endurance. True to his ascetic ways, Mahavira did not resist.

Another aspect of the Jain metaphysic is its indifference to and lack of the use of gods. Only the individual can free his soul. The means to that end is right action; outside help is of no use. In addition, there is no need for a creator, since matter always was and always will be. Gods, if they do at all, exist on a realm separate from that of humans, and they don't affect human lives. A person's search for release is solitary, far more a matter of character and self-denial than of religion. Prayer is of no use; individuals must rely on themselves for spiritual advancement, not on a transcendent being.

The Jain's only religion is a kind of ethic, a way of life. The Jains might fall into two camps: a majority, who are immersed in their material lives, who cannot give up their homes and accept the rigors of an ascetic life; and a minority, who become monks—quintessential Jains whose lives are guided by five vows.

CHAPTER 8

Another Offshoot of Hinduism: Buddhism

The teachings of dharma and the Four Noble Truths were to become the essence of Buddhism. Buddha taught that the supreme good of life is nirvana, which is "the extinction" or "blowing out" of suffering and desire and awakening to what is most real. A Sanskrit term, Buddha literally means "awakened." Buddhism also teaches pacifism and nonviolence.

Buddhism

Buddhism originated in the sixth century B.C.E. Like Jainism, it was an alternate path that emerged from the fertile soil of Hinduism. It resembled Jainism in several respects: It rejected the authority of the Vedas and the caste system and offered a vision of salvation based on the actions of the individual and fueled by effort.

Buddhism's founder, Siddhartha Gautama, practiced the Jain teachings but did not find release in them. He also practiced extreme mortification in the form of fasting, but that did not lead to his enlightenment, either. He finally found enlightenment by creating his own path, a middle way.

Whereas Jainism was extreme in its precepts, Buddhism prescribed a more moderate path or "middle way" between the desire for worldliness on one hand and the extreme asceticism of Mahavira on the other. This middle path was appealing and helped Buddhism draw in more followers.

Within a few centuries, Buddhist missionaries traveled into neighboring Asian countries and established Buddhism as one of the major religions in China, Japan, Korea, and Southeast Asia. Even today, Buddhists reside mainly in East and Southeast Asia. While Buddhism spread into foreign lands, it lost ground to a resurgent Hinduism in India, where Muslim conquest also diminished the number of Buddhists.

Buddha is also sometimes referred to as Shakyamuni, which means "Sage of the Shakya Clan," as he hailed from Shakya.

Siddhartha Gautama

Siddhartha Gautama was born sometime around 566 B.C.E. to a royal family in the Himalayan foothills, on the border of northern India and southern Nepal. Siddhartha's mother was Queen Maya, his father King Suddhodhana, and he was a blessing to the childless couple, as they would now have a prince and heir to rule over their small but prosperous kingdom. They named their son Siddhartha, which means "every wish fulfilled."

The Birth of the Buddha

There are many mythologies and stories surrounding the birth of the Buddha, but it is generally agreed (with some variation) that when Siddhartha was but days old, his father, King Suddhodhana, invited a large group of Brahmins to a feast at the palace so they could tell the future of the newborn baby. Eight of the Brahmins concurred on the prediction that Siddhartha would either become a great and powerful ruler of all the land, or a wise and sage religious figure and spiritual teacher.

They warned that if Siddhartha left the palace in search of a spiritual life, he would endure many hardships but eventually become a Buddha. If he remained within the cloistered palace walls, he would become a great ruler of the world. However, one of these Brahmins was convinced that the young boy would become a Buddha and warned of four signs that would influence the young Siddhartha and spur him to leave his home and commence a spiritual journey.

The Raising of a King

Suddhodhana had no wish for his son to become a spiritual man and teacher; he dreamed of a son who ruled over the land, the most powerful man as far as the eye could see. He decided to protect Siddhartha from the possibilities of a hard but spiritual path, and vowed to keep him cloistered in the palace, lavishing riches and luxuries beyond imagination on the young boy.

Youth of Luxury and Pleasure

Young Siddhartha was surrounded by beautiful things, and kept captive within the palace grounds, so he would not be subjected to the sicknesses and poverty of the people of the kingdom. He had everything he could ever want: great teachers, beautiful girls, companionship, wonderful food. He grew into a talented athlete, an intelligent and charming young man. His future as a leader of the people seemed secure.

One afternoon in the young prince's childhood would affect him much later in life. He was sitting under an apple tree watching the plowing of the fields as the town prepared for the next year's crops. He noticed that the plowing had destroyed the grass and that the insects that had been nesting in these young shoots were dead. The young boy felt a sadness come over him, as if he were attached to the insects, as though he had experienced a personal loss. Yet the day was beautiful and the shade of the apple tree wonderfully cool. Joy rose up inside him, and he experienced a moment of utter perfection. Siddhartha was alive in the moment, his self set aside. The compassion and love he felt for the insects took him outside himself, and he was momentarily free. Legend has it that as the day wore on, and the shadows moved, the shadow of the apple tree continued to shield the young Siddhartha.

"Buddha" is a title, not a name. Therefore, when referring to Shakyamuni Buddha, one would say, "the Buddha."

Marriage and the Birth of a Son

When Siddhartha was sixteen, he won the hand in marriage of a beautiful young girl named Yasodhara. Yasodhara was Siddhartha's cousin and was considered the loveliest girl in the kingdom. Legend has it that he managed to win her hand in a contest by piercing seven trees with one arrow.

At age twenty-nine, Siddhartha's life was as much the life of luxury as it had been before, except his wife was pregnant with their first child, indisposed and unable to entertain him. She beseeched her husband to find his own diversion, so Siddhartha wandered outside the gates of the kingdom after overhearing someone speak of the beauty of the spring in the forest just beyond.

The Four Signs

Suddhodhana tried to ensure that life outside the palace gates was just as perfect as life inside. When Siddhartha wandered outside, everywhere he went he saw happiness, health, and good cheer. Then suddenly an old decrepit man with white hair, withered skin, and a staff to lean on crossed his path. Leaning over to his companion and servant, Channa, Siddhartha asked, "What is this?"

Channa explained that before them was an old man, and he told Siddhartha that everyone would age similarly one day. Siddhartha was saddened and shocked by the sight of the old man and wondered how he could continue to enjoy such sights as his garden when such suffering was to come later.

A second trip outside the palace grounds brought the sight of a maimed man before the young prince. Channa assured him that a similar fate would not befall him, as he was healthy and well cared for. At home, the king continued to rain luxuries on the prince, hoping to distract him from these disturbing visions and his newfound knowledge. But a third visit outside his sanctuary found him confronting a funeral procession and a corpse. Channa explained death to Siddhartha and told him it was inevitable, but he was not to worry.

Siddhartha was overwhelmed. Sickness, old age, and death—how had he missed all this suffering in life? Finally, on another excursion with Channa, Siddhartha came upon a monk in yellow robes with a shaven head and an empty bowl. Channa explained that this ascetic had renounced all worldly goods. He praised the man so highly that Siddhartha returned home pensive. That night, the opulence of the palace disturbed him deeply. The four signs had left their mark, and the veil of luxury and riches had been removed. The world now seemed a place of suffering and pain.

Finding the Path: The Renunciation

Yasodhara had borne Siddhartha a son. The cycle of birth and death seemed endless and oppressive to Siddhartha—life after life and death after death as the cycle of reincarnation and karma continued. Despite his love for his family and the birth of his new baby boy (whom he named Rahula, or "chain"), he decided to go forth into the world and stole out of the palace.

His faithful companion, Channa, followed him out into the night but was soon sent back to the castle by Siddhartha. Siddhartha was now on his way, and once outside the palace grounds, he shaved his head and donned the yellow robes of the mendicant monk.

Enormous Sacrifice

This is a remarkable occurrence in the life of a prince. He was surrounded by all that many would consider necessary for a happy life: money, fame, power, love, family, health, and endless entertainment and learning. He was safe and had a promising future and a beautiful wife and son. Yet suffering had entered his awareness and dulled his enjoyment of life. His awareness of loss, of the pain that attachment could bring, caused him dissatisfaction and stress, and he vowed to live an unfettered existence. Family was not part of the life of a spiritual seeker, so family had to be left behind.

Siddhartha's Coming of Age

Siddhartha vowed to try to save all beings from such suffering, and he set forth to change the endless repetition of the cycle of loss in the world. Awareness of *duhkha* had entered the consciousness of the young nobleman and was to change his life forever.

Duhkha means "dissatisfaction, impermanence, imperfection, suffering, disease, anguish caused by attachment and desire." Duhkha is a very difficult concept to translate into Western terms. Many use the word "suffering" as a substitute for duhkha, but suffering does not encompass all the subtleties that duhkha should convey.

The forests surrounding Suddhodhana's castle were fertile and green and housed many seekers of the holy life. To seek a holy life was a worthy cause; the yellow-robed monks were not seen as beggars and dropouts but as crusaders and adventurers. People prayed for an enlightened one to save them from a life of suffering and unease. Therefore, Siddhartha must have felt a great sense of adventure leaving his safe haven and entering the woods by his home.

The young prince set out to find himself a teacher, and he wandered far and wide over the Ganges plain, learning from the truth seekers he ran across on his travels. He practiced self-denial, meditation, self-control, and yogic exercises, searching for liberation from the ties of the material world.

The Five Ascetics

Siddhartha joined up with five ascetics and practiced the principles of asceticism in an effort to achieve enlightenment and discover liberation. Asceticism was believed to burn up negative karma and free a person from samsara. It was the ascetics' belief that if they suffered enough in this life they could perhaps save themselves in the next.

Penance

Together with his five companions, he wore little or no clothing, slept out in the open no matter the weather, starved himself, and even ingested his own waste matter. He lay on the most uncomfortable surfaces possible and inflicted much suffering on himself, convinced that external suffering would banish the internal suffering forever. He became very ill, his ribs showing through, until finally his spine could be felt through his stomach. His hair fell out and his skin became blotched and shrunken. But he was still plagued with desires and cravings.

Alone Again

As Siddhartha pondered his failure to achieve enlightenment through asceticism, a young girl passed by him and offered him some rice milk. He drank his fill, casting the ascetic life behind him. When the five ascetics saw him partaking of nourishment, they grew disgusted with their companion and hurriedly distanced themselves from him.

The Middle Way

Siddhartha slowly nursed himself back to health. He became very conscious of his movements in the world and paid close attention to how he reacted to his environment, watching his thoughts as they passed through his mind. He became aware of the movements he made while he ate, slept, walked, and squatted. Siddhartha slowly became mindful of his every gesture and thought. Mindfulness made Siddhartha aware of every craving that passed through him and of how transitory these cravings were. Everything changed; everything came and everything passed. Whether or not he worried about loss, it was inevitable, as change was inevitable. With change came fear; with fear came suffering (*duhkha*).

Enlightenment

The young traveler found a nice spot to meditate under the shade of a bodhi tree. As he sat under the tree, meditating and watching his thoughts come and go, his mind started to break free of the constraints of his ego. He entered each moment, fully present, as his thoughts dropped away.

The Arrival of Mara

Mara, the evil one, arrived, determined to distract him from his path toward Nirvana. Over and again, Mara threw all his evil power and destruction toward the implacable Siddhartha, determined to unseat the immovable man.

Finally, in desperation and rage, Mara yelled out at Siddhartha, "Rise from your seat. It does not belong to you but to me!" Mara's warriors and demons rose up beside their lord and swore that they bore witness to his right to Siddhartha's seat. "Who bears witness to yours?" Mara roared at the still-unshaken Siddhartha.

Siddhartha sat motionless and then slowly reached out for help. He put out his arm and placed his right hand on the Earth. The Earth instantly roared like thunder back at Mara, "*I* bear witness!" Mara crumbled in defeat, disappearing from Siddhartha's presence.

The Buddha

Siddhartha had achieved enlightened mind, and now in his place sat the Buddha, the Fully Awakened One. He had awoken to the true nature of the world, and everywhere was a newfound freedom and compassion that was like nothing he could have imagined.

But the Buddha could not just sit under the bodhi tree forever, enjoying his newfound freedom and basking in the lightness of Nirvana. The world was full of people who had not yet woken, suffering people, who could use the Buddha's teachings to awaken themselves. And so the Buddha listened to his heart and to his nature, got up from his seat under the bodhi tree, and ventured forth to share his teachings with the people who so desperately needed his help.

On the Road

Buddha left the bodhi tree and went in search of his earlier teachers and fellow seekers of the holy life. Remembering fondly the five ascetics he had spent so much time with and who for so long had been so supportive—regardless of the way they had parted—Buddha headed toward the Deer Park at Isipatana outside Varanasi, where they were rumored to be living. Together, they formed the first *sangha,* or order of monks. He would spend the rest of his life—the next forty-five years—sharing the message of the lessons he had learned and passing on the wisdom and beauty of awakening.

The course of his remaining years was now clearly laid out before him: he would teach an ever-growing band of disciples. In time, Buddha attracted a range of people. After he first balked at allowing women to join the sangha, he eventually allowed them to form an order of nuns. Here was a stark difference introduced by the Buddha. By Hindu standards, his teachings were heterodox; contrary to the orthodoxies of Jainism and Hinduism, Buddhism taught that women could experience enlightenment.

The Buddhist Moral Code

There are several aspects of the Buddhist code of living. Vegetarianism was not a duty for his followers; monks were allowed to eat meat. Though the same expectations were not made of lay Buddhists, it was expected they would support the monks with food, clothing, and other necessities. In addition, it was imperative that they would obey a moral code consisting of five negative rules. The prohibitions included killing, stealing, lying, engaging in improper sexual conduct, and partaking of intoxicants.

The Pali Sermons described the conduct the monks were to follow:

And How, O king, is a monk accomplished in morality?

Herein a monk abandons the killing of living things and refrains from killing; laying aside the use of a stick or a knife he dwells modestly, full of kindness, and compassionate for the welfare of all living things. This is his behavior in morality.

Abandoning the taking of what is not given, he refrains from the taking of what is not given; he takes and expects only what is given; he dwells purely and without stealing.

Abandoning incontinence, he practices continence and lives apart, avoiding the village practice of sexual intercourse. Abandoning falsehood, he refrains from falsehood; he speaks truth; he is truthful, trustworthy, and reliable, not deceiving people.

Abandoning slanderous speech, he refrains from slanderous speech; what he has heard from one place he does not tell in another to cause dissension. He is even a healer of dissensions and a producer of union, delighting and rejoicing in concord, eager for concord, and an utterer of speech that produces concord.

Abandoning harsh speech, he refrains from harsh speech; the speech that is harmless, pleasant to the ear, kind, reaching the heart, urbane, amiable, and attractive to the multitude, that kind of speech does he utter.

Abandoning frivolous speech, he refrains from frivolous speech; he speaks of the good, the real, the profitable, of the doctrine and the discipline; he is an utterer of speech worth hoarding, with timely speech and purpose and meaning.

He refrains from injuring seeds and plants.

He eats only within one meal time, abstaining from food at night and avoiding untimely food.

He refrains from dancing, singing, music, and shows.

He refrains from the use of garlands, scents, unguents, and objects of adornment; from a high or large bed; from accepting gold and silver; from accepting raw grain and raw meat.

He refrains from accepting women, girls, male and female slaves, goats and rams, fowls and pigs, elephants, oxen, horses, mares, and farm-lands.

He refrains from going on messages and errands; from buying and selling; from cheating in weighing, false metal in measuring; from practices or cheating, trickery, deception, fraud, from cutting, killing, binding, robbery, pillage, and violence.

Buddha died at the age of eighty after eating spoiled pork curry. Legend says that his final words were, "Subject to decay are all component things. Strive earnestly to work out your own salvation."

There is little if any evidence that Buddha thought of himself as inventing a new religion. He grew up under the influence of Hinduism. He rejected the authority of the ancient Hindu scriptures, the Vedas, and considered the Hindu pantheon of gods mere mortal beings that, like humans, were subject to karma. Buddha's view of the human condition, and the solution to the spiritual ills of that condition, can be found by living according to the Four Noble Truths.

Buddha's Developed Moral Doctrine

Buddha was far less concerned with metaphysics and far more concerned with how to live. To live well—as we were intended to live—we must embrace the Four Noble Truths. Coupled with the Eightfold Path to those truths, this is Buddha's philosophy for finding salvation. Buddha's list of the Four Noble Truths is as follows:

The Noble Truth of Suffering

Life is suffering (or *duhkha*). Dissatisfaction and unfulfilled desires are everywhere; sadness and sorrow are constant. Even when we experience ecstasy, it lasts only for a little while. For every joy, there is a sorrow, but for every sorrow, there may not be joy. Suffering can be found in three different categories: physical suffering, such as pain, sickness, distress, and death; suffering produced by change, such as when a joyful state of mind passes and one experiences depression, longing, or boredom; and suffering produced by conditioned states of consciousness (i.e., for every stage of existence there is a corresponding karmic effect). This is the deepest, most perennial form of suffering; the notion of self is the source of suffering. Remove the self and you will remove the suffering. Here, Buddhism differs from Hinduism and Western philosophies, which assert the existence of the self, but Buddhism holds to the idea of *anatman,* or not-self.

The Noble Truth of the Cause of Suffering

The cause of suffering is desire and craving. What for? The longing is threefold: desire for pleasure, existence, and prosperity. Seeking pleasure is imprudent and futile, for pleasure is elusive, and even when it is achieved, it turns to displeasure. Since people wish to continue in their existence, they end up clinging to life, which leads to despair. Seeking prosperity, too, ends in its own kind of despair; a person's appetite for success is insatiable. A person can hanker for more pleasure and wealth, and conclude that his well-being depends on these things, but this is unenlightened. A desire for increased status will always lead to bad karma. Karma is cause and effect; good and intelligent actions will have good effects, while bad actions will produce bad effects. This is not for a future life; Buddhism speaks about Nirvana, or enlightenment, in this life.

In Buddhist thought, the soul does not exist; people live an existence of anatman. What people think is a soul is an amalgam of the five mental or physical aggregates: the physical body, feelings, understanding, will, and consciousness. These make the human personality subject to the endless cycle of birth, death, and rebirth typical of Indian religions.

The Noble Truth of the Cessation of Suffering

The third truth concerns the cure for the suffering of life. Since the cause of suffering is desire or craving, eliminating the cause will allow you to eliminate the effect. If you can destroy desire, suffering ends.

The Noble Truth of the Path That Leads to the Cessation of Suffering

The way to achieve enlightenment is through a path of spiritual, moral, and mental exercise. The path includes eight parts:

1. Right Views (understanding)
2. Right Aspirations (thoughts)
3. Right Speech
4. Right Conduct of Action
5. Right Livelihood
6. Right Endeavor or Effort
7. Right Mindfulness
8. Right Meditation or Concentration

These eight aspects of the path fit three attributes:

- Ethical conduct (*sila*) includes universal love and compassion or tolerance. The Buddha taught his doctrine for "the good of the many, for the happiness of the many, out of compassion for the world." Right speech involves truth telling and refraining from gossip, malicious words, impoliteness, and backbiting. Right conduct includes honesty and peacemaking in a person's whole life. It also includes refraining from violence, cheating, and illicit sexual liaisons. Right livelihood also refers to earning a living through honorable employment. This excludes butchers, arms dealers, bartenders, weapons sellers, and other professions that produce more evil than good.

- Mental discipline (*samadhi*, for Hindus, "holy vision") requires that a person be disciplined, exercise self-control, and concentrate his mind on the noble truths. To achieve this end concentration, he might practice breathing and other modes of yoga or meditation.

- Attaining wisdom, and ultimately enlightenment or Nirvana, requires that a person live in universal love and discipline. The person now understands the puzzle of existence and has attained Nirvana.

The Buddha's philosophy is a practical but deeply spiritual approach to living that has led many to live peaceful, fulfilled lives.

CHAPTER 9

The Bhagavad Gita

Bhagavad Gita means "song of the blessed lord," and is sometimes translated as "the song of the adorable one." Believed to have been composed between the second and third century C.E., it is an epic poem of Indian culture and religion. It is to Hinduism what the Homeric poems are to Greek and Hellenistic culture. Like those Homeric poems, the Gita is about a great battle. Through stories of the struggles of notable heroes and gods, it relays much of the basic philosophy of life and states the guiding principles of yoga. The main theme is yoga—the attainment of union with the divine. Krishna distinguishes three forms of yoga: of knowledge, action, and devotion.

The Bhagavad Gita on Duty

The Bhagavad Gita is part of a longer poem called the Mahabharata, which is the story of the struggles between two leading families from the beginning of Indian history. These two families face off in the battle of Kurukshetra, which historians place between 850 and 650 B.C.E.

The Gita begins when the hero, Arjuna, a warrior, hesitates over entering into battle against members of his own family. Arjuna's conscience revolts at the thought of the war and the idea that it involves the killing of friends and relatives. He asks his charioteer, Krishna, to pull the chariot up between the two battling armies. It becomes apparent that the charioteer Krishna is God himself. The conversation is a revelation given by a friend to a friend, a young god to his companion, the prince Arjuna.

The eighteen chapters that comprise the Gita are divided into three sections of six chapters each. In the first section, Arjuna looks out on the battlefield and questions what part he will play in the battle:

> *When Krishna heard the words of Arjuna he drove their glorious chariot and placed it between the two armies.*
>
> *And facing Bhishma and Drona and other royal rulers he said: "See, Arjuna, the armies of the Kurus, gathered here on the field of battle."*
>
> *Then Arjuna saw in both armies fathers, grandfathers, sons, grandsons; fathers of wives, uncles, masters; brothers, companions and friends.*
>
> *When Arjuna saw his kinsmen face to face in both lines of battle, he was overcome by grief and despair and he spoke with a sinking heart.*
>
> *When I see all my kinsmen, Krishna, who have come here on this field of battle,*
>
> *Life goes from my limbs and they sink, and my mouth is sear and dry; a trembling overcomes my body, and my hair shudders in horror;*
>
> *My great bow Gandiva falls from my hands, and the skin of my flesh is burning; I am no longer able to stand because my mind is whirling and wandering.*

And I see forebodings of evil, Krishna. I cannot forsee any glory if I kill my own kinsmen in the sacrifice of battle.

Because I have no wish for victory, Krishna, nor for a kingdom, nor for its pleasures. How can we want a kingdom, Govinda, or its pleasures or even life,

When those for whom we want a kingdom, and its pleasures, and the joys of life, are here in this field of battle about to give up their wealth and their life?

Facing us in the field of battle are teachers, fathers, and sons; grandsons, grandfathers, wives' brothers; mothers' brothers and fathers of wives.

These I do not wish to slay, even if I myself am slain. Not even for the kingdom of the three worlds: how much less for a kingdom of the Earth!

If we kill these evil men, evil shall fall upon us: what joy in their death could we have, O Janardan, mover of souls?

I cannot therefore kill my own kinsmen, the sons of kind Dhritarashtra, the brother of my own father. What happiness could we ever enjoy, if we killed our own kinsmen in battle?

—I.24–37 Bhagavad Gita

QUESTION?

Is there a philosophy of karma in the Bhagavad Gita?
Yes, though the meaning of karmic action has changed from earlier texts. Krishna reveals to Arjuna that action performed out of a sense of one's duty or dharma, with no thought of selfish gain, leads to spiritual fulfillment.

With those words, Arjuna sank down in his chariot, overcome by despair and grief and lacking the will to fight. Krishna saw that Arjuna's eyes were full of tears, but he did not express sympathy. Rather, he reproached Arjuna and reminded him of his duty.

Whence this lifeless dejection, Arjuna, in this hour, the hour of trial? Strong men know not despair, Arjuna, for this wins neither heaven nor Earth.

Fall not into degrading weakness, for this becomes not a man who is a man. Throw off this ignoble discouragement, and arise like a fire that burns all before it.

—II.2–3 Bhagavad Gita

After scolding Arjuna, Krishna begins a lecture on the nature of reality. He sets out to outline several yogas that will help Arjuna fight the battle. Krishna is not only playing the part of spiritual advisor to his friend, he is also utilizing this moment to proclaim to all mankind his doctrine of salvation for the world. His doctrine, known as the "Yoga of selfless Action" (karma yoga), entails self-surrender and devotion (bhakti) to the Lord, who is identical with the self within all.

The Bhagavad Gita contains an analogy for a person who has accomplished yoga and has mastered himself: "Just as a lamp in a windless place flickers not." This is the simile traditionally used for a yogi whose mind is properly controlled and who practices the yoga of the self.

The Bhagavad Gita View of Reality

Krishna believes that Arjuna's failing is the failing of all mankind. Here, Krishna instructs Arjuna about the nature of reality. The things of this world are not lasting, are unreal, and men are too attached to the things of the senses.

These attachments include the impermanent pleasures and pain of their own bodies.

If any man thinks he slays, and if another thinks he is slain, neither knows the ways of truth. The Eternal in man cannot kill: the Eternal in man cannot die.

He is never born and never dies. He is in Eternity: he is for ever-more. Never-born and eternal, beyond times gone or to come, he does not die when the body dies.

When a man knows him as never-born, everlasting, never-changing, beyond all destruction, how can that man kill a man, or cause another to kill?

As a man leaves an old garment and puts on one that is new, the Spirit leaves his mortal body and then puts on one that is new.

Weapons cannot hurt the spirit and fire can never burn him. Untouched is he by drenching waters, untouched is he by parching winds.

Beyond the power of sword and fire, beyond the power of waters and winds, the Spirit is everlasting, omnipresent, never-changing, never-moving, ever One.

Invisible is he to mortal eyes, beyond thought and beyond change. Know that he is, and cease from sorrow.

One sees him in a vision of wonder, and another gives us words of his wonder.

There is one who hears of his wonder; but he hears and knows him not.

—II.19–26 Bhagavad Gita

Arjuna wants to know the nature of this sage from Krishna.

What is the description of the man who has this firmly founded wisdom, whose being is steadfast in spirit, O Krishna? How does the man of settled intelligence speak, how does he sit, how does he walk?

—II.54 Bhagavad Gita

Lord Krishna answers decisively.

When a man puts away all the desires of his mind, O Arjuna, and when his spirit is content in itself, then he is called stable in intelligence.

He whose kind is untroubled in the midst of sorrows and is free from eager desire amid pleasures, he from whom passion, fear, and rage have passed away, he is called a sage of settled intelligence.

He who is without affection on any side, who does not rejoice or loathe as he obtains good or evil, his intelligence is firmly set in wisdom.

The objects of sense turn away from the embodied soul who abstains from feeding on them, but the taste for them remains. Even the taste turns away when the Supreme is seen.

Even though a man may ever strive for perfection and be ever so discerning, O Son of Kunti, his impetuous senses will carry off his mind by force.

Having brought all the senses under control, he should remain firm in yoga, intent on Me; for he, whose senses are under control, his intelligence is firmly set.

When a man dwells in his mind on the objects of sense, attachment to them is produced.

From attachment springs desire and from desire comes anger.

From anger arises bewilderment, from bewilderment loss of memory; and from loss of memory the destruction of intelligence, and from the destruction of intelligence he perishes.

But a man of disciplined mind, who moves among the objects of sense with the senses under control and free from attachment and aversion, attains purity of spirit.

And in that purity of spirit, there is produced for him an end of all sorrow; the intelligence of such a man of pure spirit is soon established in the peace of the self.

For the uncontrolled, there is no intelligence; nor for the uncontrolled is there the power of concentration; there is no peace, and for the unpeaceful, how can there be happiness?

When the mind runs after the roving senses, it carries away the understanding, even as a wind carries away a ship on the waters.

Therefore, O Mighty-armed, he whose senses are all withdrawn from their objects—his intelligence is firmly set.

What is night for all beings is the time of waking for the disciplined soul; and what is the time of waking for all beings is night for the sage who sees.

He unto whom all desires enter as waters into the sea, which, though ever being filled is ever motionless, attains to peace and not he who hugs his desires.

He who abandons all desires and acts free from longing, without any sense of mineness or egotism, he attains to peace.

This is the divine state, O Arjuna, having attained thereto, one is not again bewildered; fixed in that state at the hour of death one can attain to the bliss of God.

II.55–72

Krishna's Philosophy of Action

Krishna's advice to Arjuna turns from a discussion of abandoning all desires to a philosophy of action. Persons cannot attain spiritual progress just by renunciation of desires alone; in addition to renunciation, there must be action for the attainment of our spiritual goals.

So now, Krishna instructs Arjuna in the ways of yoga.

Not by nonperformance of actions does a man attain freedom from action; nor by the renunciation of actions does he attain his spiritual goal.

For no one, indeed, can remain, for even a single moment, unengaged in activity, since everyone, being powerless, is made to act by the dispositions (gunas) of matter (prakiti).

Whoever having restrained his organs of action still continues to brood over the objects of senses—he, the deluded one, is called a hypocrite.

But he who, having controlled the sense-organs by means of the mind, O Arjuna, follows without attachment the path of action by means of the organs of action—he excels.

Do you do your allotted work, for action is superior to nonaction. Even the normal functioning of your body cannot be accomplished through actionlessness.

Except for the action done for sacrifice, all men are under the bondage of action. Therefore, O son on Kunti, do you undertake that action for that purpose, becoming free from all attachment.

—III.4–9, Bhagavad Gita

Now Krishna instructs Arjuna in the manner of selfless action. The unselfish man does an action not for its consequences or rewards, but out of devotion and for the action itself. Indeed, the Bhagavad Gita recommends that the way to escape meaningless cycles of rebirth is to perform all one's actions without egotistical concern for their fruits.

Krishna is advancing another argument in favor of the yoga of action, namely that every man has to recognize his role in the scheme of cosmic ethics and actively promote its functioning. If he fails to do so, the cosmos will be turned into chaos. This is the basic theory of early Brahmanism. A prime illustration of the value of selfless action is shown in stanza 14: "From food creatures come into being; from rain ensues the production of food; from sacrifice results rain; sacrifice has its origin from action (karma)."

Human action has cosmic significance, according to the Bhagavad Gita. Action is the force that sets the cosmic wheel in motion and keeps it going. Sacrificial action leads to rain, which in turn leads to food, which leads to creatures, who begin the process all over again.

Having, in ancient times, created men along with sacrifice, Prajapati said, "By means of this sacrifice do you bring forth. May this prove to be the yielder of milk in the form of your desired ends.

"Do you foster the gods by means of this and let those gods foster you; thus fostering each other, both of you will attain to the supreme good.

"For the gods, fostered by sacrifice, will grant you the enjoyments which you desire. Whoever enjoys the enjoyments granted by them without giving to them in return—he is, verily, a thief."

The good people who eat what is left after the sacrifice are released from all sins. On the other hand, those sinful ones who cook only for themselves—they, verily, eat their own sin.

Know action to originate from the Brahman and the Brahman to originate from the Imperishable. Therefore, the Brahman, which permeates all, is ever established in sacrifice.

Whoever, in this world, does not help in the rotating of the wheel thus set in motion—he is of sinful life, he indulges in mere pleasures of sense, and he, O son of Pritha, lives in vain.

But the man whose delight is in the Self alone, who is content with the Self, who is satisfied only within the Self—for him there exists nothing that needs to be done.

He, verily, has in this world no purpose to be served by action done nor any purpose whatsoever to be served by action abnegated. Similarly, he does not depend on any beings for having this purpose served.

Therefore, without attachment, always do the work that has to be done, for a man doing his work without attachment attains to the highest goal.

For, verily, by means of work have Janaka and others attained perfection. You should also do your work with a view to the solidarity of society.

Whatever a great man does, the very same the common man does. Whatever norm of conduct he sets up, that the people follow.

There is not for me, O son of Pritha, in the three worlds, anything that has to be done nor anything to be obtained; and yet I continue to be engaged in action.

For if ever I did not remain engaged in action unwearied, O son of Pritha, men would in every way follow in my track.

These worlds would fall into ruin if I did not do my work. I would then be the creator of chaos and would destroy these people.

—III.10–23, Bhagavad Gita

At IV.19–20, this ideal of action is described directly.

He whose undertakings are all devoid of motivating desires and purposes and whose actions are consumed by the fire of knowledge—him the wise call a man of learning.

Renouncing all attachment to the fruits of actions, ever content, independent, such a person, even if engaged in action, does not do anything whatever.

—IV.19–20

FACT

Women are treated badly—as badly as untouchables on the lower end of the caste—in the Indian tradition. In the *The Laws of Manu*, a seminal text in Indian social history written about 200 B.C.E., a chapter on women is notorious for a passage that says women should be completely submissive to men. The Bhagavad Gita relegates them to the same level.

Self-Control: The Dharma of the Ideal Man

The Bhagavad Gita presents what might be called a "prescriptive ethic," ordering a way of life for the common man. In fact, it doesn't require that one be austere in physical or mental discipline; a yoga that required such extreme behavior was beyond the reach of the common man. The Gita has but one prescription for self-discipline—temperate behavior.

Krishna explains that all that is required is self-control.

When one renounces all the desires which have arisen in the mind, O son of Pritha, and when for himself is content with his own Self, then is he called a man of steadfast wisdom.

He whose mind is unperturbed in the midst of sorrows and who entertains no desires amid pleasures; he from whom passion, fear, and anger have fled away—he is called a sage of steadfast intellect.

He who feels no attachment toward anything; who, having encountered the various good or evil things, neither rejoices nor loathes—his wisdom is steadfast.

When one draws in, on every side, the sense-organs from the objects of sense as a tortoise draws in its limbs from every side—then his wisdom becomes steadfast.

The objects of sense turn away from the embodied one [the soul] who ceases to feed on them, but the taste for them still persists. Even this taste, in his case, turns away after the Supreme is seen. . . .

Yoga, indeed, is not for one who eats in excess nor for one who altogether abstains from food. It is, O Arjuna, not for one who is accustomed to excessive sleep, nor indeed, for one who always keeps awake.

For one who is disciplined in eating and recreation, who engages himself in actions in a disciplined manner, who properly regulates his sleep and wakefulness—for him yoga proves to be the destroyer of sorrow.

When one's properly controlled mind becomes steadfast within the self alone and when one becomes free from all desires, he is said to have accomplished yoga.

Wherein the mind, restrained by the practice of yoga, is at rest; and wherein he, seeing the Self through the Self, finds contentment within his own Self;

wherein he finds that supreme bliss, which is perceived by the intellect alone and which is beyond the ken of the sense-organs; wherein, being steadfast, he does not swerve from reality;

having obtained which, he does not consider any other gain to be greater than it; and being steadfast in which, he is not shaken by even a heavy sorrow;

That state, one should know as the one called yoga—the disconnection from union with sorrow. This yoga should be practiced with resoluteness and with undepressed mind. . . .

He who does not entertain hatred toward any being, who is friendly and ever compassionate, free from all sense of "my-ness," free from egoism, even-tempered in pain and pleasure, forbearing;

He who is ever content, the yogin, possessing self-control, of unshakable resolve; who has dedicated to Me his mind and intellect—he, My devotee, is dear to Me.

He who neither exults nor hates, neither grieves nor yearns; who renounces good and evil; who is full of devotion—he is dear to Me.

He who behaves alike to foe and friend; who, likewise is even-poised in honor or dishonor; who is even-tempered in cold and heat, happiness and sorrow; who is free from attachment;

Who regards praise and censure with equanimity; who is silent, content with anything whatever; who has no fixed abode, who is steadfast in mind, who is full of devotion—that man is dear to Me.

—II.55–72, Bhagavad Gita

A passage from the Bhagavad Gita reveals the self-control of the steadfast person.

Steadfast a lamp burns sheltered from the wind;
Such is the likeness of the yogi's mind
Shut from sense-storms and burning bright to heaven.
When mind broods placid, soothed with holy wont;
When Self contemplates self, and in itself
Hath comfort; when it knows the nameless joy
Beyond all scope of sense, revealed to soul—
Only to soul! And, knowing, wavers not.

—VI.66–74, Bhagavad Gita

The Spiritual Outlook of the Bhagavad Gita

The Bhagavad Gita is a lengthy discussion on the nature of duty toward others and personal obligations, and it is also rich in metaphysical thought. The poem manages to interweave our yearning to know, to act, and to have faith.

A personal god, Krishna, emerges. Krishna's conversation with Arjuna is a call to action. The obligations and duties of life that Arjuna must observe—both in terms of his personal conduct and his duties as a warrior—are not separate from the spiritual background of life and our spiritual purpose in the universe. In this context, action is always valued and inaction is devalued, even condemned.

While spirituality deals with matters that are timeless, our ideals must be in accord with the highest ideals of the age; however, these ideals may vary from age to age. So the *yugadharma*, the ideals of the particular age, must be kept in view.

FACT

In Hindu cosmology, a Yuga, or age, is the smallest unit of cosmological time. Four Yugas make up one Mahayuga, or Great Age: the Golden Age (Krita), the Silver Age (Treta Yuga), the Bronze Age (Dvapara Yuga), and the Iron Age (Kali Yuga). We are currently in the Kali Yuga, the most corrupt of the ages.

Because the modern age is fraught with frustration and quietism, the Gita's call to action makes a special appeal to our time. It is also possible to interpret ideal action in modern times as action that is humanitarian, altruistic, and practical. According to the Gita, such categories are praiseworthy, but a spiritual ideal must lie beneath such actions. Also, actions must be performed in a spirit of detachment, rather than with a concern for the results.

Finally, the message of the Gita is not sectarian or addressed to any school of thought. Rather, it is universal in scope, intended equally for Brahmin or outcaste. "All paths lead to me," the Gita says. Because it possesses such universality, it finds favor with all classes and schools. In the roughly 2,200 years since the Gita was written, India and the world have gone through various processes of change and stagnation, prosperity and decay. No matter; each age has found something relevant to its time in the Gita. It applies to the moral, social, and spiritual problems that afflict each age.

CHAPTER 10

Hindu Metaphysics: What Exists

Metaphysics is that portion of philosophy that refers to the reality of things. Four kinds of existents are described in classic Hinduism: the creator (Brahma), the creative spirit (Ishvara), the world-soul (Hiranyagarbha), and the world. All of these entities, however, are manifestations of Brahman, the absolute.

10

Brahman

It has been said that there is nothing in Hinduism more mysterious than Brahman. It is not a physical entity that you can point to, touch, or smell. The term "Brahman" means "the one without a second" or "the one that is multiple." Unlike Brahma, Brahman is not a personal, creator god.

Yet the term Brahman is essential to Hindu metaphysics. Brahman is the divine force that sustains the entire cosmos or world order. The stage for Brahman is the Upanishads, where it is exalted above all other forms of god. Brahman is an absolute godhead—infinite, changeless, and impersonal.

The term "Brahman" was developed in the Upanishads to mean "the All" or "ultimate reality." Even each individual self or atman is identical to the Brahman. Interestingly, the different views of Brahman were both theistic, in which it is identified with a god or goddess, and nontheistic, in which the Brahman was seen as a reality that lay beneath everything else.

Brahman is often understood via illustration. Here a sage explains to a student the ultimate nature of reality.

> *No one can understand the sound of a drum, without understanding both the drum and the drummer. No one can understand the sound of a conch shell, without understanding the shell and the one who blows it. No one can understand the sound of a lute, without understanding both the lute and the one who plays it. As there can be no water without the sea, no touch without the skin, no smell without the nose, no taste without the tongue, no sound without the ear, no thought without the mind, no work without the hands, and no walking without feet, so there can be nothing without the soul.*
>
> *When you throw a lump of salt into water, it dissolves; you cannot take it out again, and hold it in your hands. Yet if you sip any part of the water, the salt is present. In the same way the soul can be perceived everywhere and anywhere; the soul has no limit or boundary.*
>
> *At present there is a duality. 'You perceive other beings: you see them, hear them, smell them, and think about them. Yet when you know the soul, and when you recognize that the soul within you is the soul of all beings, how can you perceive other beings? How can*

*you see and hear them, smell then and think about them? How can
you regard yourself as subject and other beings as objects, when you
know that all are one?'*

—Brihadaranyaka Upanishad 1:4.1–4, 8

In the Upanishads, Brahman is the Absolute One, the ground of all being
which makes all things known. According to Advaita (nondual) philosophy,
Brahman alone is real; to see duality is unreal or maya.

Advaita is a term used to describe the unitary philosophies and religious
movements in India. Instead of describing these schools as being unitary
or monistic, a negative term is employed. Thus, advaita is usually translated as "nondual." Duality would imply that there is more than one reality; nonduality implies that there is only one reality.

Knowing Brahman

Trying to understand Brahman with our limited minds is a bit like trying to
look at your own eye, with which you see everything. To know Brahman
with our limited minds is akin to feeling color or feeling pain. To know Brahman, one must rely on a special, nonsensual kind of seeing, which can be
accomplished through one of the methods of God-realization.

One can only know Brahman through a transcendent state of consciousness. In the Upanishads, the negative description of God as being *neti-neti*
(literally "not this-not this") is the method by which Brahman is explained,
a method later adopted by the medieval Jewish philosopher Moses Maimonides. In speaking of God, Maimonides claimed we can only explain
what God isn't, not what he is. He called this the *via negativa*, or the "negative way."

He who really knows must understand the ultimate nature of things,
which is akin to knowing their causes. Such is the meaning of the following
passage in the Upanishads.

Sanatkumara said: "When you attain well-being, then you can act effectively. Those who do not attain well-being, cannot act effectively. Therefore you must understand the nature of well-being." The young man said: "I seek the nature of well-being."

Sanatkumara said: "When you enjoy the beauty of the world, then you can attain well-being. Those who do not enjoy the beauty of the world, cannot attain well-being. Therefore you must understand the nature of beauty." The young man said: "I seek the nature of beauty."

Sanatkumara said: "When you discern the infinite in that which is beautiful, then you can enjoy beauty. Those who do not discern the infinite in that which is beautiful, cannot enjoy beauty. Therefore you must understand the infinite." The young man said: "I seek the nature of infinity."

Sanatkumara said: "When you understand the indivisible unity of all beings, and see and hear nothing, you discern the infinite. When you see or hear only separateness and division, you discern only that which is finite. The infinite is beyond death, but the finite cannot escape death."

—Chandogya Upanishad 7:21; 22; 23; 24.10

To understand the indivisible unity of things is, in the words of the last passage, to understand Brahman.

Brahma

Brahma is called the lord and father of all creatures, a divinity who is generally considered to be the creator of the universe. Brahma frequently arises in Indian literature in a trinity, alongside Vishnu and Shiva. Brahma is the creator god, Vishnu is the sustainer of the world, and Shiva is the destroyer of the world. It is notable that unlike the other two members of the trinity, Brahma lacks a wide following of devotees. In modern-day India, Brahmanism has diminished in importance compared to the other two members of the trinity. In fact, there are only two temples in all of India devoted solely to Brahma.

In one story of Brahma's creation, he is born from a golden egg that floated in the primeval waters. In another depiction, Brahma is born in the lotus that emerges from Vishnu's navel as he lies on the primordial milk ocean. We can conclude from this image that Brahma is the creator God, but he is subsidiary to Vishnu.

In artistic representations, Brahma is often depicted with four faces. When Brahma is born, he has only one head, but he grows additional faces so that he is always able to observe his beautiful wife, Sarasvati. In a later legend, one of these faces is destroyed.

According to one legend, Brahma and Vishnu argue about which of them created the universe. While they quarrel, a large *lingam*—"phallus" in Hindu terminology—rears its head out of the ocean, crowned with flame. Brahma and Vishnu see a cave within the phallus in which the god Shiva resides. Overwhelmed by the sight of Shiva, Brahma and Vishnu agree that Shiva is the creator.

Hindu mythology includes not only a creation myth, but a destruction myth, too. The current age is called the Kali-Yuga, the final stage of a *kalpa* or time begun eons ago. This dark age is approaching its end, in which the world will be destroyed and prepared for another cycle of creation.

Hiranyagarbha

Referred to as the "world soul," Hiranyagarbha is the Golden Embryo, Golden Egg, or Golden Womb identified in the Rig Veda (X.121) as the cause of the universe. It possesses both a feminine and a masculine aspect; it is referred to as "he," but it is also the "womb" of manifest reality.

From the outset of Hindu thought, Hiranyagarbha has had multiple meanings. Consider the Rig Veda X.82, where it is the cosmic egg that separates into two hemispheres at the beginning of the world, its upper portion forming the sky and its yolk becoming the Sun. But there are various visions of how this cosmology works.

Even the same Hindu traditions embrace different ideas of the cause of the universe. For instance, some say that the *purusha* (the transcendent divine), with the cooperation of prakriti (nature), made the cosmic egg from which the world emerges. In one context, we see that Brahma, the creator, emerged from the egg to create the universe. In another context, Brahma is himself the hiranyagarbha, since the word can be used as an epithet or alternate name of Brahma.

In yet another mythological context, hiranyagarbha is seen as a creation of Shiva that embodies aspects of him. Other explanations posit Vishnu as the cause of hiranyagarbha.

One can sigh and quote the Rig Veda:

> *Who knows the truth? Who can tell us whence and how arose this universe? The gods are later than its beginning: who knows therefore whence comes this creation?*

Ishvara: The Creative Spirit

As opposed to an impersonal being such as Brahman, Ishvara is a personal god, though still the creator and ruler of the universe. As a personal god, Ishvara is involved in the lives of his creatures.

Ishvara has a series of defining qualities. He is absent of *adharma* (immorality), *mithya-jnana* (false knowledge), and *pramada* (error), and full of the positive presence of dharma, right knowledge, and equanimity. He is omnipotent, though influenced in his actions by the acts of his creatures. He acts only for the good of his creatures and treats them like a father treats his children.

Ishvara also reveals grace toward his creatures by supporting the efforts of people. For instance, if a person tries to attain something special, it is Ishvara who attains it; if Ishvara does not act, the activity of the person is fruitless.

INSIGHT

The commentary on the Nyaya Kusumanjali explains: "The Earth and other objects must have had a maker, because they have the nature of objects like a jar. . . . At the beginning of creation there must be have been [a cause] with a distinguishing faculty as then existing in Ishvara."

In the fashion of Aristotle, Indian philosophy presents philosophical arguments for the existence of Ishvara. The Nyaya Kusumanjali (*nyaya* means "analysis") states that the experience of contingency, eternity, diversity, activity, and individual existence requires an *adrsta*, an unseen cause, ultimately responsible for the joys and sorrows of life.

CHAPTER 11

Hindu Epistemology

In Hinduism, there is an obvious division between two kinds of knowledge. There is "lower" knowledge, which is knowledge of the everyday things in this world. Such knowledge arises from our senses, empirically. Hinduism also considers knowledge by way of the intellect to be lower. By contrast, there is a higher kind of knowledge, which is metaphysical. At its highest, this is knowledge that apprehends the divine, changeless reality of Brahman, not with the eyes, but with the heart.

How Do We Know What Exists?

The quest to know the reality behind the appearances of things stands at the center of all Indian philosophy. It is as if Indian philosophy is always talking of two planes—the here and now and another metaphysical level of being. So what plays out is a differentiation between what is assumed to be and what really is; what exists conditionally and what exists essentially; what is apparent and what is true.

The quest for a reality beyond the appearances of things takes place in stages, of which the Upanishads usually enumerate four. These four should be thought of as different states of consciousness. The Mandukya section of the Upanishads elaborates on the process. The god Rama tells a devotee that, "the Mandukya alone is sufficient for deliverance."

Lower Stage of Knowledge

The lowest stage of awareness is *vaishnavara* (sometimes called *jagarita-sthana*), the normal state of being awake, and hence open to sense perception and rational thought. This is also a state called *maya*.

Higher and lower knowledge are subjects addressed directly in the Mandukya Upanishad (1:1.3–9). The passage begins:

> *There are two kinds of knowledge, higher and lower. The study of sacred texts, of religion, of astronomy, and of all the arts, is lower knowledge. Higher knowledge is knowledge of the soul.*
>
> *The eye cannot see the soul, and the mind cannot grasp it. The soul has no race, and it does not belong to any social class. It has neither eyes, nor ears, nor hands, nor feet. It is vast and tiny; it is eternal and changeless. It is the source of all life.*
>
> *As the web comes forth from the spider, as plants sprout from the Earth, and as hair grows from the body, the universe springs from the soul. The universe is the energy of the soul; and from this energy comes life, consciousness, and the elements. The universe is the will of the soul; and from this will comes the law of cause and effect.*
>
> *The immortal soul sees all; nothing escapes the soul's gaze. From the soul one became many; but in the soul many are one.*

Later, the Song of the Lord (Bhagavad Gita) set forth three basic paths for living: knowledge, selfless action, and devotion to God. When used today, the path of knowledge implies an awareness of reality that is one and spiritual, the Brahman, with which each soul is identical, and which is *sat, chit,* and *ananda*—pure being, intelligence, and bliss. But the entire phenomenal world—that world we apprehend with our senses—is illusion (maya), which possesses only a relative reality compared to Brahman.

INSIGHT

In the Mandukya Upanishad (3:1.1–5, 7), a verse asks us to, "Imagine two birds perched on the same tree. One bird eats the fruits of the tree, both the sweet and the bitter. The other silently looks on. The first bird represents those who are attached to the things of this world, and so experience pleasure and pain; the second, those who are detached from the things of this world, and so are free from pleasure and pain."

The philosophy of pleasure and pain is clear: "As long as you pursue pleasure, you are attached to the sources of pleasure; and as long as you are attached to the sources of pleasure, you cannot escape pain and sorrow."

What is missing in this level of knowledge is the awareness of anything higher.

The following passage from the Chandogya Upanishad (6:9. 1–3; 10.1–3; 11.1–3) shows this distinction.

The Seed and the Blindfold

"Bring me a banyan fruit," Aruni said; and his son brought him one. "Cut it in two," Aruni said; and his son cut it in two. "What do you see?" Aruni asked. "I see some very small seeds," his son replied. "Take one of the seeds, and cut it in two," Aruni said; and his son cut the seed in two. "What do you see?" Aruni asked. "Nothing at all," his son replied.

Aruni said: "Within that seed is the essence which makes the entire tree grow—yet it cannot be seen. In the same way the soul is the essence which gives life to every being in the universe—yet it can-not be seen." "Tell me more about the soul," his son said.

Aruni said: "A man was once blindfolded, taken far from his vil-lage, and abandoned. The man wandered to the east and west, to the north and south, but he had no idea which way he was going. He called out for help. Eventually someone heard his call and took off the blindfold. The man now went from one village to another, asking directions, and he found his way back home. In the same way a good teacher takes the blindfold from the spiritual eyes of his pupils. Then they are able to find their way to the soul—which is their true home."

Maya

Maya is the lowest form of knowledge there is. How low is it? So low, that the alternate term for maya is *avidya*, or ignorance. This ignorance is of a special sort. It is ignorance of the unitary nature of all reality. A person who fails to see that all reality is one is in maya. It is as if such a person looks at reality through a veil of illusion or looks out at the world through gauzy material.

Metaphors may be necessary, since we are dealing with talk about the phenomenal world and the spirit world. Maya, the world as we sense and know it, disappears like fog does when the light of knowledge of the singu-lar nature of ultimate reality moves forward in our consciousness.

A person is in the grip of an illusion when she sees the world as dual. This duality is separateness; it is the sense of a self set apart from everything that is not self. It is a sense of twoness—of self and world—rather than one-ness. Not far removed from this sense of duality are the distinctions made by sense: hot and cold, strong and weak, light and dark, pleasant and unpleas-ant, winning and losing, life and death, and on and on.

In the midst of these changes, we yearn for something changeless among all the changing things. We long for an end to this perceived division between self and not-self. The real duality is not our personal "I" separate from the universe; rather, it is our spirit separate from matter.

In Hindu mysticism, these two are called *prakriti* and *purusha*. Prakriti is the phenomenal world, the world of matter, of things that are subject to change. This change includes growth and decay, life and death. But prakriti doesn't merely describe the world of material things; it also includes energy and any other entity. By contrast, purusha is spirit, pure consciousness. This is also known as atman, our real self. But this self is not a malleable, perishable substance, such as a brain, for the brain is part of the created world, of prakriti.

Many philosophies, including Western philosophies, draw a distinction between matter and spirit. These systems of thought are dualistic. The separation gets made between unconscious matter and conscious spirit, but Hindu mysticism goes further. It actually posits a third element, which confuses the other two. This element mixes up the roles of the other two and confuses their proper categories. This third element is called maya.

Maya is often translated as "illusion," but it is much more than that. It is the mistaken idea that each of us, each self, thinks of itself as a finite, destructible being that, as Shakespeare put it, "struts and frets his hour upon the stage and then is heard no more." Maya is the mistaken notion that reality lies beyond the tip of your nose, "out there." Maya is distortion; it can be compared to trick glasses that color each perceiver's reality, tainting it until it is distinct from what it truly is.

Maya sets up an obstacle between self and world, knower and known. Maya leads each individual to see himself as just that—an individual, and not part of the seamless web of the whole. A person in the grip of maya divides the world into as many things as there are grains of sand on the beach, multiplied by the number of stars in the sky. A person in maya fractures the world, instead of seeing it as one.

But seeing the world as one is easier said than done, for duality lies behind most perceptions of the physical world. We make so many distinctions between self and not-self: Trees, cars, rainbows—all can be termed beautiful, but all are also not-self. Only a meditating mind, calm and apart from the speeding duality and separateness of momentary existence, can allow us to see life as one.

The mystical experience is a unifying experience. In this unified state of mind, life is seen to be one; outside that state, it is infinitely diverse. It seems odd that the world can be both, but it can be. It all depends upon the mind that is doing the perceiving. It is the distorting lens of maya that makes us see the one as many.

There are reasons enough to adopt this view of life. The world that physics describes is a world of things. We see trees and mountains, sand and rocks, refrigerators and footballs. We see these objects as many, not one, and this makes sense. After all, each makes a different sense impression on us. Greek philosophers in the sixth century B.C.E. viewed nature as multifarious and sought to explain the source of this multiplicity. Later philosophers called this the problem of "the one in the many." Simply put, this was the problem of how a single substance—such as water or air—accounted for nature's many features.

In Hindu philosophy, this mode of perceiving separateness is maya. Maya is active, not passive. It is a creative force and one that interprets the world. It is the creative power of consciousness or *shakti*. One reason this maya has such a tight grip on us is because of our desires. We see things and people in the world that we desire; the world is a material place, a cornucopia of sights, sounds, shapes, and smells that we desire to experience and possess. These objective realities we perceive to be transient, changing, and finite, in opposition to a self that is eternal and changeless. It is this confusion over what is real and what is passing that characterizes maya.

Mystics in several traditions maintain that there is no relationship between matter and spirit. We are the self, pure spirit, and once the veil of maya falls, the illusion of being involved with this world and its creatures falls away. But this spiritual monism leaves matter out of the picture entirely. The Shvetashvatara Upanishad holds a different view:

Conscious spirit and unconscious matter
Both have existed since the dawn of time.
With maya appearing to connect them,
Misrepresenting joy as outside us
When all these three are seen as one, the Self
Reveals its universal forms and serves
As an instrument of the divine will.

But what is this self of ours? It is the whole of life, nothing more and nothing less. It is not separate from the world. On the contrary, it is a self united with all, *Jaganmata*, "Mother Universe," alive with the power of God.

This is a frequent vision of mystics. The Blessed Angela of Foligno had a similar experience, which was related in her *Book of Visions*. She wrote:

> *The eyes of my soul were opened and I beheld the fullness of God, in which were comprehended the whole world, both here and beyond the seas, and the abyss and ocean and all things. In all this I saw nothing but the divine power, in a way beyond the power of words to explain; so that my soul, through excess of marveling, cried out with a loud voice, This whole world is full of God!*

This vision isn't merely a matter of spiritual preference. The recognition that we are not separate creatures but all one means that we are not living for ourselves but for all. To reach this state is to be awake. That is the meaning of the name Buddha—"the awakened one." According to the mystics, once we are awake, we never fall asleep again. Our environs—our complete world—is the same as it has always been, but we look at it anew. We never lose sight of the unity underlying the apparent separateness.

Lower Knowledge in the Twelve Verses of the Mandukya Upanishad

In the Mandukya Upanishad the self—described as being Brahman, which in turn is all—has four states of consciousness. The first of these is called vaishnavara, in which:

> *One lives with all the senses turned outward,*
> *Aware only of the external world*
> *Those who know this,*
> *Through mastery of the senses, obtain*
> *The fruit of their desires and attain greatness.*
> *The waking state is unexpectedly praised here, but the only kind of success that awaits this state of consciousness is material success. For here, all of the human spirit is poured out and spent on*

a multitude of objective things, bound to space and time and to the laws of the physical universe.

The philosophy here is an echo of the Mandukya Upanishad, where it says:

Rituals and sacrifices are expressions of lower knowledge. If you wish to become wise, ignore all rituals and sacrifices, and go in search of all higher knowledge. In crossing the sea of birth and death, rituals and sacrifices are like leaking rafts.

And again, in the Brihadaranyaka Upanishad (2:4.7–9, 11–14), there is a discussion of two states of consciousness, a lower and a higher:

The sage continued: "As human beings we have two states of consciousness: one in this world, and the other in the world beyond. There is a third state between these two; in this third state we are aware of both worlds, with their sorrows and their joys.

"When we die, it is only the physical body which dies; we continue to have a non-physical existence, in which we retain the effects of our past lives. These effects determine our next life. During this period between lives we experience the third state of consciousness.

"In this third state of consciousness there are no chariots, no horses drawing them, and no roads on which they travel; we make up our own chariots, horses and roads. In this third state there are no joys and pleasures; we make up our own joys and pleasures. There are no ponds filled with lotus flowers, no lakes and no rivers; we make up our own ponds, lakes and rivers. That which we make up, is determined by the effects of our past lives."

Those who practice meditation and who conquer their senses and passions purify their hearts, thereby acquiring knowledge of the soul—which is the source of all light and life.

The Dreaming State: Taijasa, the Second State of Consciousness

In the dreaming state of consciousness (sometimes *taijasa* or *svapna-sthana*), the senses are "turned inward," which helps "one to enact the impressions of past deeds and present desires." This is higher than the second state of consciousness, because the human spirit is no longer subject to the laws of the physical world or bound to space and time.

A person here steps out of the limitations of physical nature by creating whatever the mind conceives. Consciousness in this state takes flight, leaving the physical world of matter and limited objects to the workings of a person's own mind. In Sanskrit, the term *taijasa* means "full of light."

A passage from the Katha Upanishad (4.1–5, 10–11) illustrates what it means to "turn the senses inward."

> When God created human beings, he fashioned the senses to perceive external objects and events. But wise people turn the senses inward, in order to perceive the soul.
>
> Foolish people chase outward pleasures; and so they fall into the snare of death. Wise people know that outward pleasures are fleeting, so they ignore them; they want only that joy which is eternal.
>
> Foolish people are enthralled by bright clothes and happy songs, by sweet perfumes and loving kisses. Wise people are concerned only with what lies behind all these things. Just as bees fly from one blossom to another, looking only for the essence of each one, wise people look only for the essence of every person they meet.
>
> Wise people, who know and understand the soul, are indifferent to both pleasure and pain; they have risen above sensations. They are indifferent to the past and the future; they have risen above time. They are indifferent to danger; they have risen above fear.
>
> Wise people know what is here is also there; that what was will also be. They see unity, not division.

The consciousness of a dreaming person generally creates mental pictures and notions. These ideas formed are not identical with those created during the waking state—which are sensations—but originate in the mind and are independent of material objects.

The Deep Sleep State: Prajna, the Third State of Consciousness

The stage of deep sleep is one where a person "neither dreams nor desires," it says in the Upanishads. In this state (called *prajna* or *susupti*), there is no separateness. In fact, it is a state of unification in which the spirit is no longer scattered over a profusion of objective and subjective things.

What keeps this state from being the highest of all is that the sleeper is not conscious of this unification and bliss. Since the subject is not conscious of this, prajna is not the highest of all states.

The Superconscious State: Turiya, the Fourth State of Consciousness

The highest of all states of consciousness is *turiya*, for it goes beyond the other three. This is a transcendent state, far beyond conventional awareness or apprehension. In this elevated state, the agent realizes Brahman, or ultimate reality.

In some of the early Upanishads, the two last states of prajna and turiya are combined, but the two states—of deep sleep and superconsciousness—are not the same. Similar to the state of mind of mystics through the ages, turiya is a state beyond describable qualities. In this sense, it is ineffable; that is, it cannot be expressed in precise words. Nonetheless, an attempt can be made.

The Upanishads call this a state that is none other than the Lord. He, Brahman, is the supreme of life. He is infinite peace and love, so he ought to be realized. In a passage from the Svetavatara Upanishad (6.1–10) this is referred to as "knowing God." The passage reads:

Some say that life created itself; others say that life evolved through time. God is the ruler of creation and time; all that exists comes from him.

God is pure consciousness. He is everywhere; he possesses all power; he sees every event. He created time; and living beings evolve at his command.

Those who act without thought of personal gain, and who control their actions, will eventually discover God; and then they will know that all forms of life are one. Those who work in the service of God are freed from the process of cause and effect.

Know God as the source of life, whose glory permeates the entire world. Know him as the one who is beyond space and time, and yet can be found within the human heart.

Know God as the one who makes the sun and the moon move across the sky. Know him as the one who determines what is right and wrong, and whose law is written in the human heart.

Know God as the king of all kings, the lord of all lords, the ruler of all. Know him as the one who never moves, and yet who is constantly active in the world.

Know God as the first cause of all things, and yet who himself has no cause. Know him as the Lord of love, who conceals himself in all living beings, as a spider conceals itself in its web.

Also, the scripture says turiya is represented by "Om." It says in the Upanishad:

Turiya is represented by AUM.
Though indivisible, it has three sounds.
A stands for Vaishvanara. Those who know this,
Through mastery of the sense, obtain
The fruit of their desires and attain greatness.
U indicates Taijasa. Those who know this,
By mastering even their dreams, become
Established in wisdom. In their family
Everyone leads the spiritual life.

M corresponds to Prajna. Those who know this,
By stilling the mind, find their true stature
And inspire everyone around to grow.
The mantra AUM stands for the supreme state
Of turiya, without parts, beyond birth
And death, symbols of everlasting joy.
Those who know AUM as the Self become the Self;
Truly they become the Self.

This is a supreme consciousness of consciousness. Our normal knowledge is knowledge of something; the knowledge of turiya is knowledge of nothing in particular, but knowledge of the ground of all-being and all-knowing. It is the self knowing itself for what it is—not the function of an isolated capacity of the mind, but pure awareness and knowledge of the subject itself.

INSIGHT

Those who search for the soul find the soul. Those who find the soul acquire all knowledge; they have no further questions to ask. They see the soul in every living being whom they encounter; thus, they serve every living being they encounter. By knowing the soul, they are united with all beings.

Spiritual advancement is made by renunciation. By renouncing worldly knowledge, you acquire spiritual knowledge; by renouncing worldly life, you attain immortality; by renouncing the pleasures of the body, you are freed from the pains of the body.

This state, sometimes referred to as jnana, is the self-consciousness of reality. Beyond this knowledge, there is no objective content of a world. There is no multiplicity, literally no thing with which this knowledge can be identified. It is not possible to have this knowledge in part; one has it all, or not at all. It is the knowledge of atman, which is indivisible.

This fourth condition of knowledge is purity. The senses are turned neither outward nor inward; there is neither wakefulness nor dreaming. This is the condition of supreme consciousness, when there is complete awareness of the soul. This fourth condition is expressed by the word "Om."

In sum, the Mandukya Upanishad distinguishes between a para, or higher, and an apara, or lower, knowledge. The lower is the knowledge of the Vedas and Vedangas, or traditional knowledge. This higher knowledge is that "wherewith the imperishable is grasped"; it is also that which leads to self-realization.

> *The eye cannot see it; mind cannot grasp it.*
> *The deathless Self has neither caste nor race,*
> *Neither eyes nor ears nor hands nor feet.*
> *Sages say this Self is infinite in the great*
> *And in the small, everlasting and changeless,*
> *The source of life.*
>
> *Mandukya Upanishad 3:2.3–8*

Another passage from the Chandogya Upanishad (6:1.1–7) includes a conversation between a twelve-year-old boy, and his father, Aruni. It illustrates this kind of "knowing the unknown" that constitutes higher knowledge:

> *When his son reached the age of twelve, Aruni, who was a priest, said to him: "It is time for you to go to a spiritual teacher, and become his disciple. Every member of our family studies spiritual knowledge." So the son went away for twelve years. During this time he learnt all the Vedas, and he returned home at the age of twenty-four.*
>
> *His father said to him: "You seem to be very proud of all the knowledge you have acquired. But did you ask your teacher for that wisdom which enables you to hear the unheard, think the unthought, and know the unknown?" The son said: "What is that wisdom?" Aruni replied: "By knowing one lump of clay, we come to know all things made of clay; and we realize that in essence they are the same, differing only in name and form. By knowing one gold nugget, we come to know all things made of gold; and we realize that in essence they are the same, differing only in name and form. By knowing one tool of iron, we come to know all tools made of iron; and we realize*

that in essence they are the same, differing only in name and form. In the same way, through spiritual wisdom we come to know that all life is one."

What falls away in this state of consciousness—this way of seeing—is the usual subject-object distinction or polarity. The knowing mind doesn't experience his mind as set apart from the world, and the world as other; rather, his mind is united with the world.

Two more passages from the Upanishads illustrate the point more clearly. In the Brihadaranyaka Upanishad (4:3.9–10) the supreme goal of life is discussed:

> *The soul is itself is free from desire, free from evil, and free from fear.*
>
> *When a man is in the arms of his beloved, he is oblivious to what is happening around him and within him. In the same way when we are in union with the soul, we are oblivious to what is happening around us and within us. In this state all desire is fulfilled, because union with the soul is the only desire; there can be no suffering.*
>
> *In this state there are no parents, no worlds, no spiritual forces, and no sacred texts. In this state there is neither thief nor murderer; there is no low caste or high caste; there is neither monk nor ascetic. The soul is beyond good and evil, and beyond all sorrows of the heart.*
>
> *In this state we see without seeing, smell without smelling, taste without tasting, speak without speaking, hear without hearing, touch without touching, think without thinking, know without knowing—for nothing is separate from us. Where there is separateness, there is a subject which sees, smells, tastes, hears, touches, thinks and knows; and there are objects. But where there is unity, there is no subject and no objects.*
>
> *This is divinity. This is the supreme goal of life, the supreme treasure, the supreme joy.*

And in the Brihadaranyaka Upanishad (4:4.6b), this same kind of higher metaphysical knowing is elaborated on:

The soul is not born, but always exists, It is the consciousness of life, and dwells in every heart; it is the master of all, the lord of all. The soul is not made greater by good actions, not diminished by bad actions. It is the supreme sovereign, and the protector of all living beings. It is the bridge between this world and the world beyond; and it is also the dike which separates them.

Those who love God, seek the soul through studying the sacred texts, through worship, through acts of charity, and through abstaining from pleasures. Those who find the soul, become sages. They demand nothing for themselves, because those who know the soul. Possess the whole world. They do not desire offspring, and nor do they desire wealth; they regard all desire as empty.

The soul cannot be defined; it is not this or this. The soul cannot be comprehended, because it is beyond comprehension. The soul cannot pass away, because it is imperishable. The soul is free, because it has no bonds of attachment. The soul is serene, because it cannot suffer or fear suffering.

Those who know the soul, feel no grief at the evil they do, nor elation at the good they do; they are beyond good and evil. They are indifferent to what is done and left undone. They are masters of themselves, and they are utterly calm and tranquil. They see the soul within themselves, and they see the soul in all beings.

This is the highest knowledge, for it is a knowledge beyond material reality.

CHAPTER 12

Philosophy and Theology

Before the beginning of the Christian era, six philosophical systems, or *darshanas,* had taken shape in
India. *Darshan* is from the Sanskrit root *drish,* meaning "to see," referring to the most important element
of Hinduism—the eye-to-eye contact between an
iconic divinity (the image of the divinity) and the devotee or worshipper. Each one of the six represents a
different, independent approach, a separate philosophical argument, and each is part of a larger plan.
The six systems are Nyaya, or analysis; Vaishesika, or
personal characteristics; Sankhya, or the count; Yoga;
Mimamsa, or enquiry; and Vedanta, or the end of
the Vedas.

Nyaya, or Analysis

The beginnings of the Nyaya systems go back to the disputations of the Vedic scholars. Nyaya philosophy is known for being analytical and logical; the word itself means "logic" or "the science of right reasoning" or sometimes the "science of discussion" or "the science of debate." Its first adherents, known as niyayikas, represent Nyaya as a means toward true knowledge of the soul and the aim of human life, so the use of this logical analysis was connected with and in the service of metaphysical knowledge.

Even in ancient times, Nyaya wove together two elements: *adhyatma-vidya,* or metaphysics, and *tarka-sastra,* or rules of debate, often called logic. The work called the Nyaya Sutra (written in the third century B.C.E. by Sage Gotama, who founded the Nyaya philosophy), included substantial sections on suffering, soul, and salvation. Nyaya is a prerequisite for those who want to attain the highest good.

The practice of Darhsan by itself can confer grace upon a seeker and result in spiritual benefit. This is why Hindus visit temples, as well as divine persons, and why Hare Krishna devotees worship statues, Swami Prabhupada, or images of Krishna. Darshan was also apparent in the throng of several hundred thousand who attended the funeral of Mohandas Gandhi.

So the work begins with a bold aphorism: "It is knowledge of the true character of the following sixteen categories that leads to the attainment of the highest good: (1) The Means of Right Cognition; (2) The Objects of Right Cognition; (3) Doubt; (4) Motive; (5) Example; (6) Theory; (7) Factors of Inference; (8) Cogitation; (9) Demonstrated Truth; (10) Discussion; (11) Disputation; (12) Wrangling; (13) Fallacious Reasoning; (14) Casuistry; (15) Futile Rejoinder; and (16) Clinchers." Modern readers will recognize most of these elements as being essential to a textbook on logic.

But Indian logic is not learned for its own sake; this is not formal logic or a mere device for correct thinking. Rather, logic is practiced for the sake of salvation. In the context of Hinduism, this is logic as a way to truth. Sage

Gotama, who founded the Nyaya school, asserted that the misery experienced by man was due to birth, which resulted in death. The reasoning is that if suffering, birth, activity, mistaken notions, and folly are cancelled out, *moksha* or liberation can be achieved.

FACT

Nyaya was taught in the ancient and medieval period and up to the present in India's schools and universities. It wasn't just that Nyaya was considered indispensable for the study of philosophy; it was also part of the mental training for educated people. It was as important to Indian education as Aristotle's logic was to European education.

The Vaishesika System

The Vaishesika system resembles the Nyaya system. "Vaishesika" is a Sanskrit word meaning "referring to the distinctions." It emphasized the separateness of individual selves and objects. In addition, it developed an atomic theory of the universe, similar to the one that Democritus had developed in Athens.

INSIGHT

Comparable to the Greek philosopher Aristotle (384–322 B.C.E.), who cited material, formal, efficient, and final causes to explain the existence of objects, Sage Kanada, the founder of the Vaishesika school, cited atoms as the material cause of the universe; God as an efficient cause.

The Vaishesika divides the broad multiplicity of nature into six *padarthas* or categories. The first is *dravya*, which is substance or matter. The second is guna, the quality or characteristic of a substance, as green is the quality of a substance such as a pine tree. The third category is karma, or activity; the fourth, *samanya,* or universality. The fifth is *vishesha,* or distinctiveness. Finally, the sixth category is *samavaya,* or inherence, the relationship between a whole and its parts. These six padarthas aren't mere concepts, but are the real essences of things in nature.

As with the Nyaya system, the Vaishesika school of thought took a stand on knowledge as a means to the everlasting good. In addition, it turned away from sacrifices and other religious rituals, opting instead to inquire into the nature of reality. Sage Kanada, who founded the Vaishesika system in the sixth century B.C.E., examined nature and the universe.

Sankhya

According to Sankhya, there is neither a personal God nor an impersonal one. In fact, neither monotheism nor monism is acceptable, either. The approach is atheistic, and this ruled out the foundations of a supernatural religion. There is no creation of the universe by a god, but rather a constant evolution of the universe in which matter and spirit interact.

The Sankhya philosophy is dualistic, called *dvaita,* because it builds its structure on two primary causes. These are prakriti, which is an ever-changing energy, and purusha, which is unchanging spirit. In fact, Sankhya, which was founded by Kapila, maintains that the universe arose through the union of nature (prakriti) and consciousness (purusha).

In considering the entities of the universe, Sankhya contends that there are as many souls and units of consciousness (purushas) as there are living beings. This is the evolutionary theory that emerges from Sankhya.

According to this teaching, cause and effect become the undeveloped and developed states of the same thing, as if there was an identity between them. Between the lowest and highest elements in the universe there is continuity and a unity; this is how the universe evolves and this is the metaphysical nature of the universe.

According to the Sankhya system, evolution is due to energy coming under the influence of consciousness, working with the principle of cause and effect, from which arises nature in all its diversity and complexity. Nature is ever changing and developing.

Yoga

The yoga system of Patanjali is a method for the discipline of the body and mind leading up to psychic and spiritual training. Yoga means "to yoke," and in the sense of Hinduism is the seeking of union with or harnessing oneself to God.

The yoga referred to as one of the six darshanas was founded by Patanjali in the second century B.C.E. Patanjali, who authored the Yoga Sutras, defined yoga as a methodical effort to attain perfection by mastering the physical and psychic elements of human nature. Through yoga, higher levels of consciousness can be reached, as well as higher knowledge for oneself, rather than arriving at some preconceived metaphysical theory of the universe. Yoga can be adopted and used by any system of philosophy—disciples of the atheistic Sankhya philosophy might employ yoga.

QUESTION?

What is necessary before the highest stages of contemplation are reached?
The body should be fit and healthy. A number of bodily exercises and ways of breathing (especially those involving deep and long breaths) are prescribed as a way to gain control over the body.

The physical body, active will, and observing mind must all be brought under control. Patanjali prescribes practices designed to free the body from its restlessness and impurity. Such practices can strengthen a person's vital power and also prolong youth and span of life. All of this contributes to self-realization and spiritual freedom. Still other practices are prescribed to clarify the mind and bring peace.

FACT

Hatha yoga was a technique taught by Patanjali. The goal is to activate the centers of psychic energy. Its main goal is to unite *ha* (the breath of the sun known as *prana*) with *tha* (the breath of the moon, known as *apana*) utilizing various bodily postures and purification exercises.

The later stages of such yoga are supposed to lead to some insight or even a condition of mystical ecstasy, but it must be stressed that Patanjali is not interested in metaphysical theory; rather, his concern is to indicate a practical way toward liberation by means of disciplined action. This is why he composed the Yoga Sutras, which includes the following eight steps:

- *Yama,* or self-control
- *Niyama,* encompassing various required ethical and moral practices
- *Asana,* or bodily posture and positions, used to find a position in which the concentration is not disturbed by the body
- *Pranayama,* or breath control, practiced because the breath greatly influences one's thoughts and emotional state
- *Pratyahara,* or withdrawal from consciousness
- *Dharana,* or concentration
- *Dhyana,* or meditation
- *Samadhi,* or meditative achievement, becoming one with the object of meditation

Mimamsa, or Enquiry

Founded by Jaimini, who lived around 200 B.C.E. and wrote the Mimamsa Sutras, the Mimamsa system is different from the other schools in its insistence that knowledge is insufficient for liberation. Mimamsa means "the old theology." According to Mimamsa, ritual remains essential, even though the system did not originally require or presuppose a belief in God. The principle contribution of Mimamsa is in providing an elaborate system for interpreting the Vedas.

It is the nature of Mimamsa to clarify the precise meaning of each of the Vedic injunctions so that devotees can reach the heavenly realm after death. Mimamsa is not necessarily theistic or oriented toward the gods in a true sense; gods may exist, but the Vedas supersede all according to Mimamsa.

To this day, Purva-Mimamsa plays a major role in Hindu life, since worship and the performance of sacrifices are held to bring about the fulfillment of every type of desire. These desires can be spiritual (for which worship is a preparatory cleansing) or everyday material desires.

Classical Mimamsa does not admit the existence of any creator or destroyer of the universe. Mimamsakas (or those who follow Mimamsa) even propose arguments that positively disprove the existence of God. In fact, the world has always been in existence and requires no God.

According to the Purva (or early) Mimamsa, the sole purpose of scripture was to set forth ordained duty, which was otherwise unknowable. This was done in all sorts of Vedic passages—those expressing injunctions and prohibitions. Since no Vedic passage could be lacking in purpose, all other passages were viewed as *arthaveda* or helpful explanations, praises, or condemnations in connection with injunction or prohibition.

Vedanta, or the End of the Vedas

The last school in this system is the Vedanta school. Arising from the scriptures of the Upanishads, the Vedanta system took many shapes and forms but always resulted in a monistic philosophy of the universe. This view represents the dominant philosophical outlook of Hinduism today.

QUESTION?

How can our finite minds understand atman?
The Upanishads described atman thus: "Whole is that, whole (too) is this; from whole, whole cometh; take whole from whole, (yet) whole remains." The individual soul is not a separate entity, but that absolute soul itself, though limited in some ways. It is compared to the space enclosed in a jar, the atman being universal space.

According to this view, the only existing metaphysical entity is the atman or absolute soul. This is the experiencing subject of the world; all else is objective. It is unclear from a logical point of view how all of the multiplicity of the world can belong to one thing, for if the absolute is one thing and indivisible, how can there be many things? Perhaps logic cannot account for it.

It says in the Brahmanas, "Desiring heaven, one should perform sacrifice." Consequently, the Mimamsakas emphasize the "desire for heaven," which is the basic rationale for performing a sacrifice.

Shankara and Other Important Thinkers

13

Shankara (788–820 C.E.) was a philosophical genius who created Vedanta—the end (or conclusion) of the Vedas. It is this philosophy that dominates Hinduism today. It rests on the wisdom of the three basic Hindu texts: the Upanishads, Vedanta Sutras, and Bhagavad Gita. Shankara's Vedanta philosophy taught that the world is illusory, or maya, and only the transcendent ultimate reality, the Brahman, is real.

The Importance of Shankara

Shankara, whose name often appears as Shankaracharya (*acharya* means "religious teacher"), was no retiring monk; he was a peripatetic, wandering all of India. Born in Malabar in the far south of India, he traveled incessantly, meeting innumerable people, arguing, reasoning, convincing, and infecting others with his tremendous vitality.

Shankara's World

Shankara was the disciple of guru Gaudapada—the Guru of Govinda—and expressed the guru's philosophy that the Brahman of the Upanishads was the only reality. The world itself was but a temporary illusion, a trifle. In fact, Shankara denounced the entire visible cosmos as an illusion superimposed on true being by man's deceitful senses and unenlightened mind. Any person trying to understand the ultimate nature of reality could not help but see the insignificance of this world of space and time.

Shankara possessed a far-reaching intellect. He wrote commentaries on the Vedanta Sutra, the Upanishads, and the Bhagavad Gita. He thought that only the path of knowledge, which culminated in knowing the Brahman, could lead to liberation; the paths of work and devotion were secondary. Further, he initiated a tradition of renunciative yogis, who sought the full realization of the Brahman in a state of being, consciousness, and bliss.

Shankara's Impact

In subsequent centuries, a number of important thinkers took different interpretations of the earliest Vedanta. Whereas Shankara leaned toward a monistic view of the identity of Brahman and atman, Ramanuja (1077–1157 C.E.) took up a qualified or modified monism. Madhva (1199–1278 C.E.) rejected monism altogether in favor of out-and-out dualistic theism.

Shankara's Life

Shankara was a Hindu philosopher who created the first widely known school of Vedanta. Little is known about his life, which lasted just thirty-two years. He was born in Kerala to a family of Nambudiri Brahmins, who were strict in their study of the Vedas. He was said to be a master of all the sciences, even at an early age. He is declared to have caused a river to divert and thereby come closer to his mother's door so she would be saved the trouble of fetching water.

When he was eight years old, Shankara wanted to become a renouncer, but his mother said no. Soon afterward, he was attacked by a crocodile. A moment before death he cried out to his mother to allow him to renounce the world so he could reach liberation from birth and rebirth. His mother consented, and Shankara was miraculously released from the mouth of the crocodile. He proceeded to tour India and debate everyone he encountered. At a very early age, he retired to the forest, where he met the sage Govinda and became his pupil. In time, Shankara became known as the most brilliant philosopher of his time.

Shankara would come to be associated with Shaivism and with the worship of the goddess through texts later attributed to him. His system of Vedanta is known as the Advaita, or nondual Vedanta.

FACT

Though Advaita, or nondual Vedanta, is attributed to Shankara, the formal school of thought known as Vedanta owes more to a man named Badarayana, a sage from the first century. It is Badarayana who receives credit for stressing knowledge as the only way to liberation.

Advaita, or Nondualism

The fundamental principles of Shankara's philosophy derive from his concept of absolute nonduality. What exactly does this mean? Those who believe in notions of plurality and cause and effect look at the world through a false set of glasses, peering out through the visor of maya. In addition, your soul, though it appears separate from other souls and from Brahman, is in reality nothing but the one unitary Brahman. The person who sees reality as dual dwells in ignorance. The only cure for this ignorance is knowledge. Religion and devotion play a subordinate role to knowledge.

Shankara's views are arguably the most widely known outside of India. He held that maya causes the mistaken conviction that reality is packaged into immutable discrete things and selves who compete for their share of those things. Persons thus accumulate bad karma, which perpetuates the round of rebirths as the only way to make restitution.

Mysticism

Mysticism means different things to different people, but it is acceptable to define it as a direct encounter with divine reality. In Hinduism, there are at least two categories of spirituality that can be called mystical. One of these is a kind of cosmic or uniting mysticism in which the person experiencing it discovers that she is not a distinct self separate from the world, but one with a cosmic reality. The other kind of mysticism is a theistic or dualistic mysticism, in which the person experiencing it and the deity are perceived as separate. The person remains herself throughout the experience and is aware of her own individuality.

Shankara is a prime exponent of uniting mysticism. In fact, one could argue that Shankara's entire system of thought derives from his meditation on the Upanishadic teaching of the oneness of the Brahman (or absolute reality) and atman (soul). For Shankara, attaining the knowledge of the complete unity of all reality is the goal of a long process of clarifying one's perceptions. If this is the goal of knowledge, another is to banish ignorance (literally, "nonknowledge" or *avidya*) that binds us in the snares of illusion.

Shankara wrote poems, some of which were meditations meant to transport the spirit through the final barrier of thought. One collection, "Morning Meditations," is a metaphysical search for the supreme essence, Brahman.

At dawn I call to mind the essence of the Self shining forth self-effulgent in my heart, the Fourth (turiya), which is existence—eternal, pure spiritual consciousness, and bliss—the goal and salvation of the "Highest Swans." [In the poem, swans are compared to wandering Vedantic ascetics, who, like swans, roam the world in homeless freedom.] The being that regards the states of dream, waking, and deep sleep—that supreme essence (Brahman) am I. It is indivisible, with-

out parts; I am not a combination of the five perishable elements. I am neither body, nor the senses, nor what is in the body. I am not the ego-function: I am not the group of the vital breath-forces; I am not intuitive intelligence (buddhi). Far from wife and son am I, far from land and wealth and other notions of that kind. I am the Witness, the Eternal, the Inner Self, the Blissful One.

Suppose that while you are walking in the forest, you become terrified at the sight of a form you are sure is a serpent. You go out of your way to avoid the danger, only to find out later that it was merely a coiled rope. According to Shankara, this is the kind of power maya has on us.

Owing to ignorance of the rope, the rope appears to be a snake; owing to ignorance of the Self, the transient state arises of the individualized, limited, phenomenal aspect of the Self. The rope becomes a rope when the false impression disappears because of the statement of some credible person; because of the statement of my teacher I am not an individual life-monad. I am the Blissful One.

I am not born; how can there be either birth or death in me?

I am not the vital air; how can there be either hunger or thirst for me?

I am not the mind, the organ of thought and feeling; how can there be either sorrow or delusion for me?

I am not the doer; how can there be either bondage or release for me?

Neither hatred and aversion nor passionate clinging have I; neither cupidity nor delusion. I am possessed of neither egotism nor self-infatuation. No claim of the ritualistic code of the duties of life (dharma), no worldly purpose (artha) no desire for any kind of enjoyment (kama), no freedom attained or released to be sought (moksha), pertains to me. I am Siva, whose being is spirituality and bliss. I am Siva, the ever peaceful, perfect being.

For me there is no death, no fear, no distinction of caste. I have no father, mother, birth, relatives, or friends. For me there is neither teacher nor pupil. I am Siva ("the peaceful One"), whose form is spirituality and bliss.

I am neither male nor female, nor am I sexless. I am the Peaceful One, whose form is self-effulgent, powerful radiance. I am neither a child, a young man, nor an ancient; nor am I of any caste. I do not belong to one of the four life-stages. I am the Blessed-Peaceful One, who is the only Cause of the origin and dissolution of the world.

For Shankara, these lines are to be repeated silently in solitary hours of meditation. The stanzas should be memorized, with the result that the person meditating is imbued with the attitude they instill. The result will be transcendent peace. The truly spiritual person purifies her desire for individuality. Uniting mysticism is about being one with the truth; in fact, Shankara recommended intense devotion to Shiva as an integral part of his teaching.

In a polemic against the logical inconsistency of Buddhism, Shankara wrote, "Buddha, by propounding the three mutually contradictory systems, teaching respectively the reality of the external world, the reality of ideas only and general nothingness, has made it clear that he was a man given to make incoherent assertions."

The Shankaracharya Order

Shankara is the founder of the first major order, known as the Shankaracharya Order. He established monasteries in four sacred cities: Badrinath in the north, Shrinagar in the south, Puri in the east, and Davarka in the west. Shankara's followers established a number of Vaishnava orders, the first of which was begun by Ramanuja, another renowned theologian. Shankara's monks learned the nondualistic Vedanta system of thought, with its mysticism.

The Shankaracharya order of renouncers was formally known as the Dashanami (Ten Names) Order. This is because the renouncers, or Sannyasins, all take one of ten names: Aranya, Ashrama, Bharati, Giri, Parvata, Puru, Sarasvati, Sagara, Tirtha, or Vana. Shankaracharya's aim was to establish a highly disciplined and intellectually capable group of mendicants who could challenge and defeat the Buddhists of his time and who would debate theistic Hindus who clung to Vedic orthodoxy.

The Dashanamis of the Shankaracharya Order are still considered the most respected group of mendicants in India. Members of the order are learned in Sanskrit and Vedanta philosophy and are often educated in English as well. The order is devoted to noninjury and nonviolence; however, they hired militant mendicants carrying tridents to defend them against attacks by militant Vaishnavite Sadhus. Battles between these groups are famous for their carnage.

Ramanuja

Ramanuja (1077–1157) was a celebrated philosopher and saint of South India. He was the founder of the philosophical school known as Vishitadvaita, or special nondualism. His highest ideal was the love of God (*bhakti*), as well as the knowledge that all creatures and all inanimate creatures are alike "forms of God."

Ramanuja's views are often set off against those of Shankara. Ramanuja thought the divinity was endowed with attributes. Shankara viewed the ultimate reality or Brahman as completely beyond characteristics or characterization. Shankara's Brahman was an inert, transcendental reality; Ramanuja believed in a "qualified Brahman"—that is, a personal god endowed with attributes to comprehend souls as things.

FACT

Ramanuja's guru felt threatened that his student developed his own view of the Sanskrit scriptures to challenge his own. The guru is said to have arranged to lure Ramanuja on a pilgrimage to the holy city of Benares so he could be killed. But Ramanuja was miraculously saved, and eventually his guru bowed at his feet and accepted Ramanuja as his teacher.

In a passage entitled "How God Is Regarded by the Ignorant and by the Wise," Ramanuja wrote, "high-minded believers worship God by paying homage to him . . . by performing the sacrifice called *jnana*." What does that mean? God is worshipped as the one underlying the individual plurality of things.

Ramanuja, the greatest bhakti theologian so far, enumerates six prerequisites for someone embarking on the bhaktimarga: a bhakta has to observe certain dietary rules; show complete disregard for worldly objects; continue all religious activities faithfully; perform puja or purification; behave virtuously; and be free from depression.

Madhva

Madhva (1199–1278), also known as Madhavacharya, and Anandatirtha, was a brilliant, prolific scholar of Vedanta. He studied the writings of Shankara, but as a proponent of dualism, he concluded by rejecting Shankara's teachings.

Born in a village in South India, Madhva became an expert on the Vedas at a young age and became a Sannyasin early on. He spent several years in prayer and meditation, and then began to teach and sermonize.

Madhva eventually wrote tracts opposing twenty-one important philosophers in order to establish his own philosophy of dvaita, or dualist Vedanta. As he traveled, he spoke out against the various existing philosophical schools. He remains the chief representative of the dualist philosophy of Dvaita Vedanta, the third of the three major schools of Vedanta thought. According to Madhva, three separate substances have existed eternally: God, the soul, and the world.

Madhva produced a massive body of work, including commentaries on all thirteen of the orthodox Vedic Upanishads, the Vedanta Sutra, and the Bhagavad Gita. In these works, he argued passionately for the idea that God and the human self or soul were completely distinct from each other, and the world was also completely distinct from God.

FACT

A Sannyasin is one who has renounced the world and lives without possessions, solely for the realization of liberation. This lack of possessions consists not only in total material poverty, but also in what Christian mysticism calls the "poverty of spirit"—freedom from such dualistic notions as good and bad, desire and repulsion, and fear and greed.

Although all three are real and eternal, the latter two are subordinate to and dependent upon God. This independent reality, Brahman, is the creator of the universe (Vishnu, according to Madhva), who manifests himself in various forms and from time to time is incarnated as an avatar.

Madhva presented a challenge to all nondualist thinkers. He argued that only the grace of God, in the form of Krishna, could save a human being from the endless round of birth and rebirth, and only bhakti or devotion to the divinity could rescue humans from the abyss of successive rebirth.

CHAPTER 14

What Morality Consists of: The Four Castes

The caste system has been an institution of Hinduism from the beginning. From the earliest Aryan times, there has been evidence of a stratification of Indian society, with the priestly class at the top of the social order. Although the caste system was officially outlawed after Indian independence from Great Britain in 1947, it had a profound impact on the formation of Indian society, and its legacy is apparent in today's India.

The Caste System

Going back to the Vedic hymns, there are references to four social orders, later known as castes. One hymn refers to ritual sacrifices performed on Earth by a priestly class. The hymn speaks of four social orders, and the passage emphasizes the magical-ritualistic origin of castes.

Caste Development

At some time after 700 B.C.E., the "modern" caste system, a system of social hierarchy, began to develop in India. In Vedic tradition, the concept of varna stratified society into four groups: Brahmins (priests), Kshatriyas (warriors), Vaishyas (common people, including merchants), and Shudras (servant classes). In addition to the four classes, a fifth class, known as Untouchables, emerged.

The Hindu tradition first distinguished between those who are twice born and those who aren't. The twice born are in the highest three stages of the social hierarchy—the Brahmins, Kshatriyas, and Vaishyas. Those not twice born are Shudras.

The Brahmins made up the highest social order, the literate intelligentsia that gave India its thinkers, law makers, judges, and ministers of state. This scholarly elite has usually been associated with the priesthood. The *Rajanyas*, later called *Kshatriyas,* or rulers, and the military class, were the second highest social order. Landowners, merchants, and moneylenders, known as Vaishyas, made up the third class. Finally, the Shudras, originally those peoples conquered by the Aryans, were workers, artisans, or serfs. The concept of Untouchables was created to refer to people whom the upper classes would not even allow to be near them or to touch them.

Before the caste system was solidified, there was evidence of social intercourse among classes. We now tend to associate the caste system in India with the four basic social groups—Brahmins, Kshatriyas, Vaishyas, and Shudras. However, these groups were once divided into many, many more. There were castes of metal workers, weavers, warriors, and priests. Other castes developed along ethnic or religious lines; tribal communities, as well as Muslims, Christians, and Jews, were incorporated into Hindu society as distinct caste groups. As a consequence, more than 3,000 castes emerged in Indian society.

The Caste System in Everyday Life

The caste system dominated every aspect of life in traditional Hindu society. Caste, more properly *jati,* or birth, is directly related in most cases to occupation, so entering a caste was not an act of merit or will; a person was born into the caste of his parents. From that moment on, a person's caste determined much of his future; caste determined diet, vocation, place of residence, and choice of mate. In addition, caste hierarchy was based on concepts of purity and pollution. The more contact a person had with the sources of pollution—blood, death, and dirt—the lower his position in the system. The sacerdotal position, or priestly work, was considered purest. At the other extreme, work that involved dealing with the dead, carrion, cleaning of sewers, sweeping, and other such tasks was considered unclean and lowly and considered suitable for and to be performed by only hereditary Untouchables.

Legacy of the Caste System

This formalized social pecking order has been defended as the best and most natural functioning division of society and a model for the entire world to emulate. On the other hand, it has been attacked as the root cause of all social evil and the root of the economic backwardness of India.

Whatever one's judgment may be, there is no doubt that the caste system has shaped Indian society throughout the last several thousand years and that it is still of large practical significance. But today in Indian society people are no longer ranked rigidly by occupation.

Brahmins: The Priests

It would not be an unusual sight to see a Brahmin in a loincloth and a sacred thread sitting before a temple in India. These are members of the hereditary priestly class of India. The term "Brahmin" derives from the Vedic word *brahman,* meaning "prayer."

The authority for the Brahmin's social place originally came from Vedic scriptures. Brahmins were responsible for the transmission of the Vedas over the centuries via oral tradition. This ensured Brahmin authority over all ritual, since it was only through knowledge of the Vedas that the rituals could be performed. As it stood, all public rituals had to be supervised by Brahmins and all private rituals could be learned only from Brahmins.

As Indian culture moved further away from exclusive reliance on Vedic ritual, Brahmins claimed that their exalted status was due to their purity. This purity implied special norms of conduct such as vegetarianism. Brahmins may give food to any group, but they will only accept food from or eat food with other Brahmins. Certain Brahmins considered the most pure will not associate with or marry anyone but other Brahmins.

The Brahmins kept their dominant role as transmitters of knowledge, so they maintained their social authority. Their knowledge extended beyond Vedic scripture; Brahmins are the reflective group, with an intuitive sense of what is right. They are the intellectual and spiritual leaders, so their class includes philosophers, artists, religious leaders, teachers, and others who live a "life of the mind."

Kshatriyas: The Kings and Warriors

The warrior and kingly class in the ancient class system of India was the Kshatriyas, second in the social hierarchy only behind the Brahmins. They shouldered the great burden of protecting and ruling. Because of their elevated function in Indian society, they were always allied with Brahmins. The importance of the rulers was symbolized by wearing sacred threads, which marked them as twice born. Their first birth is physical, the second spiritual.

Though they were always allied with Brahmins, at times the warriors competed with the them for control of the top of the social hierarchy. By the sixth century B.C.E., the heterodox movements of Buddhism and Jainism—both of which opposed Brahminical orthodoxy—were started by men of Kshatriya lineage: Siddhartha Gautama (later Buddha) and Vardhamana (later Mahavira).

QUESTION?

What is the sacred thread worn by Brahmins and Kshatriyas?
The sacred threat is a cord worn by upper-caste Hindu males over the right shoulder. The thread runs across the chest and around the left side of the body. It consists of three strands before marriage and six or more thereafter. This thread can be worn by any of the three upper castes—Brahmins, Kshatriyas, and Vaishya. In actual practice, Brahmins commonly wear the thread, while the Kshatriyas and Vaishyas wear it less often.

Further symbolic importance is bestowed on the Kshatriyas in Indian literature. Up to the Gupta era (600 C.E.), the Kshatriyas learned Sanskrit and, to some degree, the scriptures. Amazingly, the Upanishads reveal instances of Kshatriya kings teaching Brahmins the highest wisdom. Both the Ramayana and Mahabharata are Kshatriya epics that cover the issue of kingly succession. Further, these epics highlight the two Kshatriya heroes Rama and Krishna, both recognized as avatars of Lord Vishnu.

FACT

A Kshatriya who led a bad life in deed, word, or thought and who held wrong views about the world would be reborn in the pit of purgatory after parting with his body. The fates of Brahmins, Vaishyas, and Shudras would be similar.

Vaishyas: The Commoners

The Vaishyas of the caste system were typically merchants or agriculturalists. They were also known as the providers. Because this class was comprised of farmers and merchants, it was known as the backbone of the economy. To further understand their importance in the economy, we could employ a modern term: the middle class.

Shudras: The Servants

The first mention of the Shudras occurs in the ancient Rig Veda. There, they are mentioned as the lowest of all the social groups in the social division. In present-day India, the name Shudra is used for castes that are lower in the social hierarchy. These groups would include barbers, washermen, and others who perform personal services. The concept of Shudra is by no means inflexible, however; each region of India has its own idea of what makes up a Shudra.

Untouchables

Below the Shudras, in what is now an informal caste hierarchy—the caste system being abolished after Indian independence in 1947—are the Dalits or Untouchables. They are sometimes referred to as the filth and unclean sector of society. Untouchables now tend to be employed as sweepers, refuse removers, and leather workers.

The regard for Untouchables in the Indian caste system was so low that they were considering a polluting influence and were not allowed to touch any person of the upper classes. In certain parts of South India, the concept of Untouchables went as far as demanding certain people stay out of the sight of the upper castes.

The idea of Untouchables dates to the rise of Aryan cultural domination in India. Evidence suggests that some tribal groups and people last integrated into India became "outcastes" or "the fifth caste." The Aryans had embraced a fourfold class system since antiquity.

Today's Dalit

Almost all of the freedom fighters in India who agitated for independence from Britain denounced the idea of caste and called for the permanent abolition of the Untouchable designation.

Chief among those abolitionists was Mohandas Gandhi. Instead of referring to people as Untouchables, he coined the term *harijan* (meaning "born of God") to relieve the stigma of Untouchables. The constitution of India was written by an Untouchable, Dr. Babasaheb R. Ambedkar (1891–1956).

When it came to setting up India's central and state governments, Untouchables were given designated quotas of positions, including parliamentary seats, to guarantee their advancement.

FACT

The word "caste" is a Portuguese derivative; *casta* means "race." It has come to mean the multiple classes into which traditional Indian society has been divided. The Sanskrit word that Indians have traditionally accepted is *jati* or "birth."

By now, India's Untouchables have taken an increasingly militant political stance. They prefer to call themselves *Dalit,* meaning "the oppressed." Many of them have converted to Buddhism, following Dr. Ambedkar's conversion in later life. Buddhism was always opposed to caste notions and preached equal spirituality.

The Caste System Today: Is It Still Practiced as Much?

There are 67 million Dalits in India, and more than 250 million around the world. In order to escape from the clutches of the caste system, some of them have converted to Buddhism, Jainism, Sikhism, Islam, and Christianity. Dalits account for 17 percent of the total population of India, of which 81 percent live in villages.

In some places, the caste has lost some force. Intercaste marriages are on the rise, especially in the urban areas. However, the caste system is still practiced with a vengeance in rural areas.

Dalits and Democracy

Democracy has been the hallmark of independent India for the last six decades, since independence in July 1947. Democracy is supposed to guarantee its citizens justice, liberty, and equality; however, the benevolent ideas that were meant to bridge the gap between the Dalits and the other castes have, in some instances, worked in reverse.

First of all, the political process of elections works to perpetuate the caste system rather than wipe it out. Candidates who run for elective offices invariably select a constituency where their caste is the majority. Caste solidarity comes to the forefront; it is necessary for the political survival of both the candidate and the constituents.

Secondly, the government has introduced some affirmative action programs to amend the wrongs done to the Dalits over the centuries. These programs are supposed to eradicate the root causes of economic, educational, and social disadvantages. Instead, these programs sometimes serve to perpetuate the system. In order to get the quota of services, a person has to prove that she is a Dalit, and thereafter she is identified as part of the lowest of all classes.

A Different View of Caste: Past and Present

Let us consider the history of the caste system from a pragmatic view, as opposed to traditional explanation.

The people of the lowest caste were called Dravidians by the Aryan conquerors. In fact, they were known as Adi Dravidian, emphasizing the fact that they were the original indigenous people of India.

The Vedic Brahmins called the Dravidians Untouchables and expelled them from their locales, saying they were polluters and unclean people. Dravidians did not accept the social hierarchical system devised by the Brahmins; they were the defeated people and yet were too proud to submit. The Brahmins expelled them, and the Dravidians in turn expelled the Brahmins.

There was a custom among the Dalits that if a Brahmin set foot in their area, the women would break up the cow-dung pots, or degrade him on sight to cleanse the area because the Brahmin's presence polluted their space. In other words, segregation and the concept of Untouchables were practiced by both sides—victors and vanquished.

The Dravidians were a proud people and rejected the names others tried to force on them, even Gandhi's name for them, Harijans ("children of God"). The Dravidians considered this a degrading and condescending name, and declared they wanted to be identified as Dalit, oppressed or broken people.

Rejecting the Caste System: The Sikhs

Sikhism was started in 1519 by Guru Nanak (1469–1538) in Punjab. He was born a Hindu but reared in the democratic doctrine of Islam. He rejected the caste system of Hinduism and founded his faith as a doctrine of loving devotion to "one God, the Creator" whose name was Truth (Sat). He spoke of his belief in one deity, discounting the lesser gods and goddesses of Hinduism. The deity of Sikhism was not a human figure; rather, it was an overarching idea that encompassed the infinite reaches of the universe. Nanak taught that meditation and repetition of the deity's name was essential to becoming one with the deity. Sikhism shared with Hinduism its belief that the soul was stuck in a cycle of birth and rebirth until its eventual enlightenment allowed it to become free.

FACT

There are now 19 million adherents of Sikhism in India, roughly 2 percent of the country's population, most from the state of Punjab. There are 25.8 million Sikhs worldwide. Great Britain, Canada, the United States, and Malaysia have the largest numbers of Sikhs outside of India. East Africa is also home to a large population of Sikhs.

Nanak rejected all of the impurities of Hinduism, speaking out against the caste system and Hindu practices such as female infanticide and the burning of widows. He believed that one's destiny was predetermined. One was fated to perform certain actions, good or bad, and there was no way to change one's place in the cycle of birth and rebirth. Nanak decried both the elaborate ceremonies and extreme asceticism of Hinduism. Instead, he preached that people could find salvation by embracing unselfish ways and following an enlightened guru. His message was especially appealing to the lower castes, who seized upon the idea that all people should be equal in society.

CHAPTER 15

Life's Four Stages

There is a sense in Hinduism, as in other philosophies, that a well-lived life must have a certain structure. The idea of living out four stages originated in the raja yoga of Patanjali, but lasted well beyond his time.

Dharma

Dharma is a terms with many meanings in the Hindu tradition. In fact, it can be interpreted as "religious law," "right conduct," "duty," and even "social order." In this instance, it applies to the appropriate stages of a person's life.

The root of the word itself is *dhri,* which means "to hold up." The social idea of dharma most likely got its foothold from the Vedic notion of *rita,* or "cosmic order." The social order, or dharma, is maintained by a second sense of dharma—right conduct and the fulfillment of duty and the religious law.

There is another sense of the term that determines our true essence. The righteous life, which lies at the basis of human morality and ethics, should be practiced. For individuals, dharma is inseparable from one's karma, since dharma can be realized by the individual only to the extent permitted by one's karmic situation.

Part of this dharma is the notion that an ideal religious life is broken down into four stages or stations. The first of these is the student stage (Brahmacharya). By the late teens, one becomes a householder and marries (Grihastha). After bringing up a family, one retires to solitude and lives as a forest dweller (Vanaprastha). The final stage involves the renunciation of all material goods (Sannyasis).

Brahmacharya

As with the idea of dharma, the concept of Brahmacharya is broad enough that it literally means "conducting oneself in accord with Brahman." It refers to the ancient practice of celibacy for men, considered essential to advanced spiritualists and novices alike who wish to break the bonds of worldly existence. It also refers to the student stage of a man's life. This is the definition that has meaning with relation to dharma. At the Brahmacharya stage, a boy studies the scriptures with his guru. He also learns the meaning of service, waiting on and serving his guru.

In the Brahmanical tradition of stages, or ashramas, the student was expected to remain celibate during the twelve years—from the age of twelve to the age of twenty-four—of Vedic learning with his guru. At that time, it was expected he would take up the household life.

FACT

A student studied the Vedas for twelve years, or until he had properly learned it. The student lived with his teacher or guru and helped him with religious observances. He begged food in the morning and in the evening, both for himself and for his teacher.

Householders

The second stage, reached in his late teens, was the onset of his maturity. He married the woman his parents had chosen for him and became a householder.

In many Hindu texts, the householder's life is considered the greatest of the four stages of life. Hinduism does not hold up monasticism as a common ideal for all; rather, the struggles and challenges of household management, family life, and social obligations are expected to contribute to the strengthening of a man's will for the life of retirement and the spiritual life to follow.

ESSENTIAL

The ashramas were the four traditional stages of life that Brahmin males were expected to follow according to the authoritative Hindu texts. Others from twice-born castes, such as warriors or merchants, could opt to follow the ashramas. Shudras and Dalits (Untouchables) were not included in this system.

The householder stage is often characterized as the basis and support for the other three. In fact, the householder stage affords a man an opportunity to realize the first three ends of man—pleasure (kama), material gain (artha), and virtue (dharma). In order to do this, the scriptures say, "One should give his daughter in marriage to a young man endowed with intelligence. One should marry a girl who possesses the characteristics of intelligence, beauty, good character, and freedom from disease."

The status of women is a curious matter here. One view says they should be shown the utmost respect, yet another says they deserve no freedom. In fact, the ethics stressed that a woman's father protects her in childhood, her husband protects her in youth, and her sons protect her in old age—so a woman does not need independence according to the stations of life.

The duty to provide has been called the highest duty of all, and this falls on husbands, who must strive to protect their wives. In protecting his wife scrupulously, he is also protecting his own offspring, character, family, and self. A husband should engage his wife in the collection and expenditures of his wealth, in cleanliness, in duty, in cooking food for the family, and in looking after the necessities of the household.

Retirement

Following the householder's stage, a man is expected to give up his belongings and retire from active family and social life to seek seclusion from the world. His wife can come with him or be left behind with her sons. According to the Laws of Manu, "When a householder sees his skin wrinkled and his hair gray and when he sees the son of his son, then he should resort to the forest." In addition, he should be available to offer advice and guidance to family and society.

In this stage, a man should be engaged in study and should be willing to give more than he receives. He should strive to be self-controlled, friendly, spiritually composed, and compassionate. Finally, the Law of Manu dictates, "Having consigned the sacred fires into himself in accordance with the prescribed rules, he should live without a fire, without a house, a silent sage subsisting on roots and fruit."

CHAPTER 16

Important Thinkers of the Last Three Centuries

In the last three centuries, several major Hindu philosophers have emerged to enrich Hindu thought. The following six men were poets, philosophers, religious figures—in a word, men of thought and action who brought a new understanding to Indian philosophy. Some even straddled Eastern and Western thought. In addition, they moved comfortably between different literary genres—essays, poems, and books. They also fought in the enduring struggle for India's independence from Great Britain.

Mysticism

This chapter reminds us that there is a Hindu tradition of mysticism. Mysticism is generally understood as a doctrine that claims you can have an immediate spiritual intuition of truth believed to transcend ordinary understanding of a supreme being. Mysticism allows an unmediated and intuitive union of the soul with God through contemplation or spiritual ecstasy. Thus, the main goal of mysticism is to obtain greater knowledge of God and unite the soul with Him.

This mystical phenomenon is found in all major religions. Since the sacrificial cult of the Rig Veda did not wholly meet the needs of the people, and since the texts of the Upanishads didn't satisfy head and heart, people needed something else for their religious craving—both knowledge of God and a way to commune with God. The mystic actions of the ascetic came close to fulfilling this aspiration. Even though mystical union was not possible for all, there was a chance for all to practice.

By the time of the Upanishads, asceticism had become widespread, and it was through the ascetics rather than the orthodox sacrificial priests that the new teachings developed and spread. Most of the new developments in thought were about mental and spiritual exercises of meditation. The original motive of Indian asceticism was the acquisition of magical power. If asceticism had its charms even for the less spiritual, they were still greater for the questing souls who took to a life of hardship from truly religious motives. As a person's mystical exercises developed, his psychic faculties enhanced, and the ascetic obtained insight no words could express.

The metaphysical interpretation of the ascetic's mystical knowledge varied from sect to sect, but the fundamental experience was the same, and was not appreciably different from that of the Western saints and mystics, whether Greek, Jewish, Christian, or Muslim. But Indian mysticism is unique in its elaboration of techniques for inducing ecstasy, and in complex metaphysical systems built upon interpretations of that experience. Where in other religions mysticism is of varying importance, in those of India, it is fundamental.

The Smartha philosophy defines mainstream Hinduism as allowing for the veneration of numberless deities, but this worship proceeds with the understanding that all of them are but manifestations of the one divine power. That ultimate power is termed Brahman or atman, and is believed to have no specific form, name, or attribute.

The system prevalent in Hinduism is defined by the Smartha philosophy; this theory allows the veneration of numberless deities, but on the understanding that all of them are but manifestation of one divine power (a belief that is sometimes called soft polytheism).

Ramprasad Sen (1718–1775)

Ramprasad Sen, who is often referred to simply by his first name, was a beloved Bengali poet and saint, the author of odes and composer of Hindu devotional songs. His work reveals a mystical approach to Hinduism. A good portion of his body of work reveals his devotion to Kali, a four-armed Hindu goddess associated with death and destruction.

Ramprasad was likely born to a higher-caste Vaidya family of traditional physicians. His education included a study of Sanskrit, not to mention Bengali and Persian. He lived on the banks of the Ganges, near Calcutta. He started out as a clerk for a wealthy household in Calcutta, but despite his occupation, was constantly distracted by thoughts of the goddess Durga, or Kali. Legend has it that one of his employers, upon seeing his beautiful verses to the goddess in his account books, told him to stop being an accountant at once, and offered him a salary to continue writing devotional verse.

When Ramprasad was just past sixty years old, he proclaimed that on the very day the goddess was to be submerged in the Ganges (which turned out to be Kali or Durga Puja day), he would be immersed with the Divine Mother. He then descended slowly into the river, singing some of his farewell songs. He died singing an ode to the goddess Tara.

Many of Ramprasad's poems involve themes of death and an afterlife. In "Death at Hand," he writes: "Vain are thy wanderings on the Earth. Two days or three, then ends this Earthly life; yet all men boast that they are masters here. Time's master, Death, will come and overthrow such masterships."

QUESTION?

What is shakta?
Shakta refers to both the practitioner and devotee and to the faith of a female-centered religious tradition that evolved out of prehistoric Mother Goddess worship, found in civilizations across the globe.

The poem "Death at Hand" reflects a clear understanding of the short-lived quality of Earthly existence. Ramprasad is considered a central figure in the revival of Shaktism, or goddess worship, in late eighteenth-century Bengal.

Sri Ramakrishna (1836–1886)

The connection between the supernatural and Ramakrishna started before his birth. His mother, Chandramani Devi, was said to have had a vision of light entering her womb before his birth. Sri Ramakrishna was just six years old when he had his first spiritual experience. This mystical experience accorded him, without his wishing it, a spiritual status that his contemporaries could have envied.

Many in his village of Kamarpukur considered the child Ramakrishna to be an incarnation of God. He entered into trancelike states throughout his childhood. Henceforth he neglected his studies, preferring instead to spend his time in solitary meditation, singing and performing Hindu stories. For much of his life he served as priest at the Kali Temple at Dakshineshwar, near Calcutta. There he lived a life of renunciation, but he would stop performing his priestly duties whenever the "divine madness" took over his conscious awareness.

He married Sarada Devi, whom he viewed as the goddess incarnate. In turn, she looked upon Ramakrishna as her spiritual teacher. He would lead no movement, nor establish any society for the faithful; however, he remained devoted to the goddess Kali throughout his life. He benefited from the teachings of Tota Puri, who taught him Advaita Vedanta and the practice of absorption in the formless, which he quickly achieved.

Union with God

Ramakrishna sought to turn his whole life into an uninterrupted contemplation and union with God. In part, his doctrine was that the revelation of God can take place at all times and that God realization is not the monopoly of any one religion or faith.

In "The World as Seen by a Mystic," he shows his method of reaching a state of God realization.

> *I practiced austerities for a long time, I cared very little for the body. My longing for the Divine Mother was so great that I could not eat or sleep. I would lie on the bare ground, placing my head on a lump of Earth and cry out loudly: "Mother, Mother, why dost Thou not come to me?" I did not know how the days and nights passed away. I used to have ecstasy all the time. I saw my disciples as my own people, like children and relations, long before they came to me.*

Ramakrishna then relates how he attained a state of continuous ecstasy and "gave up all external forms of worship." In referring to the time of joyous illumination that immediately followed his enlightenment, he exclaimed:

> *What a state it was! The slightest cause aroused in me the thought of the Divine Ideal. One day I went to the Zoological Garden in Calcutta. I desired especially to see the lion, but when I beheld him, I lost all sense-consciousness and went into Samadhi. Those who were with me wished to show me the other animals, but I replied: "I saw everything when I saw the king of beasts. Take me home." The strength of the lion had aroused in me the consciousness of the omnipotence of God and had lifted me above the world of phenomena.*

It is said there are two levels of Samadhi: samprajnata Samadhi, in which the yogi is still aware of a degree of worldly differentiation; and asamprajnata

Samadhi, in which there is a full realization of the self or *purusha* and its consciousness and no involvement in worldly differentiation. Ramakrishna had reached the second stage.

Vivekananda (1863–1902) was a disciple of Ramakrishna. One of the outstanding achievements of his life was the establishment of Ramakrishna Missions in India, involved in philanthropic activities. Once, he encouraged his audience in Madras, saying, "We must conquer the world through our spirituality and philosophy. There is no other alternative; we must do it or die." He wanted to promote a universal religion based on a Vedanta that might be adapted to the needs of our time.

The first stage is said to contain the seeds of awareness of the external world of differentiation, while the second stage is said to be "seedless"; that is, it no longer engenders thoughts tied to the external world. Neither of these states can be described precisely because both take consciousness beyond language and into indescribable realms.

Ramakrishna's entire life was spent longing for uninterrupted contemplation and union with God. Both his life and teaching appeal to seekers in all religions, as he taught that the revelation of God can take place at all times and that God realization is not the special possession of any one religion or faith. He took up various disciplines associated with other religions, specifically Christianity and Islam, and maintained that the paths of all lead to God realization; all religions have the common goal of God consciousness.

Hinduism is a decidedly theistic religion. A difficulty lies in determining whether it is polytheistic, pantheistic, or perhaps even a monotheistic religion. The difficulty of labeling it lies with the Western thinkers, because for Indian thinkers, divergent views both complementary and contradictory can coexist, and are acceptable to all.

Ramakrishna had several mystical experiences, which accorded him spiritual status. His devotion is characterized by an unrestricted nonsectarian Hinduism; the cult of the Mother seemed to predominate his religious beliefs. He performed several miracles as the result of mystical rewards from the Mother Goddess.

Sri Ramakrishna died on August 16, 1886; he was an inspiration for a generation of Hindus. In time, his influence spread throughout the world through the Vedanta societies founded by Swami Vivekananda.

Raja Rammohun Roy (1772–1833)

Raja Rammohun Roy, sometimes referred to as Rammohun, was a reformer at heart. The upshot of his life's work was to make Hinduism a more tolerant religion. He was best known for the abolition of *suttee*, the immolation of widows on their husband's funeral pyre. But he also denounced the disadvantages of polygamy and challenged the authority of the Hindu priesthood.

Roy was born in Radhanagar, Bengal, on May 22, 1772, to a Bengali Brahmin. Despite his father's rank, he was raised in a religiously diverse family. His father worshipped Vishnu, while his mother was a devotee of the Goddess. Raised in Patna, a center of Muslim learning, he was influenced by Islamic teaching against images; later, in Calcutta, he was exposed to Christianity. He became quite a scholar, soon learning Bengali, Sanskrit, and other Indian languages as well as Arabic, Persian, Hebrew, Greek, and Latin. As a consequence of his broad, liberal education, he was inclined to reject the traditional orthodoxy of Hinduism and to accept the common aspects of different faiths, including Buddhism, Jainism, Hinduism, and Christianity.

Roy was well read in many of the world's scriptures, having read most in their original language. He sought a way to free his own Hindu tradition from a rigid adherence to superstition and prejudice. He turned to the ancient texts of the Upanishads and advocated that other Indians do the same. He also recommended that Indians relearn their tradition, as well as science, philosophy, and newer perspectives.

Because of his attachment to learning, Roy was not susceptible to foolish beliefs, choosing to reject image worship and the burning of widows.

It was with this last barbaric practice that Roy's name was forever associated. His denunciation of *suttee,* the practice of burning a widow alive on her husband's funeral pyre, was a constant on his list of practices to protest. In 1828 alone, some 309 widows were burned alive within the jurisdiction of Calcutta. In time, it was clear that Roy would be a champion of women's rights like no other.

FACT

As a social reformer, Roy protested vehemently against the social rigidity of the caste and dowry systems. A dowry is a sum of money, goods, or an estate that a woman brings to her husband in marriage. This sexist practice led to abuse of women, and at times, death at the hands of husbands and in-laws trying to extort larger dowries.

Women were often murdered—frequently by hanging or fire, known as "bride burning"—in countries such as India, Pakistan, and Bangladesh. Some took their own lives because of continuous harassment and torture by husbands and in-laws trying to extort larger dowrys.

Dowry deaths still occur today. The Indian national crime bureau reported 6,787 dowry deaths in 2005 alone. Far from dwindling in number, dowry deaths actually increased by 46 percent over the 4,648 reported in 1995.

Social Reform

Roy's passion for reformed Hinduism led him to become founder and leader of the Brahmo Samaj (a Brahmo is someone who worships Brahman), also known as "The Society of Worshippers of One God." This was a community of likeminded reformers who met regularly to worship the Supreme Being—Brahman—rather than practice religious idolatry. Thus began the "Renaissance of Hinduism."

The Brahmo Samaj adhered to a set of doctrines. The Samajists placed no faith in any scripture as an authority. Likewise, they had no faith in avatars and denounced polytheism and idol worship. They also made it optional for their members to believe in the doctrines of karma and rebirth.

The Brahmo Samaj society, established in 1828, aimed to reform Hinduism by banishing the caste system, idolatry, and other features of Indian life it considered debased. The Samaj—including Roy, Devendranath Tagore (1817–1905), and Keshub Chunder Sen (1838–1884)—were theists who stressed the worship of one God, omniscient and omnipotent. All truth is from God, and the prophets of all religions were to be respected.

As such, Roy sought to bring fresh air to Hinduism. In sum, he became a voice of tolerance and reason and a continuing influence on traditional Indian practices. It was the first prime minister of India, Jawaharlal Nehru, who called Roy a "pioneer of modern India," and Swami Vivekananda extolled Roy's love, which extended to Muslims as well as Hindus.

Rabindranath Tagore (1861–1941)

Rabindranath Tagore was a man of parts. Lyrical poet, novelist, dramatist, and essayist (not to mention a musician and artist), Tagore was a prominent representative of a new Indian humanism. He fought for social reform and was probably the first modern Indian writer to earn a worldwide reputation, in part because he was the first Asian to win the Nobel Prize for literature.

Beyond that, Tagore was fresh air. He was a liberated thinker and one well outside the box of traditional Hindu categories. In fact, he preached of a harmony of the cultures of the Orient and the Occident, and tried to awaken in men a kind of spirituality beyond the strictures of precise beliefs. The spirituality he stressed was based on an understanding among peoples and a longing for human equality.

Tagore was born on May 7, 1861, in Calcutta. His father's father had been a prominent, highly educated businessman and a supporter of the Brahmo Samaj, the reform sect founded by Raja Rammohun Roy.

Rabindranath was the youngest of fourteen children, all of whom were well educated, including the girls, in keeping with the newly emerging Bengali tradition. In fact, the children were educated in Bengali and English and used their knowledge to publish magazines, write plays, and sponsor the arts. Rabrindranath's own talents grew in the fertile soil of rich surroundings.

He married at age twenty-two and the couple had five children. By then, he had begun something of a literary reputation, based on a long poem. In 1890, he began managing the family estates at Shelaidaha, what is now Bangladesh. He lived modestly on a houseboat, writing essays, plays, and short stories.

By 1901, he set out on a pioneering educational experiment in west Bengal, championing the outdoor class, run in the ancient Indian way with one teacher and very few students. Today, this school is run by the government of India under the name Vishva Bharati. That year, at the age of forty, Rabindranath wrote *Naivedya* and other works. That same year his wife died as well as a son and a daughter.

The grief he felt affected the tone of his writing. Still, he developed a large following among Bengali writers and in 1912, while reading his poetry in England, he was heard by William Butler Yeats. The English version of *Gitanjali* (*Song Offerings*, 1915) was later published by the India Society with an admiring preface by Yeats.

FACT

In November 1913, Tagore was awarded the Nobel Prize in literature, based on the attention that the English translation of *Gitanjali* (*Song Offerings*) had drawn. The work was a collection of 103 poems, mostly metaphysical in nature.

His literary fame firmly established by the time he was sixty, Tagore began to paint and exhibit his paintings in India and Europe. He would become the only person to compose two national anthems, India's and Bangladesh's. His love for India was well known, and he did what others of his generation did to contribute to the mother country's struggle for independence. He carried on a correspondence with Mohandas Karamchand Gandhi, a mutual admirer.

Because of Tagore's literary and national interests, refined aesthetic sensibilities, and extensive travels, he developed a philosophy of universal brotherhood and cultural exchange. He believed that the divinity was immanent and the reflection of that divinity was in human beings. His reputation is one of philosopher and literary figure.

Sri Aurobindo (1872–1950)

Aurobindo Ghose, later named Sri Aurobindo, was one of the great sages of modern India. Following his influential political career in the cause of Indian independence, Aurobindo turned to the spiritual realm and developed integral yoga, which managed to combine yogic practices from different historic Indian yogas.

Ghose was born on August 15, 1872, in the Indian state of Bengal to a surgeon, Dr. Krishnadhan Ghose, and his wife Swarnalata Devi. His father sought to Anglicize his son and packed him off to Manchester, England, to study, where he would be isolated from Indian influences.

In 1889, he entered Cambridge, where he distinguished himself in Latin, Greek, and French. At twenty-one, he returned to India and taught English and French at Baroda College. He eventually became vice principal, and at age twenty-nine married a fourteen-year-old girl, Mrinalini Rose. He had also begun his political activity in support of Indian independence. Aurobindo was frequently absent from home, and was devoted to spiritual pursuits. His marriage produced no children and his wife died at thirty-two, right before their planned move to the Pondicherry Ashram Aurobindo had established.

In 1903, a spiritual event occurred that shaped his life. He realized, through the aid of a teacher, the nondual nature of the divine, Nirguna Brahman.

When Aurobindo moved to Bengal in 1906, he thrust himself into revolutionary political activity on behalf of India's independence, years in advance of Gandhi's return from South Africa. He wrote journal articles and was arrested on a charge of sedition in 1907. He was arrested again the following year and spent a year in Alipore jail awaiting trial.

In Alipore jail Aurobindo experienced a spiritual epiphany and turning point. There he read the Bhagavad Gita, practiced yoga, and had a vision of Krishna that was powerful and transformative. Not long after he was released from jail, he headed to the French protectorate of Pondicherry, in part to avoid arrest by the Indian police.

In 1914, a Frenchman by the name of Paul Richard persuaded Aurobindo to write philosophy for a monthly journal called *Arya*. Aurobindo had developed a reputation as a yogi and Richard was interested in this philosophy. So was his wife, Mirra Alfassa, who found in Aurobindo the fulfillment of her spiritual calling. In 1920, she left her husband and joined Sri Aurobindo in his spiritual quest. In time, she would be dubbed "the Mother."

Aurobindo's ashram would flourish with the arrival of Mirra Alfassa. In 1928, he released his book *Mother,* where he affirmed to the skeptical that the Mother's consciousness and his consciousness were one and the same. In 1939–1940 the ashram released the book *Life Divine*, one of Aurobindo's masterpieces. Aurobindo and Alfassa developed a kind of yoga with unique characteristics. Aurobindo had argued that each of the yogas developed in India had its own important and positive elements, but that practicing any one of them solely would lead to an unbalanced spiritual development.

In his book *Synthesis of Yoga,* Aurobindo outlined how yogas of the Bhagavad Gita, particularly, could be harmonized into a synthesis that would serve the whole human being—the physical, emotional, mental, psychic (soul), and spiritual levels. The term Aurobindo used for the yoga that would involve all levels of the human being was *integral yoga.*

Sri Aurobindo argued that the world was real, in opposition to many Indian philosophers who maintained that the material world was illusory. Moreover, he was not engaging in metaphysics for its own sake; he believed that the world was evolving toward a state of perfection. He reasoned from science that since life emerged from matter, and consciousness from life, that superconsciousness or the "supramental" stage must develop from ordinary consciousness.

Aurobindo's yoga aimed at accelerating the advance of this evolution toward "Supermanhood." He and the Mother focused entirely on engendering what they called the Supramental manifestation, which would transform not only all human beings, but all life and even all matter. They desired to unlock the divine within matter itself; thus, they referred to their philosophy as Divine Materialism. This was the vision that he developed in his massive book *The Life Divine*.

Sri Aurobindo, who provided a reinterpretation of the Vedas and commentaries on the Upanishads, had this to say on polytheism: "Indian polytheism is not the popular polytheism of ancient Europe; for here the worshipper of many Gods still knows that all his divinities are forms, names, personalities and powers of the One; his gods proceed from the one Purusha, his goddesses are energies of the one divine Force."

He acknowledged at his death in 1950 that he had not yet achieved "the descent of the Supramental." He said this would occur through the efforts of the Mother. In 1956, she announced that the descent had occurred, and in 1968 she inaugurated Auroville, a new utopian city in Southern India dedicated to the realization of her goals. She intended it to be a truly international city, belonging to "no one in particular" and therefore to everyone. Along with the ashram in Pondicherry, the city flourishes to this day, still developing and working out the principles of Aurobindo's and Mother's philosophies. She attended to the ashram until her own death in 1973.

INSIGHT

In a speech called "The Resurrection of Hinduism," Aurobindo said, "That which we call the Hindu religion is really the eternal religion, because it is the universal religion which embraces all others. If a religion is not universal, it cannot be eternal. A narrow religion, a sectarian religion, an exclusive religion can live only for a limited time and a limited purpose."

Aurobindo and the Mother never desired to foster a cult or new religion; theirs was the loftier goal of the transformation of the consciousness and existence of all humanity. As a consequence, no successor was appointed to follow the Mother. Yet, the work of Aurobindo and the Mother lives on, due in large part to a devoted group of admirers who have continued to practice yoga in creative and ever-changing ways. Ashrams devoted to Sri Aurobindo have been established at three sites in the United States: Dr. Haridas Chaudhuri's California Institute of Integral Studies in San Francisco, founded in

1951; Matagiri—which means "Mother's mountain" in Sanskrit—founded in the Catskill region of New York in 1968; and a third ashram founded in Lodi, California, in the 1990s.

Sarvepalli Radhakrishnan (1888–1975)

Sarvapalli Radhakrishnan is one of the most remarkable philosophers and religious thinkers of modern India. His philosophical and religious ambitions were far reaching. He tried to establish a connection between Indian thought (based on Vedanta and Buddhism) and Western thought, without sacrificing any of the main Hindu theories. As with many of his contemporaries, he participated in the movement for India's independence and held several distinguished positions in the new government of independent India, including the post of president.

Radhakrishnan was born on September 5, 1888, at Tituttani, near Madras in South India. His early years were spent there and in Tirupati, both renowned pilgrimage centers. As was customary, he married young. He and his wife Sivakanuamma had five daughters and one son. He graduated with a master's degree in arts from Madras Christian College in 1908 and wrote a thesis called *The Ethics of the Vedanta and Its Metaphysical Presuppositions,* which was a reply to the charge that the Vedanta system had no room for ethics. The thesis was published as a book when he was just twenty years old.

It was just the beginning of a philosophical career in which he moved easily between Eastern and Western philosophy. In 1909, when he was twenty-one, he took a position in the department of philosophy at the Madras Presidency College. He followed that distinction with an even greater one, first being appointed professor of philosophy in the University of Mysore, and three years later being appointed to the most important philosophy chair in India—King George V Chair of Mental and Moral Science in the University of Calcutta.

The honors kept getting greater for the philosopher and political figure. He represented the University of Calcutta at the Congress of Universities of the British Empire in June 1926 and the International Congress of Philosophy at Harvard University. In 1929, he took a post at Manchester College, Oxford, and from 1936 to 1939 served as Spalding Professor of Eastern Religion and Ethics at Oxford. In 1939, he was elected fellow of the British Academy. From 1939 to 1948, he was the vice chancellor of Banaras Hindu University.

An academic career then blossomed into politics. Among myriad posts, he was the leader of the Indian delegation to UNESCO from 1946 to 1952, and served as ambassador to the Soviet Union 1949–1952. He was also vice president of India from 1952 to 1962. From May 1962 to May 1967, he was the president of India. He passed away on April 17, 1975, at the age of eighty-six.

Radhakrishnan's greatest philosophical contribution was taking the philosophical and religious riches of India beyond her shores. He translated and commented on the Upanishads, Vedanta Sutra, and Bhagavad Gita. In addition, he compared Eastern and Western philosophies.

In the same open spirit that allowed him to bridge Eastern and Western thought, Radhakrishnan, like Gandhi, was not restricted by social conventions adverse to freedom and justice. He criticized India's caste system and customs that degraded women, and he fought to establish a pluralistic and democratic society that would fulfill the highest ideals of Indian tradition.

CHAPTER 17

The Life and Thoughts of Mohandas K. Gandhi (1869–1948)

Mohandas K. Gandhi is better known as Mahatma, a title that means "great soul." In his long and accomplished life, Gandhi became the unofficial leader of India. The philosophy of nonviolence, which he embraced and used to protest British rule of India, would become his legacy.

The Concept of Nonviolence

Nonviolence was a concept developed by Mahavira (540–468 B.C.E.) for Jainism; it is also found in Buddhism. Hinduism assimilated this idea into its scriptures, making Buddha an avatar of Vishnu and thus incorporating Buddhism and Jainism.

Ahimsa (nonviolence) within Hindu thought surely means abstaining from killing, but it also includes developing a positive attitude toward all living things. Jainism is both a philosophy and a religion, and it is central to both theory and practice. Nonviolence and nonkilling are synonymous first principles in the dharma of the sages and saints.

Mohandas Gandhi drew upon New Testament teachings and ideas from Ruskin and Tolstoy, and combined them with Vedic ideas to come up with his own brand of nonviolence. He called his technique *satyagraha* ("holding to the truth"), and he attempted to use this idea against a vastly superior occupying power—the British.

However, nonviolence was more than a technique to be used by the weak against the strong; it was primarily a way of life, of which political freedom was but one manifestation. Gandhi's nonviolent tactics of civil disobedience came to dominate politics in India. His technique proved successful in the political arena against a very formidable enemy. In time, the idea that had germinated in India grew and expanded to become known all over the world.

FACT

The Reverend Dr. Martin Luther King Jr. embraced Gandhi's interpretation of nonviolence, and it influenced his crusade to bring about social change in the United States. While King was a student at a theological college in 1948, he became convinced that this was one of the most potent weapons available to oppressed people in their struggle for freedom.

Gandhi's view of nonviolence was not a Hindu religious idea, but a political idea. It was a powerful concept, and it has been used frequently as a successful technique to resolve conflict since Gandhi proved its effectiveness.

Gandhi's Life

Mohandas Gandhi (1869–1948) led a fascinating life, but he was not always a champion of the Indian struggle for freedom. Married young, he became a lawyer, but was not satisfied. His travels to South Africa and across India opened the world to him, and he found his calling in the fight for the lives of ordinary Indians. In time, his courage and leadership—and his philosophy of nonviolence—resulted in India's independence from Great Britain.

In his *Autobiography: The Story of My Experiments with Truth*, Gandhi recalled several incidents from his childhood. In an elementary school in Porbandar, where he was born, he misspelled the word "kettle." He was the only one in his class who had made a mistake; all of the other boys had copied the word from each other. The teacher had failed to catch the others copying, but he didn't fail to bring Gandhi up for public ridicule. Gandhi never criticized the teacher, and his evaluation of the teacher didn't diminish one bit, "for I had learned to carry out the orders of elders," he said, "not to scan their actions."

FACT

At this time of his life, he was a shy boy, avoiding all company. "My books and my lessons were my sole companions," he wrote. "To be at school at the stroke of the hour and to run back home as soon as the school closed—that was my daily habit."

Another incident involved a book that Gandhi's father had purchased for the boy to read. He rarely read anything outside of his schoolwork, but his eyes fell on *Shravana Pitribhakti Nataka*, a play about Shravana's devotion to his parents. There was even a picture of him carrying his blind parents on a pilgrimage by means of slings fitted for his shoulders. The book and that image left an indelible image on the young Gandhi, who also remembered the agonized lament of the parents when their child died.

Gandhi on Early Marriage

"If I am a worshipper of truth," Gandhi said, then "it is my painful duty to record my marriage at the age of thirteen." Later on, he would see youngsters of the same age and feel "inclined to pity myself and to congratulate them on having escaped my lot." He admitted that he saw "no moral argument in support of such a preposterously early marriage."

Of the Hindu custom of marriage in general, Gandhi was highly critical. His parents insisted on the arranged marriages of his older brothers and himself, all of which occurred at roughly the same time. "There was no thought of our welfare," Gandhi recalled. "It was purely a question of their own convenience and economy." The three Gandhi weddings were to be held simultaneously. A date was set, extravagant plans were made, and his father, who worked in Radjkot, had to rush to the wedding in Porbandar, 120 miles away. He was severely injured when the coach he was traveling in toppled over. The date of the nuptials could not be changed, so Gandhi's father bore his painful injuries in order to attend his sons' marriages.

Gandhi would recall his parents fondly and could not criticize them for staging three weddings at once. "Everything on that day seemed to me right and proper and pleasing," he said. "There was also my own eagerness to get married."

QUESTION?

What special rituals were performed at the wedding of Gandhi and his wife Kasturbai?
There was one ceremony typical of Hindu weddings at that time. The *saptapadi* was a seven-step walk that a Hindu bride and bridegroom took together while making promises of mutual fidelity and devotion. After this, the marriage became irrevocable.

He recalled the uneasiness of his own actions and those of his thirteen-year-old bride on their wedding night. Little, inexpensive booklets distributed at the time discussed conjugal love, thrift, child marriages, and other subjects. Gandhi read them cover to cover. "Lifelong faithfulness to the wife, inculcated in these booklets as the duty of the husband, remained permanently imprinted on my heart. Furthermore, the passion for truth was innate in me, and to be false to her was therefore out of the question."

Kasturbai was illiterate and had none of Gandhi's literary ambitions, so he had no connection with her through his studies. She was not the kind of girl to be restrained; Gandhi was jealous, and she could go nowhere without his permission. This led to quarrels, but his wife brooked none of his orders and went out whenever and wherever she liked.

As he grew more cross with her, she took more liberties. "Refusal to speak to one another thus became the order of the day with us, married children," said Gandhi. He later realized how possessive and jealous he had been and reasoned that if she had no right to restrain his behavior, then he had no right to restrain hers.

FACT

During the first five years of marriage, parents do not allow couples to stay long together. This is one of those protections that Hindu society constructed against lustful love. So the child-wife spends more than half her time at her father's house. Gandhi estimated that during the first five years of their marriage, they spent less than three years together.

Though married, Gandhi was still in high school. At the age of eighteen, he went to England, signaling what he called "a long and healthy spell of separation." By the time he got the call to go to South Africa, he was "fairly free of his carnal appetite."

The Method of Nonviolence Is Born

Nonviolence first entered Gandhi's mind as the result of one particular incident. He would later read and be influenced by American philosopher Henry David Thoreau's ideas on civil disobedience.

The Incident

By age twenty-four, Mohandas Gandhi was a barrister. He passed the London matriculation examination, and after three years, he returned to

India. However, he knew nothing of Indian law and because he was shy, was not suited to argue cases in court. In 1893, he agreed to assist a South African firm in a case.

As he set out for Pretoria, the capital of Transvaal in South Africa, Gandhi looked the part of a fashionable dandy, dressed in a frock coat, pressed trousers, shining shoes, and a turban. First-class accommodations were purchased for him, and he boarded the train at Durban for the overnight journey. But he had not counted on the reaction of his fellow passengers, all of whom were of European descent.

FACT

From 1860 to 1890, some 40,000 laborers had come from India to serve European landlords in South Africa. Following their period of servitude, many Indians settled in South Africa. White rulers imposed petty restrictions and heavy taxes on them. Jingoistic newspapers perpetuated the stereotype that Indians were a dirty, uncivilized people. They didn't enjoy freedom of movement on the railways, nor could they stay at hotels reserved for Europeans.

Gandhi's train pulled into Martizburg, the capital of Natal, and Gandhi related that a white man entered his compartment and "looked me up and down" and "saw that I was a colored man." This disturbed the man, who charged out of the compartment and returned with two officials. Gandhi was ordered to the third-class compartment. He refused to leave, protesting that he had a first-class ticket. The official persisted, Gandhi dug in his heels, and eventually a constable was summoned to forcibly remove Gandhi and his luggage from the train.

It was winter, and bitterly cold in the waiting room at the train station. Gandhi sat shivering through the night and drifted into philosophical reverie. He examined the very nature of his life and his duties in it. He decided he must press on to Pretoria, and in the morning his employer used his influence to get Gandhi reinstated as a first-class passenger. He suffered more abuse on the way to Pretoria. On one leg of the journey, he had to travel by stagecoach, but was not allowed to sit inside with the other passengers. Instead, he had to sit on the coach box and was humiliated when the coachman asked him to stand on the footboard. The ordeal gave Gandhi a sense of the conditions of Indians in South Africa and strengthened his resolve to do something about it.

Gandhi decided that being thrown off the train to Pretoria for sitting in a "white only" section was "only a symptom of the disease of color prejudice" and that "I should try if possible, to root out the disease and suffer hardships in the process." It was the beginning of his struggle for the rights of ordinary Indian citizens.

A Leader for Civil Rights

Within a week of his arrival in Pretoria, Gandhi had summoned all the Indians of the city to a meeting. He was twenty-four years old, and was making his first public speech. The audience consisted of Muslim merchants interspersed with a few Hindus. His goal was "to present to them a picture of their condition."

At this time, the Natal legislature was taking up a bill to deny the vote to Indians. The Indian community wanted Gandhi to lead the opposition to this bill. He could not stop the bill from passing, but he drew attention to the grievances of Indians in South Africa. In 1894, he formed the Natal Indian Congress to fight for the rights of Indians, which became a great force in South African politics. In 1897, he was attacked and nearly lynched by a white mob.c.e. His response to the incident was more ethical than legalistic, and showed that a change had come over him; he refused to press charges against his aggressors.

At the beginning of the South African War (better known as the Boer War) in 1899, Gandhi thought Indians must support the war effort to legitimize their claims to full citizenship. Thus, he helped organize an ambulance corps of 300 free Indians and 800 laborers. But when the war ended in 1902, conditions for the Indians had not improved.

In 1906, the Transvaal government passed a measure compelling the colony's Indian population to register. This included a strip search of women in order to identify any birthmarks. In Johannesburg that year, Gandhi held a mass protest. For the first time, he articulated his philosophy of satyagraha or "truth force," asking his fellow Indians to oppose the new law using non-violent methods. Over a period of seven years, Gandhi was imprisoned several times, and many other Indians were jailed, beaten, or shot for defying the registration order.

Until the time of the voter registration law, the thought of civil disobedience had never struck Gandhi, but he realized that by being a nuisance and opposing the law peacefully, he could engender change in the opposition. The British government was forced to negotiate a compromise with Gandhi because of the negative publicity the campaign had generated against them.

Gandhi's years in South Africa were pivotal for his political and spiritual development. He resided there from 1893 until 1914; he was twenty-four when he arrived and forty-five when he left. He studied the Bhagavad Gita, and he corresponded with and was influenced by the Russian novelist Leo Tolstoy (1828–1910), who cultivated his own interest in Indian philosophy. In addition, he pored over the writings of a philosophical predecessor and kindred spirit, Henry David Thoreau. Thoreau (1817–1862) had been an American transcendentalist and literary figure in the nineteenth century. His suggestive essay "Resistance to Civil Government or Civil Disobedience" shaped Gandhi's own philosophy of resistance to government.

Indians Against the British Occupiers

By 1914, at the outbreak of the World War I, Gandhi returned to India to bring his political ideas to bear on the Indian struggle for independence. At first, Gandhi supported the British effort in World War I and the effort to recruit Indians into the British army. But that changed when the British passed the Rowlatt Act in 1919, a measure that allowed the government to imprison Indians without a trial. Gandhi launched his first call for satyagraha, or nonviolent disobedience, on Indian soil.

On April 13, 1919, the British answered the show of civil disobedience with violence, in what has become known as the Amritsar Massacre. General Dwyer of the British Army gave the order to fire into a large crowd of people who were listening to a speech. The British machine guns killed 379

Indians and wounded 1,137. The firing would have continued, but the British ran out of ammunition.

The violence shocked Gandhi, and he halted any political agitation, but the larger point was that he had succeeded in getting Indians to stand up against British rule. His star was on the rise.

Economic Pressure Against the British

In 1920, Gandhi was elected president of the All-India Home Rule League; in 1921, he became the head of the Indian National Congress. The Congress under Gandhi's leadership was more militant, adopting the goal of self-rule in its new constitution. Now Gandhi practiced a policy of boycotting all foreign-made goods, especially British goods.

FACT

Aware of the effect of his behavior on that of his fellow Indians, Gandhi could often be found at his spinning wheel, which he used to spin thread for cloth for all his own clothing. He wanted all Indians to use homespun cloth in place of foreign-made fabric. He became the symbol of the Indian independence movement.

In time, foreign clothing was cast into giant bonfires. The boycott of all things foreign expanded to British education facilities, and even to a refusal to pay taxes. The British quelled the agitation and sentenced Gandhi to six years in prison for sedition. For health reasons, Gandhi served just three years and was released in 1924. By 1928, the British had appointed a constitutional reform commission with no Indians on it. Gandhi countered by launching another nonviolent resistance campaign, this time against the tax on salt.

Gandhi's famous Salt March in 1929 was a campaign against the salt tax levied by the British. This campaign was a piece of political theater, the highlight of which was the 250-mile Dandhi March from Ahmedabad to the seaside village of Dandhi. There, Gandhi made his own salt, a powerful symbolic image. The march, which took about a month to complete, picked up new participants as it passed through each village.

FACT

The Salt March gained international attention, but it had its own price. Some 60,000 Indians were imprisoned during the protest. The government agreed to free all prisoners in return for suspension of the agitation. Gandhi was invited to the Round Table Conference in London as the only representative of the Indian National Congress.

By 1932, Gandhi had turned his attention inward, beginning a campaign to improve the lot of India's Untouchables. He continued to struggle for Indian independence, and also tried to stop the brutal animosity between Muslims and Hindus.

Gandhi renamed the Untouchables harijans or "children of God." In 1933, he fasted for twenty-one days to protest the Indian government's treatment of Indians, which was the first in a series of important political fasts.

By 1934, Gandhi resigned as the party leader of the Indian National Congress because he found a lack of commitment to his program of nonviolence as a way of life for the new India by members of the Congress. Jawaharlal Nehru became the new leader; meanwhile, Gandhi devoted himself to the goal of educating rural India. He fought against the institution of Untouchables, and worked to promote the manufacture of homespun clothing and other village-level cottage industries. The British jailed Gandhi from 1942 to 1944 for this agitation.

Quit India Movement and Independence from Britain

An essential part of Gandhi's practice of civil disobedience was the Quit India Movement. The movement had begun because of Gandhi's call for immediate and total independence from Britain.

Quit India

During his "Quit India" speech in August 1942, Gandhi made the clarion call "do or die"—either we must free India from British rule or die trying. Still, the method was passive resistance, not violence. The resolution to quit India was passed at the Bombay session of the All-India Congress Committee. In response, the British detained Indians and arrested more than 10,000 people. Gandhi fasted, hoping for the release of the prisoners.

INSIGHT

In his "Quit India" speech, Gandhi said, "I know the British government will not be able to withhold freedom from us, when we have made enough self-sacrifice. We must, therefore, purge ourselves of hatred. Speaking for myself, I can say that I have never felt any hatred."

By 1946, the prisoners were set free, and the British conferred with the Indian National Congress to make arrangements for India's independence. Gandhi believed in cooperation between the Hindu and Muslim communities in India and maintained relationships without regard to religious affiliation; he did not believe in segregation of the two faiths. Nonetheless, the Indian National Congress agreed to a partition agreement that cleaved two states out of British India: India and Pakistan. The transfer of power was effected in August 1947, and people celebrated in the streets. But Gandhi wondered, "Why are they rejoicing—I see only a river of blood."

With hunger strikes—one more variety of civil disobedience—Gandhi was able to quell terrible riots between Muslims and Hindus on the eastern border between India and the new Pakistan. The process of partition was very violent—several million people were forced to flee their homes, and at least 1 million were slaughtered in communal riots.

Gandhi sought peace between the two religious groups and between the two new countries, but when he visited New Delhi in an attempt to pacify the two communities on January 30, 1948, a gunshot rang out and the champion of nonviolence fell. Nathuram Godse, a Hindu radical who opposed Gandhi's acceptance of Muslims, had pulled the trigger. It was the irony of ironies—the world's greatest champion of nonviolence, killed by a gunshot. As he expired, Gandhi uttered the word "Rama," an Indian word meaning God.

Gandhi's Legacy

Gandhi was a man of action every bit as much as a man of religion. He was critical of all organized religions. He explained that he was a Hindu, a Christian, a Muslim, and a Jew. Gandhi was deeply spiritual, and his spirituality was never unworldly. He searched for truth and pursued nonviolence in every area of life. He believed these two aspects were the most important on the way to understanding God. Thus, the name Mahatma—really a title of honor—was bestowed on him by India. He is considered the father of the modern Indian nation, but his influence transcends borders, for he was a great soul on the world stage, too.

CHAPTER 18

Other Disciples of Civil Disobedience and Nonviolence

The idea of civil disobedience has been intriguing to philosophers, spiritualists, and political thinkers down through the ages. It began with Socrates, who faced a jury of his peers and was found guilty of two charges: corrupting the youth and inventing new gods not of the state.

Socrates

Socrates (469–399 B.C.E.) is shown facing these charges in Plato's dialogue *Apology*, which is the Greek word for defense. Socrates tells his cross-examiners (29d) that if the court were to discharge him conditionally upon his giving up engaging in philosophical inquiry and debate, he would disobey such an order. "Suppose that you said to me 'Socrates, on this occasion we shall disregard Anytus and acquit you, but only on one condition, that you give up spending your time on this quest and stop philosophizing. If we catch you going on in the same way, you shall be put to death.'" If such an arrangement were offered, Socrates proclaims he would not accept the offer. "I should reply, Gentlemen, I am your very grateful and devoted servant, but I owe a greater obedience to God than to you, and so long as I draw breath and have my faculties, I shall never stop practicing philosophy and exhorting you and elucidating the truth for everyone that I meet."

Socrates remains the living example of the view that the life of the philosopher is the good life, that a life of questioning and engaging in philosophical discussion is the way to pass the days. In short, he proclaimed, "The unexamined life is not worth living."

INSIGHT

Socrates was responsible for making the statement, "The unexamined life is not worth living." He thought that questioning one's life was the most meaningful activity. To live a full life, one must raise questions about how to live, specifically whether to prioritize the needs of the soul over those of the body.

To this point in the dialogue, Socrates is saying he would not accept an offer of freedom that required he cease philosophizing. So how can we compare the views he expresses in Plato's *Apology* with those found in the *Crito*, a dialogue named after his friend that describes his last days in jail? Here in the jail cell, it is roughly four weeks after the trial where he was found guilty and sentenced to death. In the *Crito*, Socrates treats the laws of Athens, which imply that individual citizens mustn't evade the court's judgment, including any sentences given, as legally binding.

At 50c in the *Crito*, Socrates speaks to his friend as if he were a political conservative (in the original sense of one who wishes to "conserve" the laws), and resists Crito's desperate attempt to convince his friend to escape from jail. In escaping, Socrates believes he will be "destroying the laws." It would be as unjust of him to escape as it was for the court to wrongly convict him. Not only will his escaping weaken the laws, but Socrates will be treating his beloved Athens badly. The state is like a parent, who gave us "life in the first place" and so should not be harmed, any more than one would harm one's parents.

Does this show that Socrates has committed a contradiction in the two dialogues? It is not easy to accuse great philosophers of contradicting themselves in such an obvious fashion; you must first see if there is a way of getting them out of the bind.

In the *Apology,* there is only one possible judgment Socrates is prepared to disobey—one banning him from engaging in philosophical activity in Athens. His disobedience in this case will be overt; he will practice philosophy in the open, just as he always has. That is, he will pursue the truth with whomever he meets, whether they are foreigners or citizens, professionals or craftsmen, philosophers or nonphilosophers.

By contrast, he will not disobey a lawful command—if he disobeys a legal verdict he will weaken the law—so he cannot escape as Crito wants him to do. On the other hand, his continued philosophizing in the *Apology* is right because it is grounded in the obedience to God. If he escaped from jail—because he was breaking the law—he could not claim the same God-based reasoning.

This is civil disobedience of a special sort. Socrates appeals to men's intellects, though he does not try to escape the legal consequences of his actions by violence or by fleeing. Thus, he does not injure the state by rendering null and void the laws of the land or the verdict of courts. In addition, he suffers no disrepute, which he might have suffered had he escaped jail.

In terms of civil disobedience, Socrates was the originator. His actions in fourth-century Athens were the rational model for citizens of the future. His was a method grounded in reason and persuasion, not in law breaking or violence.

Martin Luther

Martin Luther (1483–1546) was a German theologian who will forever be known as the principal initiator of the Protestant Reformation in Europe.

Dating back to the eleventh century, the Catholic Church had accepted various forms of indulgences, especially granting indulgences to those who went on Crusades. These indulgences could be obtained by saying certain prayers, or by performing specified works, such as helping the needy, worship, giving money to the church, or taking part in a Crusade.

Born in Eisleben, his upbringing encouraged an appetite for learning, music, and the Bible. He entered law school, but never practiced. He was known by friends as "the philosopher" and "the king of hops," since he loved beer.

Luther became obsessed about what to do to get deliverance from an angry God. According to a popular story, in 1505, he was returning from school during a thunderstorm when he was thrown from his horse. Terrified, he promised St. Anne, the patron saint of minors, that he'd become a monk.

At twenty-one, he entered a monastery in Ereford, shunned his worldly needs, and sought worthiness in God's eyes in all his actions. He even spent up to six hours in confession. But still he couldn't obtain spiritual peace. He learned Hebrew and Greek so he could pore over the most ancient manuscripts of the Bible. He was ordained a priest in 1507 and went to the University of Wittenberg to study and lecture on Aristotle.

In 1510, Luther was sent to Rome on business for his order, hiking to Rome over the Alps during a severe winter. When he first saw the Vatican, he dropped to his knees, proclaiming, "Hail, holy city of Rome." But Luther was shocked by the spiritual laxity he found there. Upon his return from Rome, he completed work on his theological doctorate and continued to lecture at Wittenberg. For Luther, these were times of great spiritual anxiety and physical torment. His search for quietude and spiritual peace led him further into an intense study of the scriptures. He devoted himself to the work of the church and became district vicar in 1515.

The 95 Theses and the Sale of Indulgences

The final straw for Luther was when Johann Tetzel, a German preacher of the Dominican order, arrived in Saxony in 1517 to proclaim an indulgence granted by Leo X. Luther opposed indulgences—the church's practice of accepting money for absolving people's sins. At the time, Tetzel was selling indulgences so he could raise money in Germany for the construction of St. Peter's Basilica in Rome. People brought pieces of silver to confession, happily claiming they no longer had to repent their sins.

FACT

So famed was German preacher Johann Tetzel for selling indulgences that he would speak the catchy couplet, "As soon as a coin in the coffer rings/the soul from purgatory springs." Tetzel established a kind of science of indulgences, charting the price for each kind of sin.

This was an outrage to Luther, who promptly wrote his 95 theses. He wished to expose the fraud being sold to believers: Why should they pay money for forgiveness, when forgiveness was a gift of God? Each of the theses was a proposition, a set of principles, some addressing matters of church doctrine.

QUESTION?

Why didn't the church act to eliminate indulgences?
The abuse of indulgences had been condemned by many Catholic theologians. On the other hand, indulgences produced great financial success for the church, so ecclesiastical authorities had not put an end to it.

Luther posted his 95 theses on the Wittenberg church door on October 31, 1517, hoping for a scholarly debate on the subject of the church's sale of indulgences. His actions jump-started the Reformation; October 31 is still celebrated as Reformation Day. People were inspired by his ideas, and the sale of indulgences dropped dramatically.

Luther's theses were widely distributed and read, finding a sympathetic audience among the exploited peasantry and among those civil authorities who resented the funds being sent to Rome. The propositions were brought before the pope, who feared they would cause dissention in the Augustinian order. Meanwhile, Luther also challenged the supremacy of the pope in public debates. In 1520, he was excommunicated. At the Diet of Worms in 1521, he defended his doctrines before Charles V, but he was made a pariah of the Holy Roman Empire.

Nevertheless, Luther's voice had been heard. By mid-century, a host of German and Scandinavian rulers had severed their links with Rome and set up new "Lutheran" churches in their territories. Luther's intention was not to split Christendom in this way, but he was left with little choice when his proposals of reform for the church fell on deaf ears.

Social Condition in Luther's Time

When Luther was born, nearly all of Western Europe looked to Rome as the head of the church. By the time he died, Europe was divided into Roman Christians and "protesting" or Protestant Christians. Born in Renaissance Europe, he grew up in a time of great social flux. Nearly 90 percent of the populace consisted of poor, illiterate peasants, pawns ruled by kings, nobles, and bishops. Most children died before adulthood. Plague was a constant fear. People worked the land, hoping only to survive the winter. Life for most was a dreary preparation for heaven. The Christian church gave people hope for a better life after death.

By Luther's time, the church was losing touch with people's needs. Corrupt popes and bishops lived in luxury while people struggled. The church's involvement in politics was ruining its reputation, and it had begun to pay its bills by selling forgiveness. Luther, known as the "Father of Protestantism," changed all of that in one generation. He is considered, with Guttenberg and Newton, one of the most influential people of the past millennium.

Henry David Thoreau and Civil Disobedience

It was Henry David Thoreau (1817–1862) who coined the term "civil disobedience" in his 1848 essay of that name. Thoreau's own essay is rife with acerbic wit and pointed criticism. "Unjust laws exist: shall we be content to obey them, or shall we endeavor to amend them? . . . Men generally, under such a government as this, think they ought to wait until they have persuaded the majority to alter them. They think that, if they should resist, the remedy would be worse than the evil."

Thoreau was educated in the works of Plato, Eastern philosophy, Kant, and his mentor, Ralph Waldo Emerson. He attacked social conformity; he believed that rather than choosing the more difficult path of rebellion, men quietly choose acceptance of the status quo as a way of life. "The mass of men lead lives of quiet desperation," he wrote in his essay "Economy." "What is called resignation is confirmed desperation."

Thoreau wrote his feisty essay on civil disobedience as a lecture, to be delivered at the Concord Lyceum in February of 1848. Thoreau began his bold essay with the line, "I heartily accept the motto, 'That government is best which governs least,' and I would like to see it acted up to more rapidly and systematically."

Speaking of the government, Thoreau asked, "Why does it not cherish its wise minority? Why does it cry and resist before it is hurt? Why does it not encourage its citizens to be on the alert to point out its faults? . . . Why does it always crucify Christ, and excommunicate Copernicus and Luther, and pronounce Washington and Franklin rebels?"

Some three hundred years after the death of Martin Luther, Henry David Thoreau, an American transcendentalist, established a reputation as one of the most influential figures in American thought and literature. Much of his reputation owed to his supreme individualism; Thoreau championed the human spirit against materialism and social conformity. Who else would retreat from a bustling New England to live in solitude in the woods of Concord, Massachusetts?

Walden

Several years before his essay, Thoreau built himself a small cabin on the shore of Walden Pond, near Concord. He remained there for more than two years, "living deep and sucking all the marrow out of life." He shunned materialistic pursuits and supported himself by growing vegetables and surveying and doing odd jobs in the nearby village. He devoted countless hours to observing nature, reading, and writing, and he kept a detailed journal of his observations, activities, and thoughts. It was from this journal that he distilled his masterpiece *Walden*.

The contemplation during his secluded activities at Walden Pond proved to have great mileage. The journal, begun in 1837, was also the source of his first book, *A Week on the Concord and Merrimack Rivers* (1849), as well as his posthumously published *Excursions* (1863), *The Maine Woods* (1864), *Cape Cod* (1865), and *A Yankee in Canada* (1866).

The ideas expressed in his "Civil Disobedience" grew out of an overnight stay in prison as a result of his conscientious refusal to pay a poll tax that supported the Mexican War, which to Thoreau represented an effort to extend slavery.

Thoreau's experience of solitude in jail was no doubt made more bearable by his solitude in the woods of Concord. He believed that by removing himself from the bustle of townlife, he liberated himself from an unquestioned adherence to prevailing attitudes. He was so far off the beaten path that he was unfailingly refreshing in his thought and manner of expression. "The greater part of what my neighbors call good I believe in my soul to be bad," Thoreau wrote in *Walden*. "If a man walk in the woods for love of them half of each day, he is in danger of being regarded as a loafer; but if he spends his whole day as a speculator, shearing off those woods and making Earth bald before her time, he is esteemed an industrious and enterprising citizen."

The insight shows Thoreau's ability to both surprise and teach us. He observed modern civilization—with all its fragmentation and desperation—and said we live a life of "restless, nervous, bustling, trivial activity."

INSIGHT

Writing some 150 years ago, Thoreau saw, even in his time—and no doubt for times to come—that we are in thrall to busy-ness, that we are forever dominated by the tyranny of the immediate. In "Life Without Principles," he voices one of his profoundest critiques: that our minds can "be permanently profaned by the habit of attending to trivial things, so that all our thoughts will be tinged with triviality."

He protests against addictive consumerism, unreflective philistinism, mindless mass entertainment, technology for technology's sake, and our slavish habit of turning into sheep in our daily lives. We succumb to the herd mentality of bowing before an anonymous "They," he wrote in *Walden*. Free of the mental shackles that beset so many of his peers in mid-nineteenth-century America, he criticized the Mexican War and the subjugation of Native Americans, and he gave voice to the protection of animals in wild areas. But he reserved his sharpest criticism for slavery.

To say that Thoreau was for the abolition of slavery is to understate the case severely—he participated in the abolitionist movement in almost every conceivable way. He was active in the Underground Railroad and protested against the Fugitive Slave Law, a federal law intended to enforce a section of the United States Constitution that required the return of runaway slaves.

In addition, he gave support to John Brown and his party. An abolitionist, Brown unabashedly advocated armed insurrection as a means of abolishing slavery. Brown also led the ill-fated raid at Harper's Ferry, Virginia, which led to his capture, trial for treason against Virginia, and subsequent hanging in 1859.

But Thoreau's own method of protest was antithetical to Brown's violence. Because of his principled justification of revolt and method of nonviolent resistance, he would have considerable influence on revolutionary movements over the course of the twentieth century.

Civil Disobedience

In "Civil Disobedience," originally published as "Resistance to Civil Government," he defended conscientious objection to unjust laws, which he thought should be transgressed without delay. To the undiscerning reader, Thoreau may come off as an anarchist, but this cannot be literally true, for anyone arguing for anarchy is arguing for a state of "no rule." This was not Thoreau's intention; he urged citizens to fight for a better government—one morally and practically superior to the one they have. "Let every man make known what kind of government would command his respect, and that will be one step toward obtaining it."

Indeed, Thoreau's words possess a kind of eternal relevance. He refuses to acknowledge the authority of a government that is so morally corrupt that it loses the consent of those governed.

INSIGHT

"There will never be a really free and enlightened state," Thoreau maintained, "until the State comes to recognize the individual as a higher and independent power, from which all its own power and authority are derived, and treats him accordingly." The laws of society are not sacred; in this sense, a just government could never come into conflict with the individual conscience, which ought to follow higher laws.

Thoreau's advocacy of civil disobedience has had wide-ranging impact—on the British labor movement, the passive-resistance independence movement led by Gandhi in India, and the nonviolent civil rights movement led by Martin Luther King Jr. in the United States. Above all, Thoreau's quiet, one-man revolution in living at Walden has become a symbol of the willed integrity of human beings, their inner freedom, and their ability to build their own lives.

Thoreau was prolific beyond belief—his writings, including his journals, were published in twenty volumes in 1906.

Leo Tolstoy

The Russian writer Lev Nikolayevich Tolstoy—known better as Leo Tolstoy—was influenced by the nonviolence of Christ, and he in turn would influence Mohandas Gandhi's thoughts on civil resistance, but Tolstoy (1828–1910) is surely better known for his timeless literary classics, especially *War and Peace*.

Tolstoy underwent a spiritual crisis at the age of fifty. Such was his despair that he contemplated suicide. He found solace and hope in the notion that societies ought to be—and could be—constructed on Christian principles. Tolstoy read the Gospel of Matthew and Jesus' statement that we shouldn't resist evil persons but should "turn the other cheek," and decided social Christianity was a distinct possibility. All that had to be done was to apply Christ's philosophy of love, tolerance, and nonviolence to concrete situations.

Pacifism

War is immoral, since by Tolstoy's interpretation, "Thou shalt not murder" opposes all sorts of killing. He takes the title of his work, "The Kingdom of God is Within You," from Luke 17:21, but it could be argued that The Sermon on the Mount shaped Tolstoy's understanding most of all. From that open-air sermon, Jesus delivered the "Beatitudes"—the word means "blessedness"—suggesting that those not wealthy or powerful or even favored on Earth will nonetheless experience the blessings of the kingdom of heaven. The sermon also instructs listeners to "resist not evil," but to do good to one's enemies.

To the charge leveled by those who thought that a nonviolent society is utopian and that the implementation of such a society would be worse than before, Tolstoy replied that only those that prosper as a result of the present arrangement wanted to keep up the status quo. Tolstoy wrote, "That this social order with its pauperism, famines, prisons, gallows, armies, and wars is necessary to society; that still greater disaster would ensue if this organization were destroyed; all this is said only by those who profit by this organization, while those who suffer from it—and they are ten times as numerous—think and say quite the contrary."

Tolstoy counters his detractors' objections in his second chapter, "Criticisms of the Doctrine of Nonresistance to Evil by Force on the Part of Believers and of Unbelievers." He deals first with criticisms of those believers who often make up the hierarchy of the church. "The first and crudest form of reply consists in the bold assertion that the use of force is not opposed by the teaching of Christ; that it is permitted, and even enjoined, on the Christian by the Old and New Testaments."

FACT

Tolstoy embraced pacifism and thought nonviolence could solve nationalist divisions. Gandhi's idea of satyagraha, or nonviolent resistance, is derivative of Tolstoy. They were similar in other ways, too. "You must be the change you want to see in the world," Gandhi advised, echoing one of Tolstoy's most poignant sentiments: "Everyone thinks of changing the world, but no one thinks of changing himself."

According to Tolstoy, such arguments proceed by authority merely, being made by men who have "attained the highest ranks in the governing or ecclesiastical hierarchy, and who are perfectly assured that no one will dare to contradict their assertion, and that if anyone does contradict it they will hear nothing of the contradiction."

In his ninth chapter, entitled "The Acceptance of the Christian Conception of Life Will Emancipate Men from the Miseries of our Pagan Life," Tolstoy maintains that Christians are to heed only a "divine law of life." This divine law is "implanted in the soul of every man, and brought before his consciousness by Christ, as the soul guide of his life and other men's also." What does this entail for daily living?

The Christian is independent of every human authority. And though he "may be subjected to external violence, he may be deprived of bodily freedom, he may be in bondage to his passions (he who commits sin is the slave of sin), but he cannot be in bondage in the sense of being forced by any danger or by any threat of external harm to perform an act which is against his conscience."

A life of civil disobedience must follow from this duty to conscience. This is because "For a Christian the oath of allegiance to any government whatever—the very act which is regarded as the foundation of the existence of a state—is a direct renunciation of Christianity. For the man who promises unconditional obedience in the future to laws, made or to be made, by that very promise is in the most, positive manner renouncing Christianity, which means obeying in every circumstance of life only the divine law of love he recognizes within him." Tolstoy then puts in bold relief the contradiction of heeding conscience on the one hand and temporal authority on the other: "For a Christian to promise obedience to me, or the laws of men, is just as though a workman bound to one employer should also promise to carry out every order that might be given him by outsiders. One cannot serve two masters."

Martin Luther King Jr.

The core of Martin Luther King's doctrine of civil disobedience—in his words, "nonviolent direct action"—can be found in his "Letter from Birmingham Jail." There is no question that King, similar to Tolstoy, is willing to disobey society's laws if they are unjust laws. In fact, doing so will be a necessary means to achieving social justice.

Letter from Birmingham Jail

King's "Letter from Birmingham Jail" was prompted by a letter written and signed by eight Alabama clergymen. In the usual way, the letter called for calm and patience. The men previously "issued an appeal for law and order and common sense" and urged King to let racial matters be pursued in the courts. Until that time, all decisions of those courts should be "peacefully obeyed."

In no uncertain terms, King wrote back, his letter beginning with the gentle salutation "My Dear Fellow Clergymen," and then elaborating on Birmingham's white power structure that left his community with no alternative but to act. In the letter, he calls Birmingham the "most thoroughly segregated city in the United States"; it owns an "ugly record of brutality," and black people undergo "grossly unjust treatment in the courts."

What's more, there had been more unsolved bombings of Negro homes and churches in Birmingham than any other city in the nation. Despite these facts, King finds that city fathers have always "refused to engage in good-faith negotiation." In addition, the Birmingham economic community promised to remove humiliating racial signs, and in return the Alabama Christian Movement for Human Rights consented to a moratorium on all demonstrations, but seven months later the signs remained.

With no progress on the racial front in the south, King decided to take "direct action." Direct action comprised sit-ins, marches, and other actions in which protestors would make enough of a nuisance of themselves to demand a response. In addition, if opponents rained blows on the protestors, the protestors must take the abuse without retaliation.

In using "constructive, nonviolent tension" as a means of growth, King referenced Socrates. "Just as Socrates felt that it was necessary to create a tension in the mind so that individuals could rise from the bondage of myths and half-truths," so those opposing segregation must be "nonviolent gadflies to create the kind of tension in society that will help men rise from the dark depths of prejudice and racism to the majestic heights of understanding and brotherhood." Without this sort of aggressive prodding, nothing would change, King asserted, for, "It is an historical fact that privileged groups seldom give up their privileges voluntarily. Individuals may see the moral light and voluntarily give up their unjust posture; but, as Reinhold Niebuhr has reminded us, groups tend to be more immoral than individuals."

As such, the response that urges people to wait would no longer do. The institutional violence caused by the separate and unequal arrangements in the south would no longer do. Obeying laws? There are just laws and unjust laws, and King says, "One has not only a legal but a moral responsibility to obey just laws." On the other hand, "One has a moral responsibility to disobey unjust laws." But how does a person decide which is which?

The son of a preacher, King's beliefs were grounded in the Bible and philosophy. "A just law is a man-made code that squares with the moral law of the law of God. An unjust law is a code that is out of harmony with the moral law. To put it in the terms of St. Thomas Aquinas: an unjust law is a human law that is not rooted in eternal law and natural law. Any law that uplifts human personality is just. Any law that degrades human personality is unjust. All segregation statutes are unjust because segregation distorts the soul and damages the personality." King further illustrated his meaning by comparing it to voting rights.

An example of such an unjust law is one "inflicted on a minority that, as a result of being denied the right to vote, had no part in enacting or devising the law." In the Alabama of King's day, all sorts of methods were used to prevent would-be black voters from becoming registered. There is nothing wrong with having such an ordinance on the books, but there is something wrong when it is used to "maintain segregation and to deny citizens the First-Amendment privilege of peaceful assembly and protest."

INSIGHT

Legality does not equate to morality. For as King points out, everything that Adolf Hitler did in Germany was legal; so it was illegal to aid and comfort a Jew in Hitler's Germany. Even so, King insists that if he lived in Germany at that time, he would have aided and comforted his Jewish brothers.

King made an additional point relevant to nonviolent direct action. He concluded that the greater obstacle in the achievement of equality was not the White Citizen's Councilor or the Ku Klux Klan, but the white moderate who prized order above justice and hates the tension created by protest and advises the oppressed class to "be patient" and wait for a more "convenient season." King refers to a letter he has just received from a white brother in Texas: "All Christians know that the colored people will receive equal rights eventually, but it is possible that you are in too great a religious hurry. It has taken Christianity almost two thousand years to accomplish what it has. The teachings of Christ take time to come to Earth." There is no truth to the notion that human progress will just come about on it own. It does not. Rather, it arrives from the tireless efforts of men "willing to be co-workers of God."

King also resents the term "extremism" that the clergymen have used to describe his activities in Birmingham. How could clergymen see nonviolence as extremism? King maintains that he stands between two forces in the black community: One is a force of complacency, embodied by middle-class blacks who are so used to years of oppression that they are drained of self-respect and have adjusted to segregation. The other force is black nationalism, the best known of which was Elijah Muhammad's Muslim movement, made up of people who have lost faith in America, have repudiated Christianity, and concluded that the white man is an incorrigible devil. King notes that he stayed between these two forces, advocating neither the "do-nothingism" of the complacent set nor the "hatred and despair" of the black nationalists.

King at first chafed at being described as an extremist, but was not put off after thinking about it. "Was not Jesus an extremist for love: 'Love your enemies, bless them that curse you, do good to them that hate you.' Similarly, Lincoln could be described in a similar manner, given his proclamation 'This nation cannot survive have slave and half free.'" So the important matter isn't whether we will be extremists or not, but for what cause. "Will we be extremists for the preservation of injustice or for the extension of justice?"

King gave vent to another major disappointment—the nature of the church and its leadership. He recalled being the leader of the bus protest in Montgomery, Alabama, a few years earlier and how he had thought he would be supported by white ministers and rabbis of the South. He had heard white ministers speaking of segregation and remarking, that it was "a social issue, with which the gospel has no real concern."

He also chastises the clergymen for commending the Birmingham police for "keeping order" and "preventing violence." However, the clergy seemed to miss the police dogs biting black protestors and the police who beat them with clubs. How could these same clergymen have not commended the courage of those who demonstrated? What about those who practiced sit-ins and faced jeering, hostile mobs and racial epithets? What about the seventy-two-year-old woman in Montgomery who rose up with a sense of dignity and decided not to ride a segregated bus? Others were willing to sit at lunch counters and willingly went to jail for conscience's sake.

All of them were, in reality, standing up for "what is best in the American dream," King wrote, "and for the most sacred values in the Judaeo-Christian heritage." In doing so, they were nonviolently effecting change.

CHAPTER 19

Hindu Ideas in Popular Culture

Many Westerners first became aware of Eastern spirituality in the 1960s. Transcendental meditation came to our shores and was prescribed by a peaceful Indian man with a never-ending smile, Maharishi Mahesh Yogi. At about the same time, Swami A. C. Prabhupada went to New York to begin the Hare Krishna movement. Grounded in the Hindu devotional tradition of bhakti that dated to the Vedas, "Krishna consciousness" would soon attract tens of thousands of devotees across the United States and on several continents. But would either of these figures have grabbed our attention quite as much without the spiritual curiosity of The Beatles?

Transcendental Meditation

Transcendental meditation was begun by Maharishi Mahesh Yogi (1917–2008) in 1956. It is essentially the mantra yoga that Maharishi revived and introduced to the world. TM, as it became known, stressed natural meditation and the liberating pleasures such practices could invoke. It promised a drugless state of mind with inner peace and knowledge for its practitioners.

Maharishi Mahesh Yogi

The Maharishi was born Mahesh Prasad Varma. He earned a degree in physics from Allahabad University before turning to the study of meditation. Beginning in the 1940s, he spent thirteen years in silent retreat with Swami Brahmananda Saraswati, affectionately known as Guru Dev. After the latter's death in 1958, the Maharishi moved to the United Kingdom and founded the Spiritual Regeneration Movement. He taught publicly and attracted many disciples. From him, they learned the fundamentals of yoga, breathing, and mantra meditation.

Cultural Revolution

To begin TM, the Maharishi or some appointed instructor typically asked questions of the student about his health, education, marital status, feelings, and overall evaluation of his life. Each student was prescribed a private individual mantra or sound for silent repetition. The mantra is a specially empowered spoken or chanted utterance, ranging from one syllable to a long chant, as in the mantras of the Rig Veda. The student chants the mantra for twenty minutes each morning and evening. This phrase or sound allows the individual to "become" the mantra.

Etymologically, *mantra* comes from *man* ("think") and *tra* ("instrument"), making a mantra literally an "instrument of thought" or, more accurately, an instrument of consciousness. The idea originally referred to Vedic hymns, from which one whispered brief texts or divine names.

The Maharishi—which means "great seer" in Sanskrit—brought TM from India to the West in 1959, and it became a distinct subculture within the 1960s youth movement. In meditation, the ideal was to clear the mind of the usual desires and ideas that burden it. Hunger, song lyrics, distracting smells, scientific formulas, sexual fantasies—all of this must fade into the background of consciousness in order for meditation to be effective.

The idea behind chanting a mantra is to provide, much in the way Catholics have learned to use the Rosary beads, a sort of controlled distraction. The hope is that a mantra—especially one that is chosen by the teacher—will alleviate the problems and stress in your life, and you will be a better person for it.

The person meditating must free himself from the tyranny of the immediate that dominates his ceaseless conscious thoughts. People spoke metaphorically of its benefits. Before TM, one eager student said, you look at the world through a very narrow lens. The longer you meditate, the wider your lens becomes.

In the Maharishi, the West got its first look at a quiet Indian holy man. In no time, this brand of meditation was everyone's path to inner peace and a higher state of consciousness. In very little time, TM attracted a long list of luminaries, including actress Mia Farrow, musician Donovan, cultural philosopher Marshall McLuhan, and the Beatles, who eventually rejected the Maharishi's teachings.

FACT

The Maharishi was the guest of honor on the *Merv Griffin Show* in 1975. Clint Eastwood strode onstage and walked to the couch where the Maharishi was sitting. He opened his suit jacket and reached in as if he were going to pull out Dirty Harry's .44 Magnum. Instead, he produced a flower and handed it to the Maharishi. TM initiations soared.

TM went global in just a matter of years. The Maharishi had to train thousands of his most devoted followers as TM initiators. Soon the Maharishi had a marketing bonanza; most good-sized American cities had a storefront TM center and a listing for "Meditation, Transcendental" in the yellow pages. People took to calling TM the McDonalds of meditation, making use of a McMantra. Standardized TM posters had little spaces in which the local teacher could write the name and time of the free public lecture.

It might not have provided all the spiritual answers that people were seeking, but it got them started. The man with the long dark hair who sat in the lotus position would become familiar to the world for his inscrutable calm and broad smile.

TM Methodology

The overall strategy of the Maharishi is revealed in his book *The Science of Being and Art of Living,* in which he spells out the groundwork for realizing God. When people attacked his idea, the Maharishi said, "TM is not a religion but a science." The Maharishi didn't invent meditation, but he revolutionized it. He made it simple, practicable, and enjoyable for all; he took meditation out of the realm of religious dogma. Though the technique was inspired by Vedic practices, instructors in transcendental meditation and the Maharishi do not consider the practice to be specifically Hindu, since it does not require either belief in or devotion to a deity.

TM is supposedly grounded in the Science of Creative Intelligence (SCI); practitioners maintain that their objective is scientific, not religious. The technique is described as a simple mental exercise that initiates deep relaxation and rest. Journals such as *Science, American Journal of Physiology,* and *Scientific American* find that TM produces a state of mind known as "restful alertness." The state is characterized by significant reductions in respiration, minute ventilation, tidal volume, and blood lactate. In addition, EEG measurements showed increased coherence and integration of brain functioning, implying that the physiology was alert rather than asleep.

FACT

In 1977, TM announced its Siddha program to help initiates achieve paranormal abilities, including levitation of the body. A former instructor of the Siddha program eventually sued, claiming that these and other manifestations of unusual phenomena could not be achieved. He won a judgment of $138,000.

A positive correlation has also been found between the TM technique and various health-related conditions, including reduction of blood pressure, younger biological age, decreased insomnia, reduction of high cholesterol, reduced illness and medical expenditure, decreased outpatient visits, decreased cigarette smoking, decreased alcohol use, and decreased anxiety.

The Maharishi University of Management in Iowa was awarded an $8 million grant by the National Institutes of Health (NIH) in 1999. As recently as 2004, the NIH, an agency of the United States Department of Health and Human Services responsible for biomedical and health-related research, spent more than $20 million funding research on the effects of TM on heart disease, about a sixth of its budget for researching complementary and alternative medicine in general. In 2005, an NIH study published in the *American Journal of Cardiology* showed that transcendental meditation reduced death rates by 23 percent in a random trial in which 202 men and women with an average age of seventy-one were tracked over eighteen years. That same year, *The American Journal of Hypertension* published a study that found TM might be useful in the long-term treatment of hypertension among African Americans.

Popularity of the Movement

The effects of the TM movement have been far reaching, lasting more than half a century. TM was introduced to the West through two organizations, the Spiritual Regeneration Movement and the Student International Meditation Society. The Maharishi himself purchased the defunct Parsons College in Fairfield, Iowa, and turned it into Maharishi International University, which in 1974 was renamed the Maharishi University of Management (of the Universe).

In 1972, the Maharishi revealed a World Plan to guide the nations of the world in using the insights from the practice of TM and the Science of Cognitive Intelligence. The plan included a spectrum of activities for cultural renewal, health, freedom from war, and personal development. According to the World Plan Council, TM is not a new religious group, but some observers disagreed. Significant controversy arose as TM teachers were receiving government funds to teach TM in places such as the public schools and the armed forces. In 1978, a federal district court in Newark, New Jersey, ruled that TM was indeed a religious practice and could not receive public funds; nor could government agencies promote its teachings and practices. After this ruling, the exponential upward trajectory of growth for the movement fell dramatically, though it remains a substantial worldwide movement.

FACT

The Maharishi School of Management (of the Universe) awards bachelors, masters, and doctoral degrees in consciousness-based education. At present, almost 800 students are enrolled in programs structured one course at a time in small classes over a period of four weeks. Degrees are granted in science, the humanities, and Vedic science.

The New Jersey ruling that TM was a religious practice was historically based. The ruling pointed to several religious factors. One, the use of mantras makes TM a form of japa yoga. Two, TM initiations include traditional religious acts. Three, the movement was accepted in India as a form of Shaivite Hinduism.

If you compare TM to other movements, say EST or other human potential movements, you must admit the sheer numbers are impressive. Millions of people have attended TM courses; at present, there are some 7,000 authorized teachers working at 400 teaching centers. In the United States, a Vedic City is planned on the land adjacent to the Maharishi University of Management.

During the 1980s, the council introduced *ayurvedic* medical products and opened a center adjacent to the university to promote it. The word ayurveda means "life knowledge" and is the ancient tradition of medicine in India, said to have originated in Atharva Veda. The text Ayurveda, which is no longer extant, was said to have been written by Dhavantari, the physician of the gods. The writer and physician Deepak Chopra emerged as a leading exponent of Maharishi's Ayurvedic program, but has in recent years distanced himself from the organization.

TM has hardly been immune to attack. Its claims have been attacked by Swami Prabhupada, who began the Hare Krishna movement in America, and spiritualist Jiddu Krishnamurti. The latter has gone so far as to say that the repetition of the "Om" sound—or any other mantras for that matter—might well be replaced by the repetition of "Coca Cola" and have the same effect on the mind.

The Quiet Beatle and Hinduism

George Harrison (1943–2001) met Maharishi Mahesh Yogi in the 1960s, and the meeting would have a lasting influence on his daily practices. For all intents and purposes, the Beatles' foray into TM and Eastern philosophy began because of George Harrison's curiosity about Eastern thought.

On August 29, 1966, The Beatles performed their last concert in Candlestick Park in San Francisco. It had been an unpleasant show, and each member of the group knew that public performances were now behind them. Two weeks later, George and his wife Pattie were on their way to India, declaring they were in search of spiritual peace.

"I believe much more in the religions of India than in anything I have learned from Christianity," Harrison said to a BBC correspondent in India. "The difference over here is that their religion is every second and every minute of their lives—and it is them, how they act, how they conduct themselves, and how they think." Once in India, the couple stayed with Indian musician and long-time friend Ravi Shankar on a houseboat on a lake in Kashmir overlooking the Himalayas.

Harrison's Enlightenment

Ravi Shankar was a kindred spirit to the younger George and added several books to George's spiritual library, including *Raja-Yoga*, by Swami Vivekananda. George imbibed the Swami's central message—that all persons possess innate and eternal perfection. "You are that which you seek," Vivekananda wrote. "There is nothing to do but realize it."

But one notion held a particular attraction for George. "What right has a man to say that he has a soul if he does not feel it, or that there is a God if he does not see Him? If there is a God, we must see Him . . . otherwise it is better not to believe." This was bold material; it implied that there is far more truth in being a vocal atheist than in being a docile hypocrite. As it turned out, the desire to "see" God came out in several of George's songs, including a hit single "My Sweet Lord," with its refrain, "I really want to see you Lord, but it takes so long my Lord. . . ."

Yoga was Harrison's means to seeing and knowing God. The word "yoga," he learned, meant "to link," suggestive of the English words "yoke" or "union." Yoga involved psychophysical exercises, but its goal was to link the soul with the Supreme Soul, or God. For someone such as George, who had enjoyed inestimable material success and formed many attachments to worldly goods, it was easier said than done.

INSIGHT

Vivekananda taught that true yoga did not depend on being Christian, Jewish, Buddhist, atheist, agnostic, or theist; the benefits of yoga are available to every human being through daily practice. Simply try not to eat before morning yoga, practice mornings and evenings, and control the sex drive.

Several personal traits are required to be successful at yoga. For one, to know God, you must practice yama or self-restraint. This all-embracing virtue included no killing and, by extension, a vegetarian diet; no lying; and no stealing or taking more than is needed. These could be added to cleanliness, austerity, and dependence on God. Without these fundamentals, a yogi could not achieve his ends.

From the houseboat, George could see the clouds sitting over the Himalayas. Just twenty-three, he was already looking back on his life as a guitarist in the most successful rock-and-roll band in history. As he boarded the plane after the concert in San Francisco, he had said to his band mates, "Well, that's it. I'm finished. I'm not a Beatle anymore." The group would record together in studios for several more years, but as far as live performances were concerned, he was right. Their gig at Candlestick was their last live performance. He had had enough.

Two incidents before the final concert had set George in the direction of spirituality. The first happened at a dinner party for the Beatles and their wives thrown by George's dentist. He had spiked their coffee with LSD, and the hallucinogenic effects of the drug took hold as George drove the group home. Though George drove at a crawl of 18 miles per hour, John Lennon said the LSD made it seem like a thousand. "It was terrifying, but it was fantastic," John recalled of his first experiment with the hallucinogenic. "It was like living a thousand years in ten minutes," George said of his experiences with lysergic acid diethylamide. He also said it was like "an astronaut in a spaceship looking back on Earth."

But that was just a preamble to what he said to *Rolling Stone* magazine. "Up until LSD I never realized that there was anything beyond this everyday state of consciousness. . . . The first time I took it, it just blew everything away. I had such an overwhelming feeling of well-being, that there was a God, and I could see him in every blade of grass. It was like gaining hundreds of years of experience in twelve hours." It was as if, he said, all his sensory apparatus had been previously shut off—as if he had never tasted or smelled or heard anything before. "From that moment on, I wanted to have that depth and clarity of perception."

In 1964, Timothy Leary, a Harvard professor who dispensed hallucinogenic drugs to students, wrote of the quasi-religious effects of the drugs in his book *The Psychedelic Experience*. "Such [psychedelic] experiences can occur in a variety of ways: sensory deprivation, yoga exercises, disciplined meditation, religious or aesthetic ecstasies, or spontaneously . . . They have become available to anyone through the ingestion of psychedelic drugs such as LSD, psilocybin, mescaline, DMT, etc."

Not unlike other drugs, LSD altered brain chemistry, in itself not an intrinsically spiritual process. Still, in the 1960s hallucinogens were praised as a means to enlightenment, receiving no more ringing endorsement than that given by the philosopher Aldous Huxley, who wrote *The Doors of Perception*. "To be shaken out of the ruts of ordinary perception, to be shown for a few timeless hours the outer and inner world, not as they appear to an animal obsessed with survival or to a human being obsessed with words and notions, but as they are apprehended directly and unconditionally by Mind at Large—this is an experience of inestimable value to everyone and especially to the intellectual," Huxley wrote.

Ultimately, George stopped using LSD as a means to heighten perception because he found out that other habitual users of the drug were every bit as "stupid as they were before." "You can take it as many times as you like," he told a reporter several years after, "but you get to a point that you can't get any farther unless you stop taking it."

A second chance event caused George, and ultimately the Beatles, to drink in Indian music and philosophy. He noticed a sitar on the set of the Beatles' movie *Help!* and was intrigued by the look and sound of it. George diddled away on the instrument on the universally appealing song "Norwegian Wood," which made for a very different sound. He met Ravi Shankar and got lessons on the instrument.

By early 1967, when it came to putting together their eighth album, *Sgt. Pepper's Lonely Hearts Club Band,* George was weary of the studio work—the album had already been four months in the works, but then Lennon and McCartney asked him to contribute a song. Harrison came up with "Within You Without You," a five-minute-plus tour of Indian music and philosophy. It included a *sargam* (style of Indian music) melody; a *tambura,* or unfretted lute drone; and rhythmic *tablas,* or small hand drum. His lyrics ruminated about the illusion of separateness and differences that divide us. Peace will only come when we come to see that we are one—for life and spirit are everywhere, within us and without. The album was released in June 1967, and had many musicologists falling over themselves trying to find new verbiage to praise it. One music critic, William Mann, hailed it as more genuinely creative than anything else in pop music. Others went further, saying it was the greatest song of all time.

The diffident twenty-four-year-old had laid down the gauntlet; he produced the only song on the album on which only one Beatle performed. Juan Mascaro, a professor of Sanskrit teaching at Cambridge University, heard George's Indian track and wrote to say, "It is a moving song and may it move the souls of millions. And there is more to come; as you are only beginning on the great journey."

A footnote to George's discovery of the philosophy and music of India was a trip to San Francisco. It was the "Summer of Love" in San Francisco's Haight-Ashbury district, a supposed land of ideal peace, unsurpassed love and goodwill, flowered hair, and the home office for LSD consciousness. After returning from Greece, George and Patti flew to San Francisco to sample the capital of love. He dressed to fit in—psychedelic pants, tassled moccasins, even heart-shaped sunglasses, but he had no sooner arrived than he became appalled at what he discovered. Hippies lay sprawled out on benches, garbage all around them on the streets. Under the guise of practicing peace and love, the kids begged for coins. "Horrible, spotty, dropout kids on drugs," George called them.

INSIGHT

> The depth of George's spiritual insight and commitment to Indian philosophy was evident on his album *All Things Must Pass,* the first triple album by a single artist in rock history, released after the Beatles broke up in April 1970. In the song "All Things Must Pass," George sings: All things must pass/All things must pass away/All things must pass/None of Life's strivings can last/So, I must be on my way/And face another day.

Harrison's upbringing in postwar working-class Liverpool had taught him the value of work. The hippies were hypocrites, he told a magazine reporter. "I don't mind anyone dropping out of anything, but it's the imposition on someone else I don't like. I've just realized that it doesn't matter what you are as long as you work. In fact, if you drop out, you put yourself further away from the goal of life than if you were to keep working." Indian philosophy was worth the effort; the drug scene was not.

As his car pulled away from the curb in Haight-Ashbury, George took a photo of Paramahansa Yogananda from his pocket and held it up for the hippies to see. "This is it," he told his friends in the car. "This is where it is." Following his visit, he became more serious about meditation.

On the flight home on a private jet, George sat behind the pilot. Just after takeoff, the plane stalled, shook, and went into a dive. George could see the lights in the cockpit flashing "Unsafe." "Well, that's it," he thought and started chanting, "Hare Krishna, Hare Krishna," which means, "Praise Krishna," and "Om, Christ, Om." Former Beatles press agent Derek Taylor, who sat next to George, followed suit, chanting "Hare Krishna, Hare Krishna." The plane pulled out of its stall and landed safely in Monterrey. The group recovered from their fright by heading to the nearest beach.

The Beatles and Meditation

No celebrity attention given to the Maharishi and Indian philosophy could match the interest that the Beatles created. The Maharishi had spent the '60s traveling around the world lecturing and teaching TM nonstop, but the world outside India wasn't terribly receptive at first. Then the Beatles got interested—and the interest of the West followed.

George Harrison had already made his foray into Eastern philosophy in song during and after his Beatles years. The time was ripe; in London in 1967 the counterculture was in full swing and young Britons were discovering Eastern religions for themselves, making Britain the Maharishi's largest outpost outside of India.

FACT

The Beatles first learned of the Maharishi from George's wife, Pattie, who was, like her husband, intrigued by Indian religion. Just by coincidence, the Beatles went to hear the guru's last public appearance at a London hotel in August. So impressed were the Fab Four that they departed for a course in Wales two days after the London meeting.

Their major spiritual sojourn came in 1968. On departure day, reporters and fans crowded into London's Euston Station to watch the Beatles embark on what the *Daily Mirror* described as a "Mystical Special." The train departed with the Maharishi sitting cross-legged and waving to the crowds on the platform. George, John, and Paul entered his compartment, and the Maharishi explained they would find his meditation technique quite convenient, like funds in a bank. "You don't have to carry money around with you," he said," just make a withdrawal when needed." What if you're greedy, John asked, and want another meditation after lunch, and another after tea? The Maharishi shook with laughter. "He was laughing all the time," Ringo later said. "That really struck home. This man is really happy, and he's having a great time in life."

And so the Beatles left England to join the Maharishi at his Academy of Meditation in Shankacharya Nagar in India. Pop culture royalty soon abounded in Shakacharya; the Rolling Stones, Mia Farrow, and the Beach

Boys would be on hand. But while the Beatles were away from their usual world, on retreat to explore life's meaning, the reality of that world intruded. Their manager and friend, Brian Epstein, had been found dead in his home, having taken an accidental overdose of sleeping pills.

Soon after their retreat, the Beatles introduced the Maharishi to the *David Frost Show,* which helped transform the yogi into a household name. Now the Maharishi's message could reach millions. Part of that message was that man is not born to suffer, but he does suffer. People were trapped in prisons of unhappiness. The Beatles wished to learn how to tap the springs of pure energy and intelligence, not only for their own creative purposes but also for the benefit of others, for young people everywhere. In turn, the Maharishi saw the Beatles as apostles of his message.

But the Beatles left early; according to one account because the Maharishi was putting moves on Mia Farrow that were other than spiritual. Another account said that she didn't like the fuss he was making over her, placing paper crowns on her head and insisting on so many photographs with her. That kind of adulation wasn't what she had traveled across the world for.

George referred to the Maharishi affectionately as "The Big M." Of all the Beatles, he was the most engaged with the theory and practice of transcendence. He said that if he could turn everyone on to TM and Indian music he would. He had learned that it was great to be rich and famous, but added, "We're not eternal rich men." Lennon explained to other TM students gathered that their music served as a diary of their developing consciousness.

Ringo and Paul were more reticent about their meditation experiences. Sure, they had achieved good results with it, but it was more George's thing; he had wanted to go to India and that was fine with them. George had said, "Nobody can be 100 percent without the inner life," but Ringo thought he could find that inner life and sit in the lotus position back in Liverpool, where his children and nine cats were. His wife Maureen hated the flies, and Ringo mentioned the matter to Maharishi. The Maharishi told them that for people traveling in the realm of pure consciousness, flies no longer matter very much. "Yes," Ringo replied, "but that doesn't zap the flies, does it?"

Ultimately, rumors that the Maharishi had broken his vow of celibacy circulated through the ashram. Facts were scant, but some rumors had it that he was making advances to an Australian nurse, others that he had designs on a California co-ed. Regardless of the abrupt departure, the Fab

Four took the philosophy seriously. For a band that was always seeking to open another door, the Maharishi had opened one more.

FACT

Paul McCartney objected to the Maharishi's excessive adulation of the band and its prolific work. "That bit about being the sons of God and the saviors of mankind," Paul sighed. Paul was similarly impatient with the abstractions of the yogi's metaphysics. "I get lost in the upper reaches of it," Paul explained.

The Hare Krishnas

The Hare Krishnas are a Hindu-inspired spiritual group, a contemporary version of the Hindu devotional tradition of bhakti. By reviving bhakti, which means "worship," the Krishnas are renewing a practice that goes as far back as the Vedas, to 1500 B.C.E. More specifically, bhakti involves chanting and making offerings to chosen deities.

The Krishnas got a foothold in America in the 1960s, and were still making many converts through the 1970s. Their appearance was unmistakable: They wore saffron-colored robes, and shaved their heads—though the women modestly covered theirs—and they could usually be found in popular public places, including train stations, subways, airports, and even college campuses. They played finger cymbals and chanted devotional prayers such as "Hari Krishna, Hari Rama." They usually carried copies of some religious text, such as a hardbound and colorfully illustrated Bhagavad Gita in the 1970s, in exchange for which they sought a donation.

The founder of the Hare Krishnas was Swami A. C. Prabhupada (1896–1977). The swami was a saintly, scholarly man who played a major role in interpreting Vedanta for modern Western readers and spreading the worship of Krishna outside India.

Life of the Hare Krishna Founder

A native of Calcutta, Prabhupada was born Abhay Charan De, the son of a pious cloth merchant who visited the Radha-Govinda temple daily. When

Abbay was four, his father gave him a small image of Krishna and taught him to worship the deity. He enrolled in Scottish Churches College in 1916 and entered into an arranged marriage with Padharani Sata in 1919, while he was still a student. Though he completed his college work, he refused his degree, heeding Mohandas Gandhi's call to boycott British goods.

While working as manager of a pharmaceutical company in 1922, he met his spiritual master, Bhaktisiddhanta Saraswati, and became his disciple. Saraswati encouraged his pupil to spread the teaching of Krishna worship to the West, but the student put aside the suggestion. After his guru's death two decades later, he wrote several books, including *Bhagavad Gita As It Is*. For this and other publications, the Vaishnavites honored him with the title Bhaktivedanta, meaning "devotion to the knowledge of God." In 1944, he began publishing *Back to Godhead,* a magazine which later became an invaluable periodical for promoting the movement in America.

At the age of fifty-nine, with his children grown, Prabhupada took the order of sannyasa, retiring from family life so he could spend his remaining years spreading Krishna consciousness. He left his home in 1959 to study under another teacher, Acharya Goswami, at the Radha Damodora temple in Brindavan (Krishna's birthplace), where he lived austerely in a small room. In 1965, the Bhaktivedanta, now seventy, set sail for the United States to fulfill his first guru's desire to bequeath Krishna awareness to the West. He founded the International Society for Krishna Consciousness (known as ISKCON) in the summer of 1966. With the help of a small group of disciples, he opened a storefront temple in New York's immigrant-laden East Village, which by the mid-1960s had morphed into a Hippie-Bohemian paradise. The Hare Krishnas would take root in the suddenly spiritually fertile soil of America.

Meanwhile, before leaving for Greece as a celebration of completing the *Sergeant Pepper* album, George Harrison had purchased an album of Sanskrit prayers. One prayer became the group's theme song on the boat. The back-cover notes summoned the reader's attention. "Attention all eternal wayfarers on the shores of Earth," it read. "Swami A. C. Bhaktivedanta leads his devotees in authentic rendition of the Vedic mantra Hare Krishna, better known in India as the maha-mantra, sung on the banks of the Ganges for more than five thousand years."

While sailing on the Aegean Sea, John and George strummed ukulele banjos and chanted "Hare Krishna, Hare Krishna, Krishna Krishna, Hare Hare, Hare Rama, Hare Rama, Rama Rama, Hare Hare." The two chanted for six hours, George recalled, "Because we couldn't stop once we got going. As soon as we stopped, it was like the lights went out. We felt exalted. It was a very happy time for us."

At one point, John Lennon got to meet Swami Prabhupada and discuss the philosophy of the Maharishi with him. In the conversation, the Swami had criticized the secret mantras that the Maharishi had asked people to chant. Lennon objected, saying that, "Whether it is a secret mantra or not, it is all the word of God. So it doesn't really make much difference, does it, which one you are saying?" "Drugs are all medicines for killing diseases," Prabhupada replied, "but still you have to take a doctor's prescription for taking a particular type of medicine."

Lennon was not satisfied. "How can we tell one spiritual master from the other? The Maharishi is saying that his mantra is coming from the *Vedas*, with as much authority as you. And he is probably right. Why is the *Hare Krishna* [mantra] the best one? If we were buying flowers, someone might like roses, and someone else may like carnations better. Someone might find Hare Krishna is more beneficial to his spiritual progress, and yet someone else might find some other mantra more beneficial. Isn't it just a matter of taste?" The swami was quiet. Among his devotees he was not often challenged. But Lennon was not a devotee, he was a spiritual seeker raising questions.

The followers of ISKCON made bhakti yoga famous through their ubiquitous chanting of the Hare Krishna mantra. In time, the movement became one of the most prominent of the alternative religions to emerge in the last forty years; it has now spread to every continent. Before his death in November, 1977, Srila Prabhupada (an honorific) saw the building of many temples, children's schools in rural communities, and major cultural centers around the world. Since his death, however, the movement has not drawn the same large number of committed devotees and its leadership has become fragmented.

In July of 1977, Bhaktivedanta appointed eleven of his senior assistants to act as officiating priests to initiate all future ISKCON members on his behalf, but after his death four months later, the eleven claimed they were chosen as successor gurus, causing significant confusion within the movement. Nonetheless, ISKCON members still accept the authority of Bhaktivedanta and believe that he still exerts his spiritual influence on anyone who follows his teachings. Effigies of Bhaktivedanta Swami are still installed in all ISKCON temples.

Vedic Astrology

Not a day goes by without members of the Hindu tradition coming to a priest for information on *muhurta* (the best date and time for a particular action), birth names, and other kinds of astrological advice. Nava Graha puja (ritual for the nine planets) is one of the most popular pujas or purifications performed by a Hindu priest. Therefore, it is worthwhile to have a general understanding of the Hindu astrology.

The oldest existing scripture, the Rig Veda, has references to eclipses. Vendanga Jyotisha contains passages about astrology. The legendary sage Bhrigu is said to have perfected astrology, and the highlight of his work was putting together astrological charts laying out the horoscopes of everybody born or yet to be born in the universe. The Garga Samhita is an astronomical work and contains a chapter from 50 B.C.E. titled Yuga Purana. Mathematician and astronomer Varahamihira (505–587 C.E.) is known to have written on horoscopes. Yavana-Jataka is another astrological study. Bhattopala authored the astrological work *Hora-Shastra* in the fifteenth century, and Nilakantha produced *Tajika* in the sixteenth century.

In comparing and examining an elaboration of DNA work, we understand that a minute part of the body (or microcosm) contains all the information about the whole person (the macrocosm). Once you start thinking that the whole is embedded within every part of this creation, you can start seeing a relationship between the outer world and the inner world, between the microcosm and the macrocosm. This means that by measuring the outer world, one can grasp the inner world; but even more importantly, by setting out to influence the outer world, one can influence the inner world. Thus, we have the foundation of Hindu astrology.

What Astrology Predicts

Astrology (*jyotir vigyan*) is an art used to predict one's future based on the positions or movements of stars associated with an individual. The foundation of Jyotisha is the notion of the *bandhu* (relation) of the Vedas or scripture that is the connection between the microcosm and the macrocosm. The practice of Jyotisha primarily relies on the sidereal zodiac, which is different from the tropical zodiac used in Western astrology.

FACT

Astrology remains an important factor in the lives of many Hindus. In Hindu culture, newborns are traditionally named based on their jyotish charts, and jyotish concepts are pervasive in the organization of the calendar and holidays as well as in many areas of life, such as making decisions about marriage, opening a new business, and moving into a new home.

So momentous is the occasion of marriage that several kinds of precautions may be taken to minimize the uncertainties involved in the decision. Astrology is one such means; arranging prepuberty marriage is another. All marriage plans must reckon with the supernatural forces that affect the course of every critical venture—both auspicious and inauspicious days, favorable and unfavorable omens, and the horoscopes of the couple and their astrological congruence. Through astrology, man's uncertainty about his personal fate is made more tolerable. A person's fate is seen as locked in a grand mechanism of astral spheres, which move in preordained and predictable cycles across the firmament of time.

The Branches of Hindu Astrology

Hindu Astrology has three branches:

- Siddhanta: Indian astronomy
- Samhita: Mundane astrology, predicting important events based on analysis of astrological dynamics in a country's horoscope or general transitory events such as war, Earthquakes, political events, financial positions, electoral positions, etc.

- Hora: Predictive astrology based on analysis of natal horoscopes and the moment a query is made

There are four elements in the Hindu astrology: *Rashi* (the zodiac signs); *Bhava* (the houses); *Graha* (the planets); and *Nakshatra* (the lunar mansions). In Rashi, the signs are given for twelve sectors. That is, 360 degrees of the zodiac are divided into twelve equal parts, with each part called a sign. The Sanskrit names for the twelve signs and corresponding names from Western astrology follow.

Number	Sanskrit Name	Western Name	Element
	SANSKRIT ASTROLOGY NAMES		
1	Mesa (ram)	Aries (ram)	Fire
2	Visabha (bull)	Taurus (bull)	Earth
3	Mithuna (twins)	Gemini (twins)	Air
4	Karka (crab)	Cancer (crab)	Water
5	Simba (lion)	Leo (lion)	Fire
6	Kanya (girl)	Virgo (virgin)	Earth
7	Tula (balance)	Libra (balance)	Air
8	Viscika (scorpion)	Scorpio (scorpion)	Water
9	Dhanus (bow)	Sagittarius (archer)	Fire
10	Makara (sea-monster)	Capricorn (goat-horned)	Earth
11	Kumbha (pitcher)	Aquarius (water-pourer)	Air
12	Mina (fish)	Pisces (fish)	Water

Bhava: The Houses

A house is a zodiac division according to local time and location. In Jyotisha, more than one system aligning houses with signs is recognized. Houses are numbered counterclockwise from the house on the eastern horizon.

The significance of the twelve houses are:

- Lagna—Nature, appearance, health, character, purpose of life
- Dhana—Wealth, family, domestic comforts, early education, inheritance
- Prakrama—Younger brothers and sisters, communication (talking, writing, business documents), intelligence, later education, short journeys

- Suhrda—Mother, emotions, education, home, property and land surrounding in old age
- Suta—Children, lover, recreation, devotion, speculation and gambling, creativity
- Ripu/Roga—Health, maternal uncle and aunt, litigation, servants, mental worries, enemies, foreigners
- Kama—Spouse, business partner, death, trade, agreement, honor and reputation
- Maritya—Death and longevity, failure, suffering, sexuality, occult, dowry, inheritance, imprisonment, torture
- Bhagya—Luck, higher learning, philosophy and religion, mentor or guru, father, prosperity, travel
- Karma—Profession, status, power, father-in-law/mother-in-law, government and business
- Aya—Friends, hopes, earnings, club and social activities, elder siblings, daughter-in-law/son-in-law
- Vyaya—Expenses, sleep, spirituality, travel and pilgrimage, secret enemies, imprisonment, hospitals, asylums, liberation

Graha: The Planets

Graha means any heavenly body or point that can cast an impact on human affairs. It also includes lunar nodes (Rahu and Ketu) and subplanets (*upgrahas*)—not planets but no less effective than planets; nine *grahas* or planets; two luminaries; the five visible planets; and the two lunar nodes. The extra saturnine planets (Uranus and Neptune) are not included in the category of Graha.

Sanskrit Name	English Name	Abbreviation	Gender	Guna	Represents
Surya	Sun	Sy or Su	M	Sattva	Soul, king, highly placed persons, father
Chandra	Moon	Ch or Mo	F	Sattva	Mind, queen, mother
Mangala	Mars	Ma	M	Tamas	Energetic action, confidence and ego
Budha	Mercury	Bu or Me	N	Rajas	Communication and analysis

Sanskrit Name	English Name	Abbreviation	Gender	Guna	Represents
Brihaspati	Jupiter	Gu or Ju	M	Sattva	The great teacher
Shukra	Venus	Sk or Ve	F	Rajas	Wealth, pleasure and reproduction
Shanti	Saturn	Sa	M	Tamas	Learning the hard way, Career and longevity
Rahu	Head of Demon Snake	Ra	M	Tamas	Asura who does his best to plunge any area of one's life he controls into chaos
Ketu	Tail of Demon Snake	Ke	M	Tamas	Supernatural influence

Nakshatra: The Lunar Mansions

Nakshatra is based on Vedic astrology. By calculating the positions of the moon, constellations, and other features of the night sky, you can explore your characteristics and personality. It is thought that by becoming aware of your strengths and weaknesses, you can make a conscious effort to improve your personality.

Each nakshatra represents a division of the path of the Sun, similar to the zodiac. Traditionally, the nakshatra position of the Moon is computed for the newborn's mental makeup and calculations of planetary periods (*dasha*). Each nakshatra is further divided into four equal segments known as *charan* or *pada*. Nakshatra is important in astrological matchmaking, *Muharta*, *Panchanga*, and *Praana*.

FACT

Vedic astrology differs from Western or Tropical astrology due to its use of the fixed zodiac as opposed to the moving zodiac. Most people's Western sign would be one sign back on the Vedic chart. However, if you were born in the last five days or so of the Western sign month, you will probably be the same sign in both systems.

Consulting astrologers is important for India's elite population, but not for the poor. A difference between many Western cultures and Hindu society is that most of the people in the Western world likely consult astrology for entertainment, while many in Hindu society consult it to regulate their lives

Recently, following a controversial decision of the Andhra Pradesh High Court in 2001, some Indian universities started offering advanced degrees in astrology. The University Grants Commission (UGC) in India is a powerful body that influences higher education. The UGC, with Mr. Hari Gautam as its chairman, recently decided to introduce new departments of Vedic astrology (Jyotie Vignan) as science in all the public universities, and *karmakanda* (religious rituals) as a vocational course.

But if astrology is to be classified as a science, it must be subject to scrutiny and confirmed as a rigorous discipline, just as any other science would be. At the minimum, this would include having a set of assumptions in unambiguous language that are shown to be true by experimentation. If they are proven false by empirical evidence, then they must be amenable to correction. In addition, the astrological theory must predict results accurately, and experiments must test the predictions.

According to these definitions of what makes a science, astrology should certainly not be considered a science. In mid-1970, some 186 top scientists, including eighteen Nobel laureates, signed a statement saying astrology is not a science.

CHAPTER 20

Controversies about Hinduism

The basic source for Hinduism is the ancient texts in Sanskrit; its main problem is that not many people are well versed in that language. This shortfall contributes to the misconceptions about Hinduism. In addition, while Hinduism rightly deserves its title as a religion of peace, like any other religion, there are pockets of extremism.

Specific Misconceptions and Truths about Hinduism

The misconceptions about Hinduism range across a broad spectrum of topics. Westerners often gain a somewhat incomplete knowledge of the religion because of the cultural and language barriers.

Belief in Many Gods

This is a common misconception about Hinduism. People get the idea that there are many gods and goddesses from reading legends (Puranas) and epics. But if we look at the religion philosophically, the Hindus believe in one god—Brahman—and all other gods are manifestations of this same god.

Hinduism and the Caste System

Hinduism created and sustained the caste system. This can be seen from the reading of classical works such as the Manu Dharma Shastra. The caste system kept its grip on the people for some 4,000 years, mainly because there are religious sanctions for it.

The system was legally abolished, but the custom remains much as it has been for ages in rural areas. Although progress has been made in urban centers, classified ads for those seeking a bride or groom often require their mate be of the same caste.

Inequality of Women

Many people hold tight to the idea that women are subservient to men in Hinduism. The status of women according to the sacred texts is abysmal, but their current status in modern society is very different than it was even fifty years ago—educational advancements, job availability, and general acceptance having allowed them to become upwardly mobile. The views of men about the equality of women have also changed substantially; the opinions of the sacred texts hold no sway on this issue.

This is not to say there aren't still more hurdles for women, particularly in the area of marriage and traditional domestic customs. Child marriage, though outlawed, is still practiced in some locations, and arranged marriages are not uncommon. Accepting dowry for a bride is no longer allowed, but the practice has proven difficult to eradicate. In extreme cases, brides are killed if their dowry is not substantial enough.

Another example is the plight of widows. In ancient times, women who had lost their husbands were shunned, and widows commonly sacrificed themselves on their husbands' funeral pyres. Today, the sacrificial practice of suttee is illegal, and only a few isolated cases have been reported in recent decades. However, the stigma against widows persists, and widows are still shunted to the bottom of society.

Temporary "Heaven"

The idea that those who are in *devaloka* (heaven) will enjoy their happiness only as far as their karma allows is a misconception. According to this theory, souls will return to Earth to continue the cycle of rebirth once their stores of karma have been exhausted.

Reincarnation

The belief that people will climb from a lower to a higher class before attaining moksha is wrong. It is not true that only Brahmins will have the chance of going to heaven; in fact, everyone from any class can attain the ultimate goal of moksha or liberation.

The Sacredness of Cows

Hindus consider cows as Mother; therefore, they do not want to kill them for food. Cows symbolize all other living beings, all of which are regarded as sacred. Cows provide milk, cheese, curd, and ghee, and their urine and dung are also utilized. They are also used for plowing the fields and pulling carts.

In a mythological story, when the demons poisoned all the waters, a certain cow's milk saved humanity, and therefore the cow should be protected. The story from some Puranas gave it a religious flavor and the practice became the law of the religion. Cows are considered sacred, but they are not worshipped.

Is Practicing Yoga Heretical for Christians?

It is not unusual for adherents of one religion to maintain that it is irreligious—or even blasphemous—to dabble in the practices of another. People may hold the view, for example, that practicing yoga is heretical for Christians, but this is not true. Yoga is from India, and it is a practice derived from the Hindu religion, but there is nothing religious about yoga. It is one of the six schools of philosophy; its aim is to teach practitioners to attain salvation through meditation and cleansing of body and mind.

The metaphysical ideas of yoga were originally akin to those of Sankhya, until yoga brought a deity into the picture during the Middle Ages. The god (Isvara) of yoga was not a creator, but an especially exalted soul. Thus, the god of yoga resembled the Buddha of the Lesser Vehicle (Hinayana) or the glorified Tirthankara of Jainism. Yoga was thought to give insight into the sublime purity of the soul, and thus aid meditation.

Certain practices such as yoga are religious in appearance. By bowing to the master guru, saying *namasté* ("I bow to you"), and repeating a mantra, one is aiding his meditation. However, mantras do not have to be religious; they can be completely sectarian if you choose.

Hinduism and Contemporary Science

Religion and science are often thought to be at odds with one another. What is the relation between Hinduism and contemporary science? Is there a conflict between devout Hindus and those who embrace scientific hypotheses?

Hindu scriptures recognize two types of knowledge: lower and higher. Knowledge of the rites and rituals and scholarly study of scripture is considered lower knowledge; higher knowledge is the knowledge of atman and Brahman gained through personal experience or self-realization. Of the two, higher knowledge is true, because it liberates the individual from the cycles of births and deaths. Scientific knowledge is of the lower kind.

The relationship between Hinduism and science is not easy to describe. Since Hinduism does not have a central ecclesiastical authority, as the Catholic Church does, it is difficult to get any official verdict on any position that might be controversial, such as evolution, capital punishment, abortion, stem-cell research, birth control, or human cloning.

Hindu spiritual leaders offered their unanimous opinion on human cloning to former president Bill Clinton. "It is our wish to inform the President that Hinduism neither condones nor condemns the march of science. If done with divine intent and consciousness, it may benefit and if done in the service of selfishness, greed and power, it may bring severe negative karmic consequence. The simple rule is this: cause no injury to others and let dharma—the law of good conduct and harmony with the universe and its many forces and creatures—be the guide for all such explorations. It is a sin to tinker with God's work."

Individual Hindu groups (*sampradayas*) may have official positions determined by a guru, but in general there are no large organizations that speak for major segments of the Hindu population. Consequently, one can only address the relationship between Hinduism and science in the most general terms.

Hinduism, like Judaism and Christianity, is a metaphysical system. Science, on the other hand, is nonmetaphysical and accepts no divine or "outside the system" source. Shukavak N. Dasa pointed out in his article "Hinduism and Science" that there are three different groups of Hindus.

- Conservatives believe the Vedas are the literal truth.
- Liberals believe the Vedas should not be taken literally; scientific explanation trumps the Vedas if there is a reasoned argument.
- The majority of Hindus believe the Vedas are true, but can be reinterpreted when they come into conflict with science.

All three approaches fall within theology, hermeneutics, or interpretation of sacred writing. From the perspective of the Bhagavad Gita, it is fair to say that modern science is simply a highly detailed analysis of matter and, in this sense, there is no conflict between the Gita and science.

The view that the Rig Veda and other religious texts contain so-called secret or vague references to modern ideas such as particle theory, quantum mechanics, and string theory is a misleading attempt to link science and religion. It is not possible to read such theories into the Vedas in the hopes that faith may justify actions.

Hinduism as Near to Science

There are some Hindu stories that border on the scientific realm. For example, in Hinduism there is no one creation story; numerous cosmogonies can be found in all important Hindu scriptures. Hindus tend to see metaphors in these creation myths for philosophical and spiritual truths; some stories might be conflicting, but they do not confuse Hindus because "Truth is one; the sages call it by different names." (Rig Veda 1:164:46).

One of the most sublime accounts of creation occurs in the Rig Veda 10:129. It ponders the mystery of origins and offers more questions than answers. Many other creation stories in the Hindu tradition may be seen as metaphors that convey not absolute truth, but practical paradigms for conceiving of a person's purpose in life and their connections to the universe and other life forms within it.

One hymn from the Rig Veda tells how the universe was created from the cosmic being, or *purusha*, who is described as having a thousand heads, eyes, and feet. The Brahmin was said to have emerged from the mouth of the divine being, the warrior from his arms, the ordinary people from his thighs, and the servants from his feet. It is easy to see how this is a metaphor describing the various social duties of the different classes.

The Chandogya Upanishad 3:19:104 relates how the world was nonexistent, became existent, and then became an egg. After a year, the egg broke open and a silver part and a gold part emerged. The silver part became the Earth and the gold part became the sky. The various parts of the egg became the features of the heavens and the Earth. Many see in this an analogy to the Big Bang Theory.

In the Brhadaranyaka Upanishad, the primordial being, after realizing he was alone, created a woman from his body. From their union humans were born. After this, the woman hid from the man by taking the form of a cow, but he appeared as a bull, and from their union cattle were born. She then hid as a mare, but he came as a stallion, and from their union all one-hoofed animals were born. This went on for each of the various animals, down to the ants. This cosmology illustrates that all creatures, from humans to tiny insects, come from the same source.

In some myths, creation is said to come from being, and in others, from nonbeing. The Chandogya Upanishad itself describes creation in both ways.

Indian Cosmology or the Order of the Universe

The Vishnu Purana details an elaborate map of the cosmos in which India, here called Jambudvipa (Rose-Apple Island), is the center continent. In the center of Jambudvipa is Mount Meru, said to be the abode of Brahman and other deities.

There are oceans of different substances separating the islands, the last of which separates the last island from the "golden realm," which is the end of the universe. This describes the universe horizontally, but the Purana also describes it vertically, elaborating on various heavens and hells.

Hindus see physical matter as a manifestation or product of consciousness, whereas in modern science consciousness is a product of the physical brain. Hindus differentiate between mind and consciousness; the mind is a supersubtle material used by the consciousness to perceive physical reality. Hindu scientists consider it their duty to engage in scientific activity. Science is, after all, one of the ways in which a person may come to learn the true nature of reality.

Hindu Tolerance

Hinduism seems like such a tolerant religion. In fact, a recent Pew Research poll showed that fewer Hindus (less than 10 percent) leave their religion than any of the other faiths. This is striking, of course, suggesting that Hinduism is tolerant and broadly accepting, perhaps even nonjudgmental compared to other faiths.

According to some, Hinduism is not a religion, though it adheres to a set of beliefs and practices. Unlike Christianity, Islam, or Buddhism, it was not founded by a single person, and no organized body controls or accepts or rejects practices on behalf of Hinduism.

A Positive Spin on Hinduism

Many Hindu intellectuals define Hinduism as stated previously. Having accepted this premise, one tends to wipe away the nontolerant behavior of some members of the Hindu tradition. We seem to confuse ahimsa (nonviolence or nonkilling) and tolerance as being one and the same. Ahimsa, according to Jainism, is noninjury to man or animal. By contrast, tolerance in the religious field is acceptance of all religions as equal or valid paths to salvation.

The general outlook of Hinduism favored tolerance and kindness, was not equalitarian, and recognized the needs of a society divided into many sections and classes with varying functions—a euphemism for caste distinctions.

Many Hindus blame the proselytization of Islam and Christianity as the root cause of Hindu intolerance. The Hindu-Muslim and Hindu-Sikh riots were due to political exploitations, not religious activities. Conversion is a constitutional right and should not be blamed for causing riots.

Hinduism has a deserved reputation for being highly tolerant of other religions. Hindus have a saying: "The Truth is One, but different Sages call it by Different Names." Vivekananda's words gave the World Parliament a defining focus. He began by saying he was "proud to belong to a religion which had taught the world tolerance and universal acceptance." He explained that, "we believe not only in universal tolerance, but we accept all religions as true." He said his nation had always sheltered outsiders—for instance, fleeing Israelites and Zoroastrians.

On the subject of Hindu tolerance, you can return to the theme of religious tolerance. Ram Swarup, an Indian thinker, eloquently puts the matter this way:

> *In the spiritual realm there are two categories: God and your neighbor. . . you could look at God through your neighbor or at the neighbor through your God. In the first approach. . . if your neighbor is as good as you are, his God also must be as good as yours.*

But if you look at your neighbor through your God, then it leads to an entirely different outlook. Then you say that if your God is good enough for you, it should be good enough for your neighbor too. And if your neighbor is not worshipping the same God in the same way, he must be worshipping Devil and qualifies for conversion or liquidation.

The first approach promotes tolerance, though it gives plurality of Gods and varieties of modes in worship. The other approach gives one God and one mode of worship, but breeds intolerance.

Is There Hindu Extremism?

There is no place for violence in Hinduism, but extremist factions have perverted religious teachings to allow for persecution of and violence against other religions. The Rashriya Swayamsevak Sangh (RSS) or National Volunteer Service is the Hindu community extremist organization in India.

The main concept, the driving force for this extremism, is Hindutva, a calculated scheme developed over the years along the lines of Nazism and Fascism of the 1920s. The mission of the Hindutva, in sum, is to re-establish the supremacy of one race (Brahmin caste) by insisting on Varnashram (caste system), by imposing Sashtras (Vedism), by creating a common language (Sanskrit), by devising a common culture (Bharaty Sanskrit), and by enacting common laws based on Manu and Vedanta.

The result would be to turn India into a theocracy and ensure the dominance of Brahmins (10 percent) over non-Brahmins (90 percent). The RSS has created adjunct organizations with specific focuses such as political, economical, educational, social, labor, student affairs, and so on to infuse the Hindutva ideology in all activities of communities.

Peculiar Arguments for Hindutva

The advocates of Hindutva believe that India is a land of Hindus, people who have a unique country, race, culture, religion, and language.

The basis for Hindutva is: India is for Hindus or Hindu Rashtra. It was explained by M. S. Golwalkar in his book *One Nation*, which asserts that only people who satisfy his definition of the five traits or unities can be Hindus. He describes the general concepts of nation or nationhood and exemplifies them with his pattern of Hindu examples. Consequently, he concludes that the Indian nation satisfies his brand of Hindu Rashtra India, which he calls "Hindustan," and belongs to Hindus only; all others living in India are foreigners. He further describes these people (Hindus) as the ones following the dharmas prescribed in the Vedas.

The Shakhas (Branches)

The training of youth for the RSS is done by *shakhas* or "branches." They take in youth ages fifteen to eighteen and give them military training for the sole purpose of using them in the Hindu-Muslim conflicts. The boys are expected to not ask questions about any part of the training or the authority figures imparting instructions. This is similar to the *madrasas* run by Muslim extremists in India or Pakistan. In 2000, the RSS had 45,000 shakhas all over the country.

The purpose of the Hindutva is to teach the young students a revised history, emphasizing Hindu superiority in all the fields. As such, making necessary changes to school curriculum became a top priority for the RSS.

The Victims of the Hindutva

The targets for the RSS are three groups: Muslims, Christians, and Dalits. In the view of Hindutva, Muslims and Christians are foreigners and should either leave the country or remain in India without any fundamental rights. To accomplish this, the RSS needs to amend the Indian Constitution and make India a nonsecular country. The Dalits are outside the Vedic caste system and cannot operate as Hindus.

The year 2002 saw some of the worst violence between Hindus and Muslims since 1947. A train full of Hindu pilgrims was attacked by Muslims in the town of Godhra, killing fifty-eight people. In retaliation, Hindu mobs in the state of Gujarat savagely attacked their Muslim neighbors. By the time the violence was quelled, more than 1,000 people were dead. International human rights groups criticized the Indian government, which was largely

Hindu, for not acting quickly enough to stop what became known as the Gujarat massacre.

Hinduism in Southeast Asia

Does the presence of Hinduism in Indonesia and other Southeast Asian countries suggest that Hinduism has had a missionary tradition? No. There is no proselytizing in Hinduism, for there are no missionaries to propagate the religion.

The practice of Hinduism in Southeast Asia occurred as the result of Indian traders and seafarers who remained in those countries and settled down. They married local women and raised their families and practiced their Hindu faith. Over time, Buddhism and Islam became more popular than Hinduism, so there are relatively small Hindu communities in much of Southeast Asia. However, much of Southeast Asia owes a great debt to Hindu culture and language.

Some countries where Hinduism prevailed include central Vietnam during the Champa civilization; Cambodia during Funan; Indochina during the Khmer Empire; Sumatra during the Srivijayan kingdom; Java and Bali during the Singhasari kingdom; Bali during the Majapahit Empire; and in the Philippine archipelago. All of these countries felt the Indian influence in language, scripts, calendars, and artistic aspects.

Cambodia and Laos

Today, 95 percent of Cambodia's population adheres to the tenets of Buddhism, but that was not always the case. During the reign of the Khmer Empire (802–1431), Hinduism was an official religion of the region, and Hindu culture flourished. One of the most famous examples of Hindu architecture during the Khmer Empire was Angkor Wat, built by Suryavarman II in the twelfth century. Construction on the temple took thirty-eight years, and it was originally dedicated to Vishnu. When Buddhism began to gain prominence, many of the Hindu temples were turned into Buddhist places of worship, including Angkor Wat. Despite this, many of the temples still feature Hindu art and statues of Hindu gods.

Java

In the first and second centuries, contact with India exposed Indonesia to Hinduism. As trade links between the civilizations strengthened in later centuries, both Buddhist and Hindu scholars settled in Java. Prambanam, an architecturally significant Hindu temple, was constructed around 850 C.E. Hinduism gradually declined as Islam gained a foothold in Java, although there are still some areas where Hinduism is practiced.

Vietnam

My Son, a Hindu temple complex in present-day Vietnam, is a testament to the Champa civilization that dominated the region beginning in the second century and lasting until 1832. The art and architecture reflect Hinduism's strong influence.

Monastic Hindus

Has monasticism been a significant factor in the history of Hinduism? Monasticism is a religious practice in which a person renounces worldly pursuits in order to fully devote their life to spiritual work. Many religions have monastic elements, including Taoism, Buddhism, Christianity, Hinduism, and Jainism, though the expressions differ considerably. Those pursuing a monastic life are usually called monks or brethren (brothers) if male, and nuns or sisters if female. Both monks and nuns may also be called monastics.

In their quest to attain the spiritual goal of life, some Hindus choose the path of monasticism (*sanyasa*). Monastics commit themselves to a life of simplicity, celibacy, detachment from worldly pursuits, and contemplation of God. A Hindu monk is called a *sanyasi, sadhu,* or *swami.* A nun is called a *sanyasini, sadhavi,* or *swamini.*

Such renunciations are accorded high respect in Hindu society. Some monastics live in monasteries, while others wander from place to place, as mendicants trusting in God.

A sadhu's vow of renunciation typically forbids him from:

- Owning personal property apart from a bowl, a cup, two sets of clothing, and medical aids such as eyeglasses
- Having any contact with, looking at, thinking of, or even being in the presence of women
- Eating for pleasure
- Possessing or even touching money or valuables in any way, shape, or form
- Maintaining personal relationships

Monasticism has been a part of Hindu *ashramas* (stages). The last stage of human life is becoming a reclusive sanyasin or sanyasa, giving up all worldly possessions, and leading the life of a hermit. The four stages of life are: Brahmacharya (student life), Grihastha (householder), Vanaprastha (forest dweller), and Sannyasa (hermit).

There are many Hindu monastic orders. Some of these orders might have been fashioned after St. Benedict of Nursia, a Catholic monk. The Rule of St. Benedict became a model for all later monastic orders of other faiths. Patient obedience to such rules and one's superiors became central aspects of monasticism. Other models include the Carmelite Rule of St. Albert; the Augustinian Rule; and The Order of Ramakrishna, founded in 1899 and modeled after Western monastic rule.

Hindu Attitudes about Suicide

Suicide is an act forbidden by most major religions. St. Thomas Aquinas (1225–1274), a doctor of the Catholic Church, condemned suicide as "self-murder." Is there a Hindu doctrine pertaining to suicide? What do Hindus think about suicide or critical questions regarding medical and reproductive ethics?

Hinduism does not approve of suicide, per se. Human life, according to Hindu beliefs, is very precious and is attained only after many rebirths, enabling an individual to leap to a higher plane of existence.

According to Hindu beliefs, if a person commits suicide, he goes neither to hell nor heaven, but remains in the Earth's consciousness as a bad spirit and wanders aimlessly till he completes his actual and allotted lifetime. In essence, suicide puts an individual's spiritual clock in reverse. Hindu scriptures therefore aptly describe it as murder of self (*atmahatya*).

Suicide has been condemned by Hindu scripture because it abruptly causes karma to take an unexpected turn. There are, however, some exceptions to the prohibition on suicide. Terminal diseases or great disabilities—or even religious self-willed deaths through fasting (*prayopavesha*)—are permitted.

Prayopavesha is not regarded as suicide because it is natural and nonviolent, and only for spiritually advanced people under specified circumstances. The person making such a decision declares it publicly, which allows for community regulation and distinguishes the act from suicide performed in traumatic emotional states of anguish and despair.

Ancient lawgivers cite various stipulations for allowing suicide:

- The inability to perform normal bodily purifications
- Death appears imminent or the condition is so bad that life's pleasures are nil
- The action must be done under community regulations

CHAPTER 21

Rituals and Practices: Hindu Marriage, Funerals, Food, and Vegetarianism

Hinduism places great importance on its rituals and practices. Traditional guidelines for selecting a mate and marriage remain a powerful institution in the religion today. Funerals are sacred in Hinduism, and the dead are usually cremated. Hinduism dictates how the family should honor their lost relative. Vegetarianism is common among Hindus, who believe it is wrong to eat anything that has been killed.

Marriage Selection Criteria

In Vedic times, certain criteria were established for the prospective brides and bridegrooms, and some of these are still retained according to their caste customs.

In general, the selection criteria were:

Let him [the father] first examine the family of the intended bride or bridegroom.

Let him give the girl to a young man endowed with intelligence.

Let him marry a girl that shows the characteristics of intelligence, beauty, and moral conduct, and who is free from disease.

As the characteristics are difficult to discern, let him make eight lumps of Earth and recite over those lumps the following formula: "Right has been born first, in the beginning: on the right truth is founded. For what destiny this girl is born, that may she attain here. What is true may be seen," and let him say to the girl, "Take one of these."

If she chooses the lump from a field that yields two crops in one year, he may know, "Her offerings will be rich in food."

If she chooses from a cow stable, her offerings would be rich in cattle.

If she chooses Earth from an altar, her offerings would be rich in holy luster.

If she chooses the lump from a pool that does not dry, then her offerings would be rich in everything.

If she chooses the lump from a gambling place, she would be addicted to gambling.

If she chooses the lump from a place where four roads cross, she would be wandering in different directions.

If she chooses the lump from a barren spot, she would be poor.

If she chooses the lump from a burial ground, she would bring death to her husband.

Leading her three times round the fire and the water-pot, so that their right sides are turned towards the fire, let him say to the girl, "This am I, that are thou, that are thou, this am I; the heaven I, the

Earth thou. Come! Let us here marry. Let us beget offspring. Loving, bright, with genial mind may we live a hundred autumns."

When she sees the polar star Arundhati and Ursa Major, let her break the silence and say, "May my husband live and I get offspring!"

—Kandika 5

The marriage between people with a common paternal ancestor within seven generations or a maternal ancestor within five generations was prohibited. It was recommended that while a husband should be at least twenty, a girl should be married immediately before puberty. The general view was that the ideal marriage was one in which the bride was one-third the age of the groom. Thus, a man of twenty-four should marry a girl of eight.

The Marriage Ceremony

The ceremony down the ages did not alter substantially in content. The couple was seated in a pavilion, separated by a curtain. To the accompaniment of sacred verses muttered by an officiating Brahman, the curtain was removed and the couple saw one another, perhaps for the first time. The bride's father stepped forward and formally gave her to the groom, who promised he would not behave falsely to her in respect of the three traditional aims of life—piety, wealth, and pleasure. Next, offerings of ghee and rice were made to the sacred fire. The groom then grasped the bride's hand while she offered grain in the fire, around which he then led her with their garments tied together. The couple would then take seven steps together, the bride treading on a small heap of rice at each step. The couple was then sprinkled with holy water, completing the main part of the ceremony.

Initiation

Brahmanical initiation, which marked the admission of a young boy to the prerogatives of his social class, appeared during the period between the sixth and the third centuries B.C.E.

The initiation is the consecration in accordance with the sacred texts of the Veda. When the male desires and knows the Vedas, he is ready for this rite. The person who performs this rite should belong to a family in which sacred learning is hereditary, and he himself should be well qualified. He should have studied under a teacher who did not fall off from the ordinance of the law.

> *Let this man initiate a Brahman in spring, a Kstriya in summer, a Vaisya in autumn, a Brahman in the eighth year after conception, a Ksatriya in the eleventh year, after conception, and a Vaisya in the twelfth.*
>
> *There is no dereliction of duty if the initiation takes place in the case of a Brahman before the completion of the sixteenth year, in the case of a Ksatriya before the completion of the twenty-second year, in the case of a Vaisya before the completion of the twenty-fourth year. Let him be initiated at such an age that he may be able to perform the duties, which we shall declare now.*
>
> *If the proper time for the initiation has passed, he shall observe for the space of two months the duties of a student, as observed by those who are studying the three Vedas. After that he may be initiated; after that he shall bathe daily for one year; after that he may be instructed. He whose father and grandfather have not been initiated and his two ancestors are called "slayers of the Brahman." Intercourse, eating, and intermarriage with them should be avoided*
>
> *If they wish it, they may perform the following expiation: in the same manner as for the first neglect of the initiation, a penance of two months was prescribed, so that they shall do penance for one year. Afterwards they may be initiated, and then they must bathe daily.*
>
> —*Dharma-Sutras*, Apastamba

The Funeral Ritual

What are the most common Hindu funeral practices and ways of grieving? For the people of Vedic times, the future life was a place where those who had satisfied the gods through the performance of sacrifices and living their lives according to the expected codes enjoyed pleasures. On a more sophisticated level, death was equated with a state of nonexistence (*asat*).

As a man was born in impurity, so he died in impurity. According to the Sacred Law, mourners must avoid all close contact with outsiders for fear of carrying pollution; they must submit to rigid dietary restrictions and sleep on the ground. They must not shave their hair or worship the gods. The *candelas*, who had the duty of laying out and shrouding the body and carrying it to the cremation ground, were the most inauspicious of creatures and the lowest of the low.

The funeral ceremony (*antyesti*) was the last of the many sacraments that marked the stages of a man's life. According to the ancient custom, the corpse was carried to the burning ground as soon as possible after death, followed by the mourners, the eldest son leading the funeral procession. The body was cremated to the accompaniment of sacred texts. The mourners went around the pyre, counterclockwise, then bathed in the nearest river, tank, lake, or well. The mourners returned home led by the youngest son.

On the third day after the cremation, the charred bones were gathered and thrown into a river, preferably the Ganges. For ten days after the cremation, libations of water were poured for the dead, and offerings of rice balls and vessels of milk were made for him.

Upon dying, a man's soul became a miserable ghost (*preta*), unable to pass on to the "World of the Fathers" or to a new birth, and liable to do harm to the surviving relatives. With the performance of the last antyesti rite on the tenth day, it acquired a subtle body with which to continue its journey, speeded on its way and nourished in the afterlife by the *sraddha* ceremonies. With the tenth day, the mourners ceased to be impure and resumed their normal lives.

Food in Hinduism

In Hinduism, food is so vitally important it is considered to be part of God or Brahman, as it nourishes the entire physical, mental, and emotional aspects of a human being. It is considered a gift from God and should be treated respectfully. Here is a brief description of the nuances of Hindu food.

- Food is considered an actual part of Brahman, rather than simply a Brahman symbol.
- Beef is strictly forbidden; cow is considered Mother in Hinduism.
- Pork is a strictly forbidden food in Hinduism.
- Food contains energy-like sound waves that can be absorbed by the person eating them.
- According to the Hindu religion, violence or pain inflicted on another living thing rebounds on you (karma).
- To avoid causing pain to another living thing, vegetarianism is advocated, but not compulsory.
- Prohibited animal products may be different from one area to another; for example, duck or crab may be forbidden in one location and not in another.
- Alcohol, onions, garlic, and red-colored foods such as red lentils and tomatoes are prohibited.
- Meat is not always forbidden in the Laws of Manu.
- Fasting depends on a person's caste and the occasion.
- Serving food to the poor and the needy or a beggar is good karma. Food is associated with religious activity and is still offered to God during some of the religious ceremonies. On specific days, food is offered to departed souls. Many Hindu temples distribute foods to visiting devotees.

Food Rituals

Several rituals are associated with food in Hindu tradition. A child's first solid food is celebrated as a *samskara*, or rite, known as *annaprasana*. The funeral rites involve serving food and offering food to the departed soul for his journey to the ancestral world. According to Manu, "Food that is always worshipped, gives strength and manly vigor; but eaten irreverently, it destroys them both."

Hindus practice some rituals before eating. They include:

- Cleaning the place where the food will be eaten
- Sprinkling of water around the food, accompanied by some mantras or prayers

- Making an offering of the food, then offering five vital breaths (*pranas*), namely *prana*, *apana*, *vyana*, *udana*, and *samanaya* and then to Brahman seated in the heart

Vegetarianism

People define a vegetarian diet, in general, as a diet that excludes the meat of animals but does permit eggs. Vegetarian foods include grains, fruits, vegetables, legumes, and dairy products.

FACT

Indian vegetarians are basically lacto-vegetarians, meaning they do consume dairy products. Amazingly, Hindus make up 70 percent of all vegetarians worldwide, and account for 20–42 percent of all Indians. In the United States, vegetarians form about 1–2.8 percent of the total population.

Some definitions are needed for clearer understanding of the topic. The Sanskrit word for vegetarianism is *shakahara*, and for vegetarian, *shakahari*. Similarly, the Sanskrit word for meat eating is *mansahara*, and for meat eater, *mansahari*. What do we mean by vegetarian or vegetarianism?

Some people associate vegetarianism with India's pre-eminent leader, Mohandas K. Gandhi. Gandhi was surely a vegetarian by a conscious ethical choice, and not just out of a desire to adhere to Indian culture. He was an apostle of nonviolence, or *ahimsa*, and his adherence to this philosophy entails vegetarianism because one should refrain from being harmful to any person or any living thing, even to animals.

Ahimsa, the primary basis for vegetarianism, has been central to the Indian religious traditions: Hinduism, Buddhism, Jainism, and Sikhism. Religions in India have consistently upheld the sanctity of life, whether human; animal; or, in the case of Jains, elemental. Satyagraha (truth force) was a means of resisting the British rule of India. But the essence of truth-force is the repudiation of violence and the use of ahimsa; ahimsa and truth are so intertwined that it is impossible to separate them. Moreover, satyagraha, ahimsa, and vegetarianism are all intrinsically linked to each other.

Gandhi wanted to take up the cause of vegetarianism as a mission, but he had time only for satyagraha, and the Indian masses followed his examples anyway. People practiced vegetarianism for many reasons.

Vegetarianism and Religion

The practice of vegetarianism is not essentially a religious issue. In fact, it is a myth to think so. Of course, the proponents of vegetarianism will cite scriptures:

> *"You must not use your God-given body for killing
> God's creatures, whether they are human, animal or
> Whatever." (Yajur Veda 12.32)*

> *"By not killing any living being, one becomes fit for
> Salvations." (Manusmriti 6.60)*

> *"Ahimsa is the highest Dharma, ahimsa is the best Tapas,
> Ahimsa is the highest self-control, ahimsa is the highest sacrifice.
> Ahimsa is the highest power, ahimsa is the highest friend.
> Ahimsa is the highest truth, ahimsa is the highest teaching."
> (Mahabharata 18.116.37–41)*

The opponents will also quote scriptures to strengthen their side. At the time of the Vedas, the people's lives were centered on sacrificial offerings to deities. The offerings were vegetables and meats; often, the offerings were given to the priests and others who paid for those sacrifices. In other words, the Brahmins were meat eaters, and the others, from the lower castes, were vegetarians! In the course of hundreds of years, the trend was reversed; Brahmins became vegetarians, and the others, some of them, became meat eaters.

Reasons for Vegetarianism

At present, the practice of a vegetarian diet for Hindus is based on the following categories:

- *Medical grounds*: Medical studies prove that a vegetarian diet is easier to digest, provides a wider range of nutrients, and introduces fewer burdens and impurities into the body. Vegetarianism significantly lowers risk of cancer, heart disease, and other fatal diseases. In general, vegetarian diets can aid in keeping body weight under control. This diet is typically high in carotenoids, but relatively low in long-chain n-3 fatty acids.

- *Ecological grounds*: Earth is suffering. In large measure, the escalating loss of species, destruction of ancient rain forests to create pasturelands for livestock, loss of topsoils, and the consequent increase of water impurities and air pollution have all been traced to the single fact of meat in the human diet.

- *Ethical grounds*: Many of those who have adopted a vegetarian diet have done so on the grounds of ethical reasoning. Either they have read about or personally experienced what goes on daily at any one of the thousands of slaughterhouses around the world, where animals suffer forced confinement and violent death.

- *Religious grounds*: Major paths of Hinduism hold up vegetarianism as an ethical and religious ideal. There are three reasons for adopting this view: the principle of nonviolence, or ahimsa, is applied to animals; the intention to offer only "pure" vegetarian food to a deity and then to receive it back as Prasad; and nonvegetarian food is detrimental to the mind and spiritual development. People in Tibet and Nepal, Hindu countries, are meat eaters. Cold weather warrants such a diet choice.

- *Economical grounds*: An economic vegetarian is someone who practices vegetarianism from either the philosophical viewpoint, concerning issues such as public health and curbing world starvation, or the belief that the consumption of meat is economically unsound. This may be part of a conscious simple-living strategy or just out of necessity.

- *Cultural grounds*: This involves the caste prerogatives. People from some of these castes eat meat, excluding beef, but lower-caste people (Dalits or Untouchables) will eat beef. Even Brahmins living in the states of Orissa, Maharashtra, Bengal, and Kashmir eat meat, while Brahmins from Tamil Nadu will not eat meat. In all other states, Brahmins are mostly vegetarians. All these pronouncements are to be qualified, because many Brahmins start eating meat clandestinely, outside their home, in friends' homes or at restaurants. Vegetarianism is a cultural trait; it is different from caste to caste and from state to state.

Vegetarianism was never an essential requisite for Hinduism. Ahimsa was important especially after the influence of Buddha, and some cults were more stringent than others about being a vegetarian, but it was never a universal philosophy. Gandhi was a lacto-vegetarian, as are most of the Indian vegetarians.

CHAPTER 22

How to Find a Hindu Spiritual Leader

Basically, Hindus strive for the qualities found in Lord Hanuman, one of the great personalities in the Hindu epic *Ramayana*. In the opinion of many Hindus, Lord Hanuman seems to have qualities that the spiritual leaders can emulate. He is the personification of *brahmacharya,* or celibacy, who personifies power, self-control, intelligence, selfless service, and humility.

Training

If we look at the way the chief priests are trained and selected, that will help us understand what qualities are needed in a Hindu spiritual leader. There are ashrams (seminaries) for training priests, where they are trained in scriptures, languages, and related fields for about sixteen years.

They are admitted to these institutions at an early age, sometimes after Upanayanam (holy string), "reaching an age of reason." These young men are monitored, always under the tutelage of senior gurus. When the senior gurus certify the candidates are ready for their ordinations, they are initiated into priesthood. Some of these training institutes prepare students for religious orders like Saraswathi, similar to Jesuits or Dominicans of the Catholic Church.

Adi Sankaracharya established four *mutts* (seats of Brahmanism) as repositories of Hindu scriptures and doctrines. These four mutts are situated as guarding posts at four corners of the Hindu land. They are located at Dwarka in the West; Puri in the East; Kashi in the North; and Sringeri in the South, protecting and preserving the sacredness of Hindu scriptures. At a later date, those who did not accept this directive established a fifth mutt at Kanchipuram. In other words, there are five places from where Hindus can hope to get some definite answers for their questions.

In the modern Hinduism, the chief priests for the mutts are always Saraswathis. The selection of chief priest is not done by a body of priests, but by the sitting high priest, who appoints his own successor.

Qualities of a Spiritual Leader

We should have an idea of what qualities are required in a Hindu spiritual leader. In the performance of their duties at the temple where they are stationed, people can observe and tell others about their observations. When a vacancy arises in a temple, people can approach the selecting gurus with their choice and hope they will consider their recommendations.

For the present generation, some generalized criteria for the spiritual leader are:

- Expertise in Sanskrit and Tamil (the ancient texts are in Sanskrit; the philosophy and theology have been developed by Manickavasagar and others in Tamil only)
- Expertise in scriptures and rites, rituals, etc.
- Concern for the poor and needy people (social consciousness)
- Diligent observation of celibacy and poverty, and all their actions should be transparent
- Assistants who are accountable to authorities: trustees, government agencies, and the public
- The courage to obliterate the caste system inside and out of the temples
- Willingness to reconsider the requirements regarding temple language (Sanskrit) for conducting prayer services. In Tamil Nadu, for example, Tamil should be the language of prayer.
- No indulgence for insisting on Sanskrit, saying it is the divine language; there is no such thing. When you insist on Sanskrit, you are letting others know you are working to re-establish Brahmanism, supremacy of one caste over other castes, or maintaining the caste system.
- Willingness in nonreligious matters to get the advice from lay people (Trustees and others from the community)
- Willingness in religious matters to consult with other priests who have greater wisdom and age
- The prudence to leave money matters to others. You are not there for making money!

These considerations come from personal observations of others concerning Hinduism as well as other religions.

Spiritual Pilgrimage

Is going on a pilgrimage an important practice for Hindus? The answer is yes, since pilgrimages are an integral part of Hindu worship. Family worship takes the form of puja at home or a local temple, or visiting a famous temple for a ceremony or a sacred river for a dip on specified date.

Spiritual retreats are important in the West. People often go off for a weekend to pray, to visit with priests, and enjoy the fellowship of others. Likewise, in India, a pilgrimage increases the devotions of the people and offers opportunities for them to fulfill their obligations or make new or additional petitions to the gods.

Some of the famous temple towns include Allahabad, Amarnath, Ayodhya, Benares, Chidambaram, Gangotri, Kanchipuram, Konark, Madurai, and Rameshwaram.

Some of the holy rivers are the Ganges, Sarasvati, Jamuna, Krishna, Kaveri, Vaigai, and Pallar. In a sense, all the Indian rivers could be considered holy. If someone like a Chola king—Rajendra I (1012–1044) or Gangaikonda Chola—brought a pitcher of water from the Ganges and poured it into Kaveri, Kaveri water was believed to have been transformed into holy water.

By extending this philosophy to all the rivers, one would imagine the waters of all Indian rivers as holy water worthy of a holy bath. Major pilgrimage cities were founded on the banks of these rivers. Benares is on the banks of the Ganges; Kanchipuram is on the banks of Pallar; Chidambaram is on the banks of Coleroom; and Madurai on the banks of Vaigai. Making a pilgrimage to Benares /Kashi is one of the goals of life; however, it is not complete until a pilgrimage to Rameshwaram is also made. There are five places—called *mukti smasthans* or release stations—visiting would guarantee entry into moksha, or heaven. These places are: Chidambaram, Kalahasti, Kanchipuram, Tiruvannamalai, and Tiirvannaikaval.

During festival times, long processions go around the temples. Temple elephants lead the processions, followed by musicians and priests chanting the mantras, interspersed by chariots carrying the idols of the gods. The devotees offer incense, garlands, coconuts, lamps, money, gold, and silver ornaments to the deities.

Sacraments

There are personal rites or ceremonies in Hinduism called samskaras. In actuality, they are the equivalent of Christian sacraments. According to the most orthodox calculations, there were some forty samskaras, which covered the life of man from his conception to his death, some of which were of great importance and performed by all respectable members of the Aryan community.

Jatakarma

Jatakarma was a birth ceremony that was to be conducted before the umbilical cord was cut. It welcomes the child into the family and the world. Mantras for health and longevity are whispered in the baby's ears, to be kept secret by his parents until his initiation. At birth, the child and his parents were ritually impure and therefore not entitled to participate in ordinary religious ceremonies for ten days, when the child would be given a public name.

Upanayana

The most significant rite in the life of a boy was *upanayana* (investiture of the sacred thread or *yapnoparita*), which marked a boy's transition from boyhood into manhood. In the ceremony, a boy is marked as "twice born," allowing him to fully enter his caste. There was no such rite for girls, even though during Vedic times the girls had some types of ceremonies. Boys from the fourth caste were not permitted to perform this rite. During the ceremony, a special prayer was whispered into the ears of the initiate. This prayer—Gaytri—was popular and would be said in most of the rites, similar to Our Lord's Prayer for Christians. The Gaytri goes like this:

> *Let us think on the lovely splendor*
> *of the god Savitr,*
> *that he may inspire our minds.*

Of the various personal samskaras, three of them were concerned with events before birth. They were: *garbhadhana*—to promote conception; *pumsavana*—to procure a male child; and *simantonnayana*—to ensure safety of the child in the womb.C.E.

More important, was the first feeding—*annaprasana*. In the child's sixth month, he was given a mouthful of meat, fish, or rice, mixed with curds, honey, and ghee, to the accompaniment of Vedic verses and oblations of ghee poured on the fire. The rite of tonsure or *cudakarma* took place in the third year, and was confined to boys; with various rites, the child's scalp was shaved, leaving only a topknot, which in the case of a pious Brahmin would never be cut. Another ceremony, not looked on as of the first importance, was carried out when the child first began to learn the alphabets. There was also a rite when the boy started school.

APPENDIX

Further Reading

Anthony, Susai. *The Hindutva* (Victoria, BC: Trafford Publishing, 2005).

Burtt, E.A., ed. *The Teachings of the Compassionate Buddha* (New York: Penguin, 1982).

De Bary, Theodore, ed. *Sources of Indian Tradition* (New York: Columbia University Press, 1958).

Doniger, Wendy. *The Rig Veda: An Anthology* (London: Penguin Books, 1981).

Dougherty, Jude P. *The Logic of Religion* (Washington, DC: The Catholic University of America Press, 2002).

Dundas, Paul. *The Jains* (New York: Routledge, 2002).

Easwaran, Eknath, trans. *The Upanidhsads* (Tomales, CA: Nilgiri Press, 2007).

Fischer, Louis. *The Essential Gandhi* (New York: Vintage Books, 1962).

Gandhi, M.K. *An Autobiography, or The Story of My Experiments with Truth* (Ammedaabab: Navajivan Publishing, 2003).

Greene, Joshua M. *Here Comes the Sun: The Spiritual and Musical Journey of George Harrison* (Hoboken, NJ: John Wiley, 2006).

Greenfield, Robert. *The Spiritual Supermarket: An Account of Gurus Gone Public in America* (New York: E.P. Dutton, 1975).

Hopfe, Lewis M., and Mark R. Woodward. *Religions of the World, eighth ed.* (Upper Saddle River, NJ: Prentice Hall, 2001).

Hopkins, Jeffrey. *His Holiness: The Dalai Lama* (New York: Atria Books, 2003).

Hughes, Amanda Milay, ed. *Five Voices, Five Faiths: An Interfaith Primer* (Cambridge: Cowley Publications, 2005).

Jaini, Jagmanderlal M.A. *Outlines of Jainsim* (Westport, CT: Hyperion Press, 1940).

Jaini, Padmanabh, S. *The Jaina Path of Purification* (New Delhi: Motilal Banarsidass, 1979).

Jones, Constance A., and James D. Ryan. *Encyclopedia of Hinduism* (New York: Checkmark Books, 2008).

Klostermaier, Klaus K. *A Survey of Hinduism* (Albany: State University of New York Press, 1989).

LaChance, Paul OFM. *Angela of Foligno: Complete Works* (New York: Paulist Press, 1993).

Mack, Joshua. *Karma 101: What Goes Around Comes Around and What You Can Do about It* (Gloucester, MA: Fair Winds Press, 2002).

Mascaro, Juan. *The Bhagavad Gita* (London: Penguin, 2002).

Mascaro, Juan. *The Dhammapada: Path of Perfection* (London: Penguin, 1973).

Mehta, Gita. *Karma Cola: Marketing the Mystic East* (New York: Vintage, 1979).

Muller, F. Max. *The Upanishads, Parts I and II* (New York: Dover, 1962).

Muster, Nori J. *Betrayal of the Spirit: My Life Behind the Lines of the Hare Krishna Movement* (Chicago: University of Illinois Press, 2001).

Nehru, Jawaharlal. *The Discovery of India* (New Delhi: Jawaharlal Nehru Memorial Fund, 2003).

Powell, Jim. *Eastern Philosophy for Beginners* (London: Writers and Readers, Ltd., 2000).

Renard, John. *Responses to 101 Questions on Buddhism* (New York: Paulist Press, 1999).

Renou, Louis, ed. *Hinduism* (New York: George Braziller, 1961).

Rochford, E. Burke Jr. *Hare Krishna in America* (New Brunswick, NJ: Rutgers University Press, 1985).

Shah, Bharat M.D. *An Introduction to Jainism* (New York: Setubandh Publications, 2002).

Thoreau, Henry David. *Walden and Civil Disobedience* (New York: W.W. Norton, 1966).

Van De Weyer, Robert, ed. *366 Readings from Hinduism* (Cleveland, OH: The Pilgrim Press, 2000).

Van Loon, Borin, and Richard Osborne. *Introducing Eastern Philosophy* (Lanham, MD: Icon Books, 2001).

Viswanathan, Ed. *Am I a Hindu? The Hinduism Primer* (Palm Desert, CA: Halo Books, 1992).

Yogananda, Paramahansa. *Autobiography of a Yogi* (Los Angeles: Self-Realization Fellowship, 2005).

Index

THE EVERYTHING SERIES!

BUSINESS & PERSONAL FINANCE

Everything® Accounting Book
Everything® Budgeting Book, 2nd Ed.
Everything® Business Planning Book
Everything® Coaching and Mentoring Book, 2nd Ed.
Everything® Fundraising Book
Everything® Get-Out of Debt Book
Everything® Grant Writing Book, 2nd Ed.
Everything® Guide to Buying Foreclosures
Everything® Guide to Fundraising, $15.95
Everything® Guide to Mortgages
Everything® Guide to Personal Finance for Single Mothers
Everything® Home-Based Business Book, 2nd Ed.
Everything® Homebuying Book, 3rd Ed., $15.95
Everything® Homeselling Book, 2nd Ed.
Everything® Human Resource Management Book
Everything® Improve Your Credit Book
Everything® Investing Book, 2nd Ed.
Everything® Landlording Book
Everything® Leadership Book, 2nd Ed.
Everything® Managing People Book, 2nd Ed.
Everything® Negotiating Book
Everything® Online Auctions Book
Everything® Online Business Book
Everything® Personal Finance Book
Everything® Personal Finance in Your 20s & 30s Book, 2nd Ed.
Everything® Personal Finance in Your 40s & 50s Book, $15.95
Everything® Project Management Book, 2nd Ed.
Everything® Real Estate Investing Book
Everything® Retirement Planning Book
Everything® Robert's Rules Book, $7.95
Everything® Selling Book
Everything® Start Your Own Business Book, 2nd Ed.
Everything® Wills & Estate Planning Book

COOKING

Everything® Barbecue Cookbook
Everything® Bartender's Book, 2nd Ed., $9.95
Everything® Calorie Counting Cookbook
Everything® Cheese Book
Everything® Chinese Cookbook
Everything® Classic Recipes Book
Everything® Cocktail Parties & Drinks Book
Everything® College Cookbook
Everything® Cooking for Baby and Toddler Book
Everything® Diabetes Cookbook
Everything® Easy Gourmet Cookbook
Everything® Fondue Cookbook
Everything® Food Allergy Cookbook, $15.95
Everything® Fondue Party Book
Everything® Gluten-Free Cookbook
Everything® Glycemic Index Cookbook
Everything® Grilling Cookbook
Everything® Healthy Cooking for Parties Book, $15.95
Everything® Holiday Cookbook
Everything® Indian Cookbook
Everything® Lactose-Free Cookbook
Everything® Low-Cholesterol Cookbook

Everything® Low-Fat High-Flavor Cookbook, 2nd Ed., $15.95
Everything® Low-Salt Cookbook
Everything® Meals for a Month Cookbook
Everything® Meals on a Budget Cookbook
Everything® Mediterranean Cookbook
Everything® Mexican Cookbook
Everything® No Trans Fat Cookbook
Everything® One-Pot Cookbook, 2nd Ed., $15.95
Everything® Organic Cooking for Baby & Toddler Book, $15.95
Everything® Pizza Cookbook
Everything® Quick Meals Cookbook, 2nd Ed., $15.95
Everything® Slow Cooker Cookbook
Everything® Slow Cooking for a Crowd Cookbook
Everything® Soup Cookbook
Everything® Stir-Fry Cookbook
Everything® Sugar-Free Cookbook
Everything® Tapas and Small Plates Cookbook
Everything® Tex-Mex Cookbook
Everything® Thai Cookbook
Everything® Vegetarian Cookbook
Everything® Whole-Grain, High-Fiber Cookbook
Everything® Wild Game Cookbook
Everything® Wine Book, 2nd Ed.

GAMES

Everything® 15-Minute Sudoku Book, $9.95
Everything® 30-Minute Sudoku Book, $9.95
Everything® Bible Crosswords Book, $9.95
Everything® Blackjack Strategy Book
Everything® Brain Strain Book, $9.95
Everything® Bridge Book
Everything® Card Games Book
Everything® Card Tricks Book, $9.95
Everything® Casino Gambling Book, 2nd Ed.
Everything® Chess Basics Book
Everything® Christmas Crosswords Book, $9.95
Everything® Craps Strategy Book
Everything® Crossword and Puzzle Book
Everything® Crosswords and Puzzles for Quote Lovers Book, $9.95
Everything® Crossword Challenge Book
Everything® Crosswords for the Beach Book, $9.95
Everything® Cryptic Crosswords Book, $9.95
Everything® Cryptograms Book, $9.95
Everything® Easy Crosswords Book
Everything® Easy Kakuro Book, $9.95
Everything® Easy Large-Print Crosswords Book
Everything® Games Book, 2nd Ed.
Everything® Giant Book of Crosswords
Everything® Giant Sudoku Book, $9.95
Everything® Giant Word Search Book
Everything® Kakuro Challenge Book, $9.95
Everything® Large-Print Crossword Challenge Book
Everything® Large-Print Crosswords Book
Everything® Large-Print Travel Crosswords Book
Everything® Lateral Thinking Puzzles Book, $9.95
Everything® Literary Crosswords Book, $9.95
Everything® Mazes Book
Everything® Memory Booster Puzzles Book, $9.95

Everything® Movie Crosswords Book, $9.95
Everything® Music Crosswords Book, $9.95
Everything® Online Poker Book
Everything® Pencil Puzzles Book, $9.95
Everything® Poker Strategy Book
Everything® Pool & Billiards Book
Everything® Puzzles for Commuters Book, $9.95
Everything® Puzzles for Dog Lovers Book, $9.95
Everything® Sports Crosswords Book, $9.95
Everything® Test Your IQ Book, $9.95
Everything® Texas Hold 'Em Book, $9.95
Everything® Travel Crosswords Book, $9.95
Everything® Travel Mazes Book, $9.95
Everything® Travel Word Search Book, $9.95
Everything® TV Crosswords Book, $9.95
Everything® Word Games Challenge Book
Everything® Word Scramble Book
Everything® Word Search Book

HEALTH

Everything® Alzheimer's Book
Everything® Diabetes Book
Everything® First Aid Book, $9.95
Everything® Green Living Book
Everything® Health Guide to Addiction and Recovery
Everything® Health Guide to Adult Bipolar Disorder
Everything® Health Guide to Arthritis
Everything® Health Guide to Controlling Anxiety
Everything® Health Guide to Depression
Everything® Health Guide to Diabetes, 2nd Ed.
Everything® Health Guide to Fibromyalgia
Everything® Health Guide to Menopause, 2nd Ed.
Everything® Health Guide to Migraines
Everything® Health Guide to Multiple Sclerosis
Everything® Health Guide to OCD
Everything® Health Guide to PMS
Everything® Health Guide to Postpartum Care
Everything® Health Guide to Thyroid Disease
Everything® Hypnosis Book
Everything® Low Cholesterol Book
Everything® Menopause Book
Everything® Nutrition Book
Everything® Reflexology Book
Everything® Stress Management Book
Everything® Superfoods Book, $15.95

HISTORY

Everything® American Government Book
Everything® American History Book, 2nd Ed.
Everything® American Revolution Book, $15.95
Everything® Civil War Book
Everything® Freemasons Book
Everything® Irish History & Heritage Book
Everything® World War II Book, 2nd Ed.

HOBBIES

Everything® Candlemaking Book
Everything® Cartooning Book
Everything® Coin Collecting Book
Everything® Digital Photography Book, 2nd Ed.

Everything® Drawing Book
Everything® Family Tree Book, 2nd Ed.
Everything® Guide to Online Genealogy, $15.95
Everything® Knitting Book
Everything® Knots Book
Everything® Photography Book
Everything® Quilting Book
Everything® Sewing Book
Everything® Soapmaking Book, 2nd Ed.
Everything® Woodworking Book

HOME IMPROVEMENT

Everything® Feng Shui Book
Everything® Feng Shui Decluttering Book, $9.95
Everything® Fix-It Book
Everything® Green Living Book
Everything® Home Decorating Book
Everything® Home Storage Solutions Book
Everything® Homebuilding Book
Everything® Organize Your Home Book, 2nd Ed.

KIDS' BOOKS

All titles are $7.95
Everything® Fairy Tales Book, $14.95
Everything® Kids' Animal Puzzle & Activity Book
Everything® Kids' Astronomy Book
Everything® Kids' Baseball Book, 5th Ed.
Everything® Kids' Bible Trivia Book
Everything® Kids' Bugs Book
Everything® Kids' Cars and Trucks Puzzle and Activity Book
Everything® Kids' Christmas Puzzle & Activity Book
Everything® Kids' Connect the Dots
        Puzzle and Activity Book
Everything® Kids' Cookbook, 2nd Ed.
Everything® Kids' Crazy Puzzles Book
Everything® Kids' Dinosaurs Book
Everything® Kids' Dragons Puzzle and Activity Book
Everything® Kids' Environment Book $7.95
Everything® Kids' Fairies Puzzle and Activity Book
Everything® Kids' First Spanish Puzzle and Activity Book
Everything® Kids' Football Book
Everything® Kids' Geography Book
Everything® Kids' Gross Cookbook
Everything® Kids' Gross Hidden Pictures Book
Everything® Kids' Gross Jokes Book
Everything® Kids' Gross Mazes Book
Everything® Kids' Gross Puzzle & Activity Book
Everything® Kids' Halloween Puzzle & Activity Book
Everything® Kids' Hanukkah Puzzle and Activity Book
Everything® Kids' Hidden Pictures Book
Everything® Kids' Horses Book
Everything® Kids' Joke Book
Everything® Kids' Knock Knock Book
Everything® Kids' Learning French Book
Everything® Kids' Learning Spanish Book
Everything® Kids' Magical Science Experiments Book
Everything® Kids' Math Puzzles Book
Everything® Kids' Mazes Book
Everything® Kids' Money Book, 2nd Ed.
**Everything® Kids' Mummies, Pharaoh's, and Pyramids
        Puzzle and Activity Book**
Everything® Kids' Nature Book
Everything® Kids' Pirates Puzzle and Activity Book
Everything® Kids' Presidents Book
Everything® Kids' Princess Puzzle and Activity Book
Everything® Kids' Puzzle Book

Everything® Kids' Racecars Puzzle and Activity Book
Everything® Kids' Riddles & Brain Teasers Book
Everything® Kids' Science Experiments Book
Everything® Kids' Sharks Book
Everything® Kids' Soccer Book
Everything® Kids' Spelling Book
Everything® Kids' Spies Puzzle and Activity Book
Everything® Kids' States Book
Everything® Kids' Travel Activity Book
Everything® Kids' Word Search Puzzle and Activity Book

LANGUAGE

Everything® Conversational Japanese Book with CD, $19.95
Everything® French Grammar Book
Everything® French Phrase Book, $9.95
Everything® French Verb Book, $9.95
Everything® German Phrase Book, $9.95
Everything® German Practice Book with CD, $19.95
Everything® Inglés Book
Everything® Intermediate Spanish Book with CD, $19.95
Everything® Italian Phrase Book, $9.95
Everything® Italian Practice Book with CD, $19.95
Everything® Learning Brazilian Portuguese Book with CD, $19.95
Everything® Learning French Book with CD, 2nd Ed., $19.95
Everything® Learning German Book
Everything® Learning Italian Book
Everything® Learning Latin Book
Everything® Learning Russian Book with CD, $19.95
Everything® Learning Spanish Book
Everything® Learning Spanish Book with CD, 2nd Ed., $19.95
Everything® Russian Practice Book with CD, $19.95
Everything® Sign Language Book, $15.95
Everything® Spanish Grammar Book
Everything® Spanish Phrase Book, $9.95
Everything® Spanish Practice Book with CD, $19.95
Everything® Spanish Verb Book, $9.95
Everything® Speaking Mandarin Chinese Book with CD, $19.95

MUSIC

Everything® Bass Guitar Book with CD, $19.95
Everything® Drums Book with CD, $19.95
Everything® Guitar Book with CD, 2nd Ed., $19.95
Everything® Guitar Chords Book with CD, $19.95
Everything® Guitar Scales Book with CD, $19.95
Everything® Harmonica Book with CD, $15.95
Everything® Home Recording Book
Everything® Music Theory Book with CD, $19.95
Everything® Reading Music Book with CD, $19.95
Everything® Rock & Blues Guitar Book with CD, $19.95
Everything® Rock & Blues Piano Book with CD, $19.95
Everything® Rock Drums Book with CD, $19.95
Everything® Singing Book with CD, $19.95
Everything® Songwriting Book

NEW AGE

Everything® Astrology Book, 2nd Ed.
Everything® Birthday Personology Book
Everything® Celtic Wisdom Book, $15.95
Everything® Dreams Book, 2nd Ed.
Everything® Law of Attraction Book, $15.95
Everything® Love Signs Book, $9.95
Everything® Love Spells Book, $9.95
Everything® Palmistry Book
Everything® Psychic Book
Everything® Reiki Book

Everything® Sex Signs Book, $9.95
Everything® Spells & Charms Book, 2nd Ed.
Everything® Tarot Book, 2nd Ed.
Everything® Toltec Wisdom Book
Everything® Wicca & Witchcraft Book, 2nd Ed.

PARENTING

Everything® Baby Names Book, 2nd Ed.
Everything® Baby Shower Book, 2nd Ed.
Everything® Baby Sign Language Book with DVD
Everything® Baby's First Year Book
Everything® Birthing Book
Everything® Breastfeeding Book
Everything® Father-to-Be Book
Everything® Father's First Year Book
Everything® Get Ready for Baby Book, 2nd Ed.
Everything® Get Your Baby to Sleep Book, $9.95
Everything® Getting Pregnant Book
Everything® Guide to Pregnancy Over 35
Everything® Guide to Raising a One-Year-Old
Everything® Guide to Raising a Two-Year-Old
Everything® Guide to Raising Adolescent Boys
Everything® Guide to Raising Adolescent Girls
Everything® Mother's First Year Book
Everything® Parent's Guide to Childhood Illnesses
Everything® Parent's Guide to Children and Divorce
Everything® Parent's Guide to Children with ADD/ADHD
Everything® Parent's Guide to Children with Asperger's
        Syndrome
Everything® Parent's Guide to Children with Anxiety
Everything® Parent's Guide to Children with Asthma
Everything® Parent's Guide to Children with Autism
Everything® Parent's Guide to Children with Bipolar Disorder
Everything® Parent's Guide to Children with Depression
Everything® Parent's Guide to Children with Dyslexia
Everything® Parent's Guide to Children with Juvenile Diabetes
Everything® Parent's Guide to Children with OCD
Everything® Parent's Guide to Positive Discipline
Everything® Parent's Guide to Raising Boys
Everything® Parent's Guide to Raising Girls
Everything® Parent's Guide to Raising Siblings
**Everything® Parent's Guide to Raising Your
        Adopted Child**
Everything® Parent's Guide to Sensory Integration Disorder
Everything® Parent's Guide to Tantrums
Everything® Parent's Guide to the Strong-Willed Child
Everything® Parenting a Teenager Book
Everything® Potty Training Book, $9.95
Everything® Pregnancy Book, 3rd Ed.
Everything® Pregnancy Fitness Book
Everything® Pregnancy Nutrition Book
Everything® Pregnancy Organizer, 2nd Ed., $16.95
Everything® Toddler Activities Book
Everything® Toddler Book
Everything® Tween Book
Everything® Twins, Triplets, and More Book

PETS

Everything® Aquarium Book
Everything® Boxer Book
Everything® Cat Book, 2nd Ed.
Everything® Chihuahua Book
Everything® Cooking for Dogs Book
Everything® Dachshund Book
Everything® Dog Book, 2nd Ed.
Everything® Dog Grooming Book

Everything® Dog Obedience Book
Everything® Dog Owner's Organizer, $16.95
Everything® Dog Training and Tricks Book
Everything® German Shepherd Book
Everything® Golden Retriever Book
Everything® Horse Book, 2nd Ed., $15.95
Everything® Horse Care Book
Everything® Horseback Riding Book
Everything® Labrador Retriever Book
Everything® Poodle Book
Everything® Pug Book
Everything® Puppy Book
Everything® Small Dogs Book
Everything® Tropical Fish Book
Everything® Yorkshire Terrier Book

REFERENCE

Everything® American Presidents Book
Everything® Blogging Book
Everything® Build Your Vocabulary Book, $9.95
Everything® Car Care Book
Everything® Classical Mythology Book
Everything® Da Vinci Book
Everything® Einstein Book
Everything® Enneagram Book
Everything® Etiquette Book, 2nd Ed.
Everything® Family Christmas Book, $15.95
Everything® Guide to C. S. Lewis & Narnia
Everything® Guide to Divorce, 2nd Ed., $15.95
Everything® Guide to Edgar Allan Poe
Everything® Guide to Understanding Philosophy
Everything® Inventions and Patents Book
Everything® Jacqueline Kennedy Onassis Book
Everything® John F. Kennedy Book
Everything® Mafia Book
Everything® Martin Luther King Jr. Book
Everything® Pirates Book
Everything® Private Investigation Book
Everything® Psychology Book
Everything® Public Speaking Book, $9.95
Everything® Shakespeare Book, 2nd Ed.

RELIGION

Everything® Angels Book
Everything® Bible Book
Everything® Bible Study Book with CD, $19.95
Everything® Buddhism Book
Everything® Catholicism Book
Everything® Christianity Book
Everything® Gnostic Gospels Book
Everything® Hinduism Book, $15.95
Everything® History of the Bible Book
Everything® Jesus Book
Everything® Jewish History & Heritage Book
Everything® Judaism Book
Everything® Kabbalah Book
Everything® Koran Book
Everything® Mary Book
Everything® Mary Magdalene Book
Everything® Prayer Book

Everything® Saints Book, 2nd Ed.
Everything® Torah Book
Everything® Understanding Islam Book
Everything® Women of the Bible Book
Everything® World's Religions Book

SCHOOL & CAREERS

Everything® Career Tests Book
Everything® College Major Test Book
Everything® College Survival Book, 2nd Ed.
Everything® Cover Letter Book, 2nd Ed.
Everything® Filmmaking Book
Everything® Get-a-Job Book, 2nd Ed.
Everything® Guide to Being a Paralegal
Everything® Guide to Being a Personal Trainer
Everything® Guide to Being a Real Estate Agent
Everything® Guide to Being a Sales Rep
Everything® Guide to Being an Event Planner
Everything® Guide to Careers in Health Care
Everything® Guide to Careers in Law Enforcement
Everything® Guide to Government Jobs
Everything® Guide to Starting and Running a Catering Business
Everything® Guide to Starting and Running a Restaurant
Everything® Guide to Starting and Running a Retail Store
Everything® Job Interview Book, 2nd Ed.
Everything® New Nurse Book
Everything® New Teacher Book
Everything® Paying for College Book
Everything® Practice Interview Book
Everything® Resume Book, 3rd Ed.
Everything® Study Book

SELF-HELP

Everything® Body Language Book
Everything® Dating Book, 2nd Ed.
Everything® Great Sex Book
Everything® Guide to Caring for Aging Parents, $15.95
Everything® Self-Esteem Book
Everything® Self-Hypnosis Book, $9.95
Everything® Tantric Sex Book

SPORTS & FITNESS

Everything® Easy Fitness Book
Everything® Fishing Book
Everything® Guide to Weight Training, $15.95
Everything® Krav Maga for Fitness Book
Everything® Running Book, 2nd Ed.
Everything® Triathlon Training Book, $15.95

TRAVEL

Everything® Family Guide to Coastal Florida
Everything® Family Guide to Cruise Vacations
Everything® Family Guide to Hawaii
Everything® Family Guide to Las Vegas, 2nd Ed.
Everything® Family Guide to Mexico
Everything® Family Guide to New England, 2nd Ed.

Everything® Family Guide to New York City, 3rd Ed.
Everything® Family Guide to Northern California and Lake Tahoe
Everything® Family Guide to RV Travel & Campgrounds
Everything® Family Guide to the Caribbean
Everything® Family Guide to the Disneyland® Resort, California Adventure®, Universal Studios®, and the Anaheim Area, 2nd Ed.
Everything® Family Guide to the Walt Disney World Resort®, Universal Studios®, and Greater Orlando, 5th Ed.
Everything® Family Guide to Timeshares
Everything® Family Guide to Washington D.C., 2nd Ed.

WEDDINGS

Everything® Bachelorette Party Book, $9.95
Everything® Bridesmaid Book, $9.95
Everything® Destination Wedding Book
Everything® Father of the Bride Book, $9.95
Everything® Green Wedding Book, $15.95
Everything® Groom Book, $9.95
Everything® Jewish Wedding Book, 2nd Ed., $15.95
Everything® Mother of the Bride Book, $9.95
Everything® Outdoor Wedding Book
Everything® Wedding Book, 3rd Ed.
Everything® Wedding Checklist, $9.95
Everything® Wedding Etiquette Book, $9.95
Everything® Wedding Organizer, 2nd Ed., $16.95
Everything® Wedding Shower Book, $9.95
Everything® Wedding Vows Book, 3rd Ed., $9.95
Everything® Wedding Workout Book
Everything® Weddings on a Budget Book, 2nd Ed., $9.95

WRITING

Everything® Creative Writing Book
Everything® Get Published Book, 2nd Ed.
Everything® Grammar and Style Book, 2nd Ed.
Everything® Guide to Magazine Writing
Everything® Guide to Writing a Book Proposal
Everything® Guide to Writing a Novel
Everything® Guide to Writing Children's Books
Everything® Guide to Writing Copy
Everything® Guide to Writing Graphic Novels
Everything® Guide to Writing Research Papers
Everything® Guide to Writing a Romance Novel, $15.95
Everything® Improve Your Writing Book, 2nd Ed.
Everything® Writing Poetry Book